EMBRACING TRUTH

Homosexuality and the Word of God

edited by

David W. Torrance and Jock Stein

British Library Cataloguing in Publication Data:
a catalogue record for this publication
is available from the British Library

ISBN 978-1-871828-74-0

© Handsel Press 2012

Typeset in 11 pt Minion Pro in Haddington

Printing and cover design by
West Port Print and Design, St Andrews

CONTENTS

ACKNOWLEDGMENTS

As well as all the other contributors, the editors would like to thank Paul Burgess for his help with publicity and process.

The Scottish Order of Christian Unity generously gave a subvention which enabled the price of the book to be lower than it otherwise would have been.

STUDY GUIDE

A study guide to *Embracing Truth* can be downloaded free of charge from the Handsel Press website www.handselpress.org.uk

"This is simply the most comprehensive book that I have read on the subject. Its greatest value is that it sets the whole debate on homosexuality in its proper context: the glory of God. The late John Stott challenged the church to have a faithfulness to the Word and a sensitivity to the world. The desire of such 'double listening' was clear; that God's voice would be heard and the people of God would obey."

R. Douglas Cranston, Kilmacolm St Columba's

Introduction

There is no issue in recent times which has so disturbed the churches of the Western World and seems so insoluble, as that of same sex unions and church leadership. It has already caused division where formerly churches have been united, if not in doctrine, at least in church structure and organisation. It generates division among contemporary churches and threatens to cause some churches to break with traditions of the past and reject views held throughout the centuries by the church from New Testament times.

In a situation where the debate, sadly, has become polarized, where unhelpful accusations are made by people on both sides, we need as Christians to listen to what God is saying. The church is Christ's church. It is his body and we need to ask what God is saying to us and to the churches in this situation.

The editors of this book, along with those who have contributed, feel that God is challenging the churches not only to engage deeply with the current problems but even more importantly, to reconsider their understanding of the Word of God and how we interpret the Word. The issues go much further than those currently under debate and God is challenging us to a much deeper Christ-centred view of holy scripture. It is only by doing this that the church has any prospect of really being able to help people to move beyond polarized positions to a new and more compelling understanding of the Gospel. It is only through the Word of God that we have any knowledge of God and his salvation, and that there is a church at all. All the contributors seek to listen carefully to the Word of God and its teaching in all that it has to say to us.

While they seek to uphold the traditional view of the church from apostolic times, they believe that God is challenging all in the churches to re-examine their faith and to learn more about the whole teaching of the Bible and about human relationships and sexuality. What the Bible says, it says to all, but how often have the churches had one standard for homosexuals and another for heterosexuals? We all need to stand firm on the Word of God, to listen to it and to act in expectation of being transformed into the likeness of Christ that we might have the abundant life to which he calls us.

God is challenging the churches over their lack of love and sympathy towards those of a homosexual orientation. This can cause great suffering particularly when they may wish to be transformed and are not. In this there is great need on the churches' part for repentance. For far too long homosexuals have felt rejected, both for their sexual orientation and as individuals. Yet in Christ God never rejects anyone (John 6:37). All of us need to rediscover the reality of God's love in Christ for everyone, no matter who they are, and to love and welcome all in Christ. Dr Calum McKellar movingly draws our attention to this in his article. At the same time what he says equally applies to single heterosexual people who can feel very lonely not simply in society but in the church. It is also important to recognize that the same restraints which are required of homosexuals who seek to be true to the Word and celibate, apply equally to heterosexuals who are single, just as they also apply to heterosexuals who are married and seek to be faithful to their partners in marriage.

While strongly affirming their desire to see the whole debate widened and deepened, the contributors focus on the current issue of homosexuality in the church and examine a wide range of relevant aspects, from the biblical and theological, to the scientific and pastoral. Although not necessarily agreeing on all points, the contributors are all agreed that the Bible affirms and limits sexual practice to within marriage while condemning and prohibiting it outside of it.

Nowhere in either the Old or New Testament is homosexual practice considered something good. The contributors ask that the churches have the courage to resist the pressure by secular society to change. They also ask Christians to resist secular pressures from within the church where some are motivated solely by emotion and sympathy for relatives and friends with homosexual desires, rather than listening to and obeying the Word of God.

Despite considerable recent research, no 'homosexual gene' has been found and it seems unlikely that it will be. Whereas in some cases there may be a biological factor, among the majority of those working in the field there is general agreement that there are always a number of other factors which together give rise to a person's sexual orientation. As Prof. Gagnon has said, "the most that can be claimed is that homosexuality arises from a complex interplay of genes, intra-uterine and post-uterine biological development, environment, and choice". Family and social background are important, for example, whether a person as a child has suffered some emotional trauma, been rejected by either father or mother, never affirmed in their masculinity or femininity or suffered gender confusion. It can even be a matter of choice as Peter Tatchell, leader of Stonewall (one of the major gay organizations in the UK) affirms.

Sexual transformation (where a person's sexual orientation is transformed from homosexual to heterosexual), despite the controversy surrounding it, has been demonstrated many times, although there are also cases where transformation has been short lived.

It is important to remember that homosexuality is not an illness and that prayer is asking for a person to be transformed, not healed. Yet praying for transformation is analogous to praying for healing. Healing is a gift from God which we are called to exercise in faith and through the power of the Holy Spirit. Not all for whom we pray are healed, any more than all for whom we pray are transformed. However that should not lessen our faith and expectation that all who are sick can be healed and all with a homosexual orientation can by the grace of God be transformed, if they so desire.

We are weak and sinful and have no mechanical power to transform or heal. We welcome all help from medicine, psychiatry and Christian pastoral ministry as a gift from God, acknowledging that there is much mystery which at times baffles us all. We are called simply to press on in faith seeking ever to become more like Christ, to obey the Father as did Jesus and seeking, through the Holy Spirit to exercise the gifts which God has given that all might live life "to the full" in Christ (John 10:10).

Those praying for transformation, like those praying for the sick, need to show great wisdom, care and compassion in their pastoral care, so that if a person is not transformed they are not discouraged, knowing that they are loved by God and special. As Christians we must insist that it is people's 'identity in Christ' which is the defining principle of their lives, not their experience of different sexual desires. This is supremely important. It is Christ alone who in love for us all affirms us and gives us our identity through the Gospel. Sadly, it can be because people have too often not found themselves affirmed by the Gospel that they have clung to an identity outside it.

This book is presented with the earnest prayer that it may help in a debate where there is much uncertainty and confusion and the prayer that the Church may listen to and be a faithful, courageous witness to the Word of God in a sinful world. Christ prayed to the Father that we might be one that the world might believe. We pray in Christ for the unity of the body of Christ in spirit and in truth.

David W. Torrance, *Co-editor*   Easter 2012

Clearing the ground

Chapter 1

Confusion and clarity

Andrew Goddard

Dr Goddard is an ordained Anglican and writer on ethics who has taught Christian ethics at Trinity College, Bristol and Wycliffe Hall, Oxford.

Introduction

The issue of Christian responses to those who experience same sex attraction or identify as gay or lesbian has become one of the most pressing and divisive issues in the Christian church, particularly in mainline Protestant denominations in Europe and North America. This development only makes sense once set in the context of the incredible social change that has occurred in the last half-century, particularly in Britain in the last decade.

It is easy to forget that until forty-five years ago all male homosexual acts – even consensual acts between adults over 21 in private – were criminal offences throughout the United Kingdom. This led to a hidden gay sub-culture given the risks of social stigma, blackmail and even imprisonment for those whose sexual attractions were for other men. The law changed in England and Wales in 1967 but it was clear that there was no desire for this to result in a more public gay identity with Lord Arran, the leading peer who had pressed for change, using his speech in the Lords to tell those no longer treated as criminals – "I ask those who have, as it were, been in bondage and for whom the prison doors are now open to show their thanks by comporting themselves quietly and with dignity. This is no occasion for jubilation; certainly not for celebration. Any form of ostentatious behaviour now, or in the future, any form of public flaunting, would be utterly distasteful and would, I believe, make the sponsors of the Bill regret that they have done what they have done".[1]

---

1 Hansard, 21st July 1967, cols 522-3.

When, in 1976, the Labour government produced a Bill to consolidate sexual offences law in Scotland, it sought to retain criminalisation and the Commons approved. This was despite the fact that the Lord Advocate had made clear that, if a homosexual act was legal in England and Wales he would not prosecute and "there is no record of any prosecution in Scotland in any of the last 10 years for homosexual activities between consenting adults in private".[2] It was not until 1980 that Scottish law followed English law (keeping the age of consent at 21, despite a 1979 Policy Advisory Committee on Sexual Offences proposing 18). The situation in Northern Ireland did not change until 1982 (following a ruling by the European Court of Human Rights that it was a violation of Article 8 of the European Convention on Human Rights to criminalise homosexual acts between consenting adults) while the Isle of Man and Gibraltar did not change until 1992.

Despite this apparent 'liberalisation', the 1980s and most of the 1990s, lived under the dark shadow of the spread of AIDS, saw the resurgence of legislation and political campaigns opposed to homosexuality. The most famous example was the 1988 local government legislation (known as Section 28/Clause 28/Section 2A) which prevented local authorities promoting homosexuality including "the teaching in any maintained school of the acceptability of homosexuality as a pretended family relationship". This led to the formation of Stonewall in 1989 which became a highly effective pressure group, particularly following the 1997 election.

The last ten years have seen major legal changes. The age of consent for homosexual acts had been reduced to 18 in 1994 and, after long battles, was equalised at 16, the age for heterosexual acts, in 2001. Section 28 was repealed in Scotland in 2000 and the rest of the UK in 2003. Legal recognition, equivalent to that of marriage, was given to same sex couples through the Civil Partnership Act 2004 and subsequent equality legislation outlawed discrimination on the basis of sexual discrimination.

In the last forty years there has therefore been a sea-change in the position of gay and lesbian people in the United Kingdom. On 27th November 1970 the first gay rights demonstration in Britain took place in Highbury Fields. One hundred and fifty members of the Gay Liberation Front held a torchlight rally against police harassment and their demands – the claims of a small group viewed as extremists – have now become our social reality. They drew up this list of immediate demands:

---

2   Hansard, 18th October 1976, cols 264-5. Quoted in McManus, 80.

- that all discrimination against gay people, male and female, by the law, by employers, and by society at large, should end.
- that all people who feel attracted to a member of their own sex be taught that such feelings are perfectly valid.
- that sex education in schools stop being exclusively heterosexual.
- that psychiatrists stop treating homosexuality as though it were a sickness, thereby giving gay people senseless guilt complexes.
- that gay people be as legally free to contact other gay people, through newspaper ads, on the streets and by any other means they may want, as do heterosexuals, and that police harassment should cease right now.
- that employers should no longer be allowed to discriminate against anyone on account of their sexual preferences.
- that the age of consent for gay males be reduced to the same as for straight.
- that gay people be free to hold hands and kiss in public, as are heterosexuals.

The securing of these changes was not achieved by widespread public agitation for reform. It often initially occurred in the face of strong, some-times sadly unpleasant, opposition from politicians, religious leaders and other bodies. Nevertheless, these developments in part reflected and in part facilitated a major change in social attitudes. The 2010 Scottish Social Attitude Survey reported:

> The biggest and most rapid change in discriminatory attitudes in the last decade has been in views of gay men and lesbians. In 2000, 48% felt sexual relationships between two adults of the same sex were always or mostly wrong. By 2010 this figure had fallen to just over a quarter (27%). At the same time, support for same sex marriage increased from 41% in 2002 to 61% in 2010, while more people said a gay man or lesbian would be a suitable primary school teacher in 2010 compared with 2006 (56% comp. with 48%).[3]

In this context it is unsurprising that redefining marriage to include same sex couples is being proposed and that traditional Christian teaching is increasingly challenged not just in wider society but within the churches.

---

3   Rachel Ormston, John Curtice, Susan McConville & Susan Reid (Scottish Centre for Social Research), Scottish Social Attitudes Survey 2010: Attitudes to discrimination and positive action, 9.

The danger in this situation is that Christians respond primarily – or even solely – on the basis of their responses to these social changes. Those who are more socially conservative can then appear bitter and reactionary, others can argue that God is teaching us new things which are part of his work of inclusion and welcoming the outcasts. Perhaps the majority of Christians, aware of their own and the church's past failings in relation to sexuality (particularly their treatment of those who are same sex attracted), simply become confused and lose the confidence they previously had in traditional Christian teaching once it becomes counter-cultural to express such views.

This book argues that there is much wisdom in the church's traditional teaching about human sexuality, based on the witness of Scripture, and that it would be unwise to abandon this in the light of such rapid and untested social change. At the heart of this teaching is not a stance against homosexuality. The Christian position is rather a stance for a number of goods. Firstly, the goodness of God's will for human beings and their flourishing as revealed in Christ and the biblical witness of both Old and New Testaments. Secondly, the goodness of humans being made male and female in the image of God as described in Genesis 2. In the words of Oliver O'Donovan, if the church is asked "to adopt some alternative myth of creation-order to replace that in which Adam acclaims Eve as 'bone of my bone and flesh of my flesh', it can only refuse".[4] Thirdly, the goodness of marriage as a created institution in which one man and one woman pledge themselves to each other for life and give expression to and strengthen their love through their sexual union. This pattern of life is the best and proper context for procreation and the upbringing of children, provides wider society with a supporting structure of mutual society, help and comfort between the couple, and offers what was traditionally described as "a remedy against sin" and the destructive effects of sexual sin on both individuals and communities. This leads to the fourth good which Christians seek to uphold and commend – the virtue of chastity through which we are enabled to direct our sexual desires in a manner that enables human flourishing through faithfulness to a spouse in marriage and abstinence from sex in non-marital forms of friendship.

In the context of this positive vision the specific biblical prohibitions against homosexual behaviour – the consistent moral judgment of Scripture in both Old and New Testaments – can be seen as not isolated and

---

4   Oliver O'Donovan, "Homosexuality in the Church: Can there be a fruitful theological debate?" in Timothy Bradshaw (ed), *The Way Forward?* (SCM, 2nd edn, 2003), 30.

dispensable but integral and still applicable to contemporary culture. There are, however, a range of understandable objections increasingly raised against those who articulate this view. Many of the chapters in the book present a defence of the traditional view but before their detailed discussion it is helpful to identify and offer short (and so limited) responses to nine of the most common criticisms, grouped under the broad headings of Scripture, Science and Reason, and Contemporary Culture.

Scripture

Objection 1: "When you really look at the biblical texts, they are about bad sex not good sex and so they do not condemn all homosexual practice but only some – that which is abusive. Sexual expression within loving, permanent, faithful and stable same sex relationships such as civil partnerships or 'gay marriage' is simply not addressed."

This objection rightly calls for careful exegesis of the relevant biblical texts and awareness of their social and literary contexts. It faces, however, a major challenge: all the biblical texts relating to homosexuality are negative. In relation to the role of women in the church, the church faces the challenge of doing justice to both restrictive texts and texts which affirm women's leadership and gifts. A similar challenge relates to other contentious subjects such as war or remarriage after divorce. Here, however, there is an unambiguous consistency and coherence in the biblical witness. Walter Wink, who argues Christians should affirm same sex sexual relationships, admits that "Simply put, the Bible is negative towards same sex behaviour, and there is no getting around it."[5] When a reader of Scripture asks whether the biblical writers disapprove of those same sex activities to which they refer, then "the answer is a straightforward and uncontroversial 'Yes.'"[6] The question is, therefore, whether or not we can limit the same sex activities to which Scripture refers.

A strong case can be made for such limitation in what sadly became the classic biblical text on the subject – Genesis 19 and the story of Sodom. This is clearly a narrative about the planned homosexual gang rape of strangers and if that were the only biblical text then this objection would be highly persuasive. There are, however, the two Levitical texts

---

5   Walter Wink, "To Hell with Gays?" Christian Century 119.13 (2002): 33. Online (with Gagnon's responses) at http://www.robgagnon.net/Reviews/homoWinkExchanges.pdf

6   Walter Moberly. 2000, "The Use of Scripture in Contemporary Debate about Homosexuality", Theology 103 (July/August): 251.

(Lev 18:22 and 20:13). Although it has been argued these refer to cultic acts of homosexual temple prostitution, the wording is much more generic and the surrounding prohibitions (for example in relation to incest, bestiality etc) would not normally be seen as applying only when the acts occur in the context of idolatry.

Furthermore, there are the two Pauline texts in 1 Corinthians 6:9 and 1 Timothy 1:10. The claim is that these too are limited in scope, to similar cultic acts related to idolatry or to sexual relationships between older men and young boys (pederasty). Although not impossible, there is nothing in the terminology (Paul does not use standard words for those engaged in homosexual activity but coins a term drawn from Leviticus) or the context (whether textual – the structure of the list in 1 Tim 1 likely relates this sin to the Decalogue's prohibition against adultery – or social) to support such restrictions. The fact the ancient world knew a variety of patterns of homo-sexual behaviour, all of which Jews rejected, makes it difficult to accept (or recognise) such limitations. The even more serious difficulty is that presented by Romans 1. Paul's negative judgment on homosexual conduct is here set within a wider theological framework that looks back to creation and its disordering – in relation to God and in relation to male and female – as a result of human sin. This passage also includes female as well as male same sex behaviour, and it is much harder to argue that prohibition of the former is limited to abusive, cultic or inter-generational forms of homosexuality.

Even were all the texts explicitly addressing forms of same sex sexual behaviour conclusively shown to be narrower in their scope than tradition-ally understood, this would simply leave the Bible silent on the specific issue. The wider and deeper issue is that of the positive vision of Scripture in relation to sexuality which is summarised above. This more general teaching about sex would still entail a strong presumption against commending sexual expression even in loving and faithful same sex relationships.

Objection 2: "We do not believe the Old Testament law – particularly most of Leviticus – is applicable to Christians. We therefore eat shrimps and wear polycotton shirts despite Leviticus 11:9-12 and 19:9. Why then should we continue to object to homosexual practice?"

If the traditional Christian position relied solely on the two texts in Leviticus for its rejection of homosexual behaviour this argument could have some weight. Even then, however, it would not be conclusive. In the first place, the Christian church has from the early centuries distinguished between Old Testament laws which are no longer in force (such as the cultic laws relating to sacrifice or the food laws) and those which do continue to provide norms for the believer in Jesus. Those relating to sex are generally held to be in the latter category. Secondly, we not only uphold many (though not all) of the sexual prohibitions in Leviticus but also appeal to Leviticus in other situations, most notably the recent Jubilee 2000 campaign against international debt which was based on Leviticus 25 and the fundamental command to love our neighbour as ourselves (Lev 19:18 – the chapter between the two texts condemning sex between men).

Of course, love of neighbour is important because of its repetition and centrality in the New Testament (for example, Gal 5:14) but the rejection of homosexuality is also repeated in the New Testament, unlike the laws relating to eating sea food or wearing mixed fibres. This is the reason that, on its own, this objection collapses. But the reply may be given that not only Paul but Jesus himself teaches us to love our neighbour and the same cannot be said in relation to negative comments about homosexuality.

Objection 3: "Christians are marked out as followers of Jesus. What did Jesus have to say about homosexuality? Nothing!"

Although Jesus' teaching is clearly central to Christian discipleship, there are a number of problems with using this argument to challenge the church's traditional sexual ethic. Firstly, a good case can be made that Jesus' references to *porneia* – sexual immorality – would have included same sex sexual activity within that term.[7] Secondly, there are other important ethical areas where, in the gospels, Jesus appears to be silent. This includes not only various forms of sexual behaviour (such as incest and rape) but also as fundamental an issue as idolatry. This points to the third problem that arises with any attempt to base on argument on silence – in the case of Jesus, his silence is at least as likely to point to his acceptance of the established Jewish understanding based on the Torah (as in relation to idolatry). This would suggest the silence supports rather than undermines the traditional teaching, particularly since he reaffirms the vision of marriage based in Genesis (for example in Matthew 19). Such a view is confirmed by the fact that Jesus was not averse to challenging the moral vision of Judaism when he believed it was distorted. We have however no record of him saying something such as "You have heard that it was said a man shall not lie with a man as a woman but I say to you that when

---

7   See, for example, John Nolland, "Sexual Ethics and the Jesus of the Gospels", Anvil Vol. 26, No. 1 [2009], 21-30.

the men are expressing covenantal love they are blessed." The silence of Jesus is, therefore, a poor criticism. As the Church of England's bishops have stated, "It is therefore impossible to conceive that Jesus would have endorsed homosexuality had this been an issue that had arisen during his ministry."[8] Interestingly, this assessment is shared by leading non-Christian gay journalist Matthew Parris who has written, "Nothing in the Gospels suggests any departure from Judaic wisdom on sex and marriage, a pretty robust sense of which we gain from the Old Testament. Jesus was never reluctant to challenge received wisdoms that he wanted to change. He gives no impression that he came into the world to revolutionise sexual mores."[9]

Objection 4: "A focus on the Bible's central themes such as love, liberation, justice and inclusion of the outsider – most notably in the New Testament, the inclusion of Gentiles – should lead us to accept gay relationships."

This critique raises an important corrective to an undue focus on the question of same sex relationships. It emphasises the need to address the issue by more than simply the exegesis of the relatively small number of texts that refer to same sex behaviour. However, the problem is that none of the bigger themes rightly highlighted here can lead to the conclusion that same sex sexual behaviour and relationships are acceptable to God and to be commended and blessed by the church.

In relation to love, there is no doubting that self-sacrificial *agape* love is shown within same sex partnerships but this does not tell us how to interpret such relationships or entail that sexual expression within them is legitimate. There are various forms of loving relationship where sexual expression is wrong – notably within the family and among friends. The fact that a relationship is clearly loving and committed does not mean that all aspects of the relationship are therefore holy or that the relationship is a form of marriage. To make judgments in these areas requires a wider account of the divine order of creation and the various goods within it. Any appeal to 'love' needs to be clear that 'love' is defined not by contemporary cultural usage but by the God who is love and who has made himself known as love in his self-revelation.

In relation to liberation and justice, again there can be no doubt that people do suffer forms of oppression and injustice related to their sexuality

8   *Some Issues in Human Sexuality*, Church House Publishing, 2003, Para 4.3.63.

9   Matthew Parris, "No, God would not have approved of gay bishops", The Times, August 9th, 2003.

or sexual conduct. However, these key themes only have purchase in discussions of sexuality when combined with an account that must be given on other grounds of the evils from which we need liberation and of what is just and right. So, the language of 'gay liberation' began with secular, post-Christian and even anti-Christian groups in the 1960s and 1970s but the main network of those offering forms of healing to those with same sex attraction is called 'Exodus' as they view liberation in terms of 'coming out' of the captivity experienced by embracing a homosexual identity and pattern of life. Similarly, Oliver O'Donovan has critiqued the whole appeal to 'rights':

> The language of rights is completely impotent to resolve this kind of issue. "Right", it used to be said, "flows from the spring of righteousness". Rights are not foundational; they derive from that fabric of right (in the singular) that belongs to the network of relations that constitutes reality. Until there is agreement upon what is real, any discussion about what is right remains floating in the air. The rights that some claim to be deprived of appear to others as no more than the moral furniture of a fantastic and make-believe world.[10]

Finally, the language of inclusion and appeal to the church's inclusion of the Gentiles certainly critiques those who would reject and exclude those who identify as gay from the church but it does not entail that same sex sexual behaviour is acceptable. This can be questioned, first, on biblical grounds. The inclusion of the Gentiles in Acts 15 included certain demands on their conduct, including refraining from sexual immorality and it is very likely – particularly if the restrictions draw on Leviticus 17–18 which apply certain laws to "the alien who sojourns in your midst" – this would include non-marital sexual intercourse.

Second, on theological grounds, the indiscriminate invitation and welcome of all as sinners needs to be combined with the call to costly discipleship which seeks to enter the narrow gate and experiences the transforming power of the Spirit. The debate about the standards of sexual behavior and what forms of sexual relationship are holy and to be blessed relates to this latter area and so the pattern of Christian life cannot be defined simply by appeals to inclusion.

---

10 Oliver O'Donovan, "Homosexuality in the Church: Can there be a fruitful theological debate?" in Bradshaw (ed), *The Way Forward?* (SCM, 2nd edn, 2003), 36.

Third, this shows the deeper problem that the argument makes the error of arguing from the inclusion of people to the approval of practices. The fact that the church should welcome people from all walks of life – and indeed the fact that genuine Christians can be found in a particular vocation or social group – does not mean that pattern of living is acceptable. For example, the fact that the church should not exclude those serving in the military does not entail that war is right and pacifism is illegitimate.[11] Once again, such questions need to be decided on other grounds than appeal to a general principle.

Objection 5: "The church has changed its position on interest, slavery, divorce, women in ministry and countless other issues. This question of gay relationships is just the same."

This objection is a timely reminder that we recognise that the church has erred in the past in its understanding of biblical teaching, humanity and the pattern of Christian discipleship and that it remains imperfect, holding a mixture of truth and error. This should not be a problem to those who believe that the church, having been reformed, should always be open to further reformation (*ecclesia reformata semper reformanda*). This principle is, however, once again being made to do too much if it is claimed that it guides us clearly in relation to the church's teaching on sexuality.

The most fundamental problem is that it is impossible to argue that because the church has been wrong on certain issues in the past it is follows that it is therefore currently wrong on one particular issue. The most that could be claimed is that it always needs to be open to the Spirit showing it is in error on any particular issues. Whether or not it is actually in error and the nature of any such error requires argument about the particular issue not appeal to this principle.

The argument would, of course, be strengthened if it could be shown that the errors which have been discerned in the past are being repeated in this particular case but that faces a major challenge in relation to homosexuality. In other areas, those arguing that the church was in error appealed to biblical texts that challenged the church's traditional teaching and questioned its use of some other biblical texts to defend that teaching – usury was only prohibited between Jews, Paul's letter to Philemon and Galatians 3:28 undermined slavery, Moses tolerated divorce and remarriage

---

11 For a more detailed discussion of this argument see Andrew Goddard, *God, Gentiles and Gay Christians* (Grove Ethics Books No. 121, 2001).

and Jesus permitted it according to the Matthean exception etc. In contrast, as noted above, there are no biblical texts which speak of same sex sexual behaviour in other than strongly negative terms.

Furthermore, although often reduced to *semper reformanda* and then sometimes interpreted in a progressive, historicist manner, the principle's opening clause is a reminder that ongoing reformation should respect and be in some form of continuity with the reform that took place in the sixteenth century. Church historian David Wright has dealt with this issue in an excellent article.[12]

Although some arguments calling for a revision of the church's teaching on sexuality do attempt such entering into Reformation principles, others explicitly abandon the Scripture principle to argue that our knowledge and culture require us to move beyond what it is accepted as the Bible's teaching against homosexual behaviour.

Science and Reason

Objection 6: "Homosexuality is natural – it is found in the animal kingdom and has a biological, perhaps genetic, basis in humans – and so must be accepted rather than rejected by the church."

This argument seeks to take the traditional categorisation of homosexuality as 'unnatural' and challenge it on the basis of empirical evidence. It is weakened by its misuse of both the language of 'natural' and the scientific evidence we have relating to sexuality.

A Christian appeal to 'nature' (itself not uncontentious within the Reformed tradition) is not an appeal to patterns of behaviour we discover in other creatures, although it cannot be denied that sometimes such claims have been made in natural law defences of heterosexuality. It is, rather, an appeal to God's ordering of creation and the particular nature, calling and *telos* of human beings as creatures made in God's image. There are clearly many patterns of sexual and other behaviour which are perfectly 'natural' in the sense of being exhibited by other creatures but which are not thereby held to be conducive to human flourishing or morally acceptable in human society.

More serious, though, is the claim that we now understand homosexuality among humans to be biologically based and thus to be welcomed and celebrated as part of the diversity of God's creation. Even if true, this

---

12 David Wright, "The Homosexuality Debate and the Reform of the Church", Anvil Vol. 15 No 1 (1998), 22-33 (here 23).

would, of course, not be a knock-out blow to traditional Christian teaching. A strong doctrine of the fallen and disordered character of creation as we experience it today explains why simply demonstrating a biological basis for any pattern of human desire or action is not equivalent to showing it to be a created good. But the problem for the challenge is that it is much less well-founded scientifically than its proponents acknowledge or perhaps realise.

Although it is often claimed that homosexuality is genetic, or mostly genetic, in origin, this is, in the words of David de Pomerai, author of a major 2008 study[13] and associate professor in the School of Biology, University of Nottingham – "scientifically unfounded". He goes on to note that Bailey, the author of one of the twin studies often cited in support of a genetic basis, explicitly said that his work "did not provide statistically significant support for the importance of genetic factors for sexual orientation" and so de Pomerai concludes that "There is no 'gay gene' as such, and media reports to this effect have been very misleading".[14]

There may, of course, be biological factors other than the genetic involved and various studies have been carried out exploring hormonal effects, birth order and the brain. Here, however, de Pomerai, concludes that "The evidence for all of these biological 'nature' explanations is weak, but neither is it so negligible as to be dismissed out of hand. It seems more likely that different nature factors contribute in varying measures to homosexual tendencies, and that nurture factors play at least as important a role (possibly more so)."[15]

In summary, not only is it unclear what theological and ethical implications could or should be drawn from the scientific evidence,[16] that evidence itself is far from certain. In fact, the situation in relation to the origins and causes of homosexuality is still very similar to that described over a decade ago by Edward Stein in his important study *The Mismeasure of Desire*. Having begun with the narrative concerning the source of human attractions found in Plato's *Symposium*, after over 300 pages mapping

---

13 De Pomerai, D. (2008). "Biological Mechanisms in Homosexuality: A Critical Review" in *The Anglican Communion and Homosexuality: A Resource to Enable Listening and Dialogue*, edited by P. Groves. London: SPCK: 268-92.

14 Letter to Church of England Newspaper from the Revd Dr David de Pomerai, associate professor in the School of Biology, University of Nottingham, 9th December 2011.

15 *Ibid.*

16 For a good discussion of this see Jones, Stanton L., and Mark A. Yarhouse. (2000), *Homosexuality: The Use of Scientific Research in the Church's Moral Debate*. Downers Grove, IL: IVP.

contemporary metaphysical and scientific views about sexual orientation and sexual desires he concludes the book with a warning: "Our confidence that we have advanced a great deal in our understanding of sexual orientation compared to Aristophanes and his fellow celebrants in *The Symposium* is premature . . ."[17]

Objection 7: "It is wrong to blame someone for expressing who they are by nature and, although most people are heterosexual, we now know that a significant minority of people are naturally homosexual and so we need to support permanent, faithful and stable same sex partnerships".

This objection clearly builds on the previous one in some respects and, in so far as that objection has a poor evidential base, it too is therefore weakened. The concern about 'blame' highlights that part of the problem in current debates is that traditional teaching is often heard as seeking to blame, shame and stigmatise certain people and thus is antithetical to the good news the church is called to proclaim. To claim, however, that we are not to be blamed for expressing who we are by nature is – whatever its applicability to issues relating to homosexuality – at best an ambiguous half-truth from a theological perspective. This is because the 'nature' we are called to give expression to is that human nature which is created and redeemed in Christ. Our experiences however – including our desires and so what might subjectively feel 'good' or 'right' – are not an infallible guide to that true human nature due to human sin. The biblical witness is that, in Jesus' words, "out of the heart come evil thoughts – murder, adultery, sexual immorality, theft, false testimony, slander" (Matt 15:19). As a result, the Christian vision is not one of self-expression but rather one in which there is conflict between the Spirit and the flesh (Gal 5:17).

In addition to the theological difficulties with this objection there are also problems with its assumption that "we now know that a significant minority of people are naturally homosexual". This remains an area where more work needs to be done but it is now widely recognised that human sexual attraction is best understood in terms of a spectrum rather than a simple division between homosexual and heterosexual. Once this is accepted, the evidence suggests that many more people experience a mix of both same sex and opposite sex attraction (what might be

---

17 Stein E., *The Mismeasure of Desire: the Science, Theory and Ethics of Sexual Orientation* (New York: Oxford University Press, 1999), 348.

labelled 'bisexuality') than only same sex attraction. This is particularly the case among women and is increasingly becoming evident in terms of the identity labels that people use for their sexuality. In a UK-wide 2010 Integrated Household Survey by the Office of National Statistics (ONS) which sampled nearly quarter of a million people slightly more women identified as "bisexual" than "lesbian". Overall, only 0.9% of the sample identified as "gay or lesbian" and 0.5% as "bisexual". Although the "1 in 10" figures derived from Kinsey are still sometimes cited and widely known, it is clear that these greatly exaggerate the proportion of the population who are exclusively, or even predominantly, sexually attracted to people of the same sex.

Contemporary Culture

Objection 8: "Gay and lesbian people are a significant minority group who have been persecuted and excluded and the church should always be sympathetic to minorities and inclusive. Opposing same sex relationships is simply homophobic and prejudiced."

It cannot be questioned that those experiencing same sex attraction have been mistreated both by wider society and the church and that, where this continues, there is the need for ongoing repentance and reform. What is much less clear is the nature and scope of the reform that is necessary. As discussed earlier in relation to the fourth objection and appeals to Acts 15, the missional commitment to include cannot be separated from the call to transform and cannot on its own tell the church what patterns of life it should expect of those it includes.

Although prejudice and hatred or homophobia may be present in some of those who oppose same sex relationships, taking such a moral stance is not in itself evidence of such sinful attitudes. To equate the two both fails to do justice to the biblical, theological and other arguments against same sex relationships and, by broadening the term 'homophobia', risks drawing attention away from those attitudes and behaviours which all Christians should reject and challenge within both church and society.

It must also not be forgotten that there are many people who experience same sex attraction (perhaps the majority of Christians who have this experience) who hold traditional views of God's purposes for us as sexual beings and so reject same sex relationships. Their voice is increasingly ignored not only in society but even within church discussions and yet they offer a unique and powerful witness. They often challenge holders of traditional views to become more aware of the experience of same sex attraction and undermine the claims of revisionists that all gay and lesbian people seek affirmation of same sex relationships.

Objection 9: "People today – especially young people – are much more accepting of different patterns of sexuality, and the church should move with the times."

As noted in the Introduction, our society has seen a major and massive shift in attitudes in relation to sexuality. Although there is still a significant proportion of people unhappy with this development – a major survey from 2008 found that just over a third of people (36%) thought sexual relations between two adults of the same sex were "always" or "mostly" wrong – this group is rapidly reducing in number. It is also increasingly cautious about expressing its views lest it be attacked by pressure groups or even face legal challenge. With little sign that this trend is going to be significantly or rapidly reversed, this new social reality is something that the church needs seriously to consider. If it continues to uphold its traditional teaching and practice it will face accusations – both from within and without – that it is out of touch with our society and damaging its mission.

The fact of social change is, however, never a sufficient reason for theological change. The history of Christianity contains numerous warnings of the dangers in embracing social movements as the work of the Spirit, especially when this involves abandoning, ignoring or downplaying the wisdom of Scripture and Christian tradition. In relation to various areas – not least in regard to other issues of sexuality such as pre-marital sex, cohabitation and abortion – the movement into a post-Christendom missional context seems to be requiring the church to become more intentional and distinctive in its patterns of moral formation and discipleship.

Conclusion

Clearly the Christian church in this country cannot respond to homosexuality as it has done in the past. Society has changed and most Christians now know and respect people, including fellow Christians who identify as gay or lesbian and are in civil partnerships or other forms of same sex relationships. That reality does not, however, entail that the church must simply adapt and 'move with the times'. Rather, it signals that we need to continue to engage with this issue.

Some of those who wish to uphold the church's traditional stance may wish this was not the situation but it is a reality that will not go away, even if the church divides over it. There is the challenge to find new ways of persuading both wider society and a younger generation of Christians, that such a position is both right and pastorally feasible.[18] That requires, as has been attempted here, serious engagement with the objections to the traditional Christian position. On the other hand, those seeking to revise the church's teaching need to do so in a way that goes beyond pragmatic adaptation to social change or an appeal to experience. They have to offer a theologically robust and biblically based vision that addresses the concerns of those committed to traditional teaching and not dismiss them as homophobic or fundamentalist.

In short, we are wrestling with this question because there is a serious task of corporate ecclesial discernment required. In the past, the issue of homosexuality generally lacked a public face and so was usually dealt with privately and within a general consensus that homosexuality was wrong. That began to change in the 1960s and our social reality is now one of a very public and political framing of the questions and a new general consensus – if there is one – which has moved to accepting homosexuality. We need, therefore, to find for this new situation a public Christian discourse which can interpret same sex attraction, offer pastoral guidance and order the public life of the church as expressed in its liturgies and ordination requirements. One challenge is that there is 'a conversation waiting to begin'.[19] It is a conversation which wider society – by handling the questions through such categories as 'rights', 'freedom' and 'equality' and by means of political lobbying – has largely failed to have. In engaging this conversation – both internally and missionally – the church needs to be conscious of its new context but it must also refuse to lose its nerve. We must, in other words, wrestle with the issues theologically, guided by the authority of Scripture and respectful of Christian tradition, so that we offer a vision of human flourishing – prophetic and so possibly counter-cultural – that, through being faithful to Christ and his gospel, offers hope and life.

---

18 For a discussion of some of the pastoral issues see Andrew Goddard and Glynn Harrison, *Unwanted Same-Sex Attraction: Issues of Pastoral and Counselling Support*. London 2011 Christian Medical Fellowship.

19 Oliver O'Donovan, *A Conversation Waiting to Begin: The churches and the gay controversy* (SCM, 2009). The text of this originated in online articles and is fully available at http://www.fulcrum-anglican.org.uk/page.cfm?ID=130.

Chapter 2

Same sex science: the social sciences cannot settle the moral status of homosexuality

Stanton L. Jones

Stanton L. Jones is provost and professor of psychology at Wheaton College. An expanded version of this essay is available at www.christianethics.org. We are grateful to the magazine First Things, published by the Institute on Religion and Public Life, for permission to reprint this article from the February 2012 edition (www.firstthings.com).

Many religious and social conservatives believe that homosexuality is a mental illness caused exclusively by psychological or spiritual factors and that all homosexual persons could change their orientation if they simply tried hard enough. This view is widely pilloried (and rightly so) as both wrong on the facts and harmful in effect. But few who attack it are willing to acknowledge that today a wholly different, far more influential, and no less harmful set of falsehoods – each attributed to the findings of 'science' – dominates the research literature and political discourse.

We are told that homosexual persons are just as psychologically healthy as heterosexuals, that sexual orientation is biologically determined at birth, that sexual orientation cannot be changed and that the attempt to change it is necessarily harmful, that homosexual relationships are equivalent to heterosexual ones in all important characteristics, and that personal identity is properly and legitimately constituted around sexual orientation. These claims are as misguided as the ridiculed beliefs of some social conservatives, as they spring from distorted or incomplete representations of the best findings from the science of same sex attraction.

Today we approach same sex attraction with views grounded in social and biological scientific perspectives that are only partially supported by empirical findings. Until the early decades of the twentieth century, moral disapproval of 'sodomy' guided public policy, but that grounding was displaced by a psychiatric model that viewed homosexuality as a mental illness. Once homosexuality came to be seen not as a sin but as a sickness, it became a simple matter for social science to overturn the opposition to homosexual acts. Alfred Kinsey's studies of male and female sexuality, published in 1948 and 1953, portrayed homosexual behaviour of various kinds as a normal and surprisingly common variant of human sexuality. In 1951, Clellan Ford and Frank Beach published *Patterns of Sexual Behavior*, their famous study of diverse forms of sexual behaviour, including same sex behaviour, across human cultures and many animal species. They suggested a widely shared 'basic capacity' for same sex behaviour.

But the decisive blow to the mental-illness construal of homosexuality came from a single study in 1957. Psychologist Evelyn Hooker published findings that convincingly demonstrated that homosexual persons do not necessarily manifest psychological maladjustment. On the basis of Hooker's work, and the findings of similar studies, in 1973 the American Psychiatric Association amended its designation of homosexual orientation as a mental illness.

To avoid misunderstanding the phenomenon of homosexuality, we must grapple with the Achilles heel of research into the homosexual condition: the issue of sample representativeness. To make general characterizations such as "homosexuals are as emotionally healthy as heterosexuals," scientists must have sampled representative members of the broader group. But representative samples of homosexual persons are difficult to gather, first, because homosexuality is a statistically uncommon phenomenon.

A recent research synthesis by Gary Gates of the Williams Institute, a think tank at UCLA Law School dedicated to sexual-orientation law and public policy, suggests that among adults in the United States, Canada, and Europe, 1.8 percent are bisexual men and women, 1.1 percent are gay men, and 0.6 percent are lesbians. This infrequency makes it hard to find participants for research studies, leading researchers to study easy-to-access groups of persons (such as visible participants in advocacy groups) who may not be representative of the broader homosexual population. Add to this the difficulty of defining homosexuality, of establishing boundaries of what constitutes homosexuality (with individuals coming in and out of the closet, and also shifting in their experience of same sex identity and attraction), and of the shifting perceptions of the social desirability of embracing the identity label of gay or lesbian, and the difficulty of knowing when one is studying a truly representative sample of homosexual persons becomes clear.

With this caution in mind, we can now approach the broad beliefs shaping our culture. First, are homosexual persons as psychologically healthy as heterosexuals? Many believe so, and public representations of the scientific evidence support the belief. For instance, in 1986, in its *amicus curiae* brief for the Supreme Court case Bowers v. Hardwick, the American Psychological Association (APA) stated, erroneously, that "extensive psychological research conducted over almost three decades has conclusively established that homosexuality is not related to psychological adjustment or maladjustment." Today, twenty-five years later, the association's website still declares, after decades of research to the contrary, that "being gay is just as healthy as being straight."

Evelyn Hooker, in her 1957 study, was careful to reject only the claim that homosexuality is always pathological. She never made the logically distinct assertion that homosexual persons on average are just as psychologically healthy as heterosexuals. It is well that she did not, because the consistent findings of the best, most representative research suggest the contrary, despite a few scattered compatible findings from smaller studies of less representative samples. One of the most exhaustive studies ever conducted, published in 2001 in the American Journal of Public Health and directed by researchers from Harvard Medical School, concludes that "homosexual orientation . . . is associated with a general elevation of risk for anxiety, mood, and substance-use disorders and for suicidal thoughts and plans." Other and more recent studies have found similar correlations, including studies from the Netherlands, one of the most gay-affirming social contexts in the world. Depression and substance abuse are found to be on average 20 to 30 percent more prevalent among homosexual persons. Teens manifesting same sex attraction report suicidal thoughts and attempts at double to triple the rate of other teens. Similar indicators of diminished physical health emerge in this literature.

Social stigma is the popular explanation, both in scientific studies and in mass media, for heightened psychological distress among homosexuals. The possibility that the orientation and all it entails cuts against a fundamental, gender-based given of the human condition, thus creating distress, is not raised. The correlation between social stigma and psychological problem is real, but the empirical case for the first causing the second has yet to be made. This has not stopped advocates, however, from battling alleged stigma by increasingly framing all 'anti-gay sentiment' as a form of prejudice. This has led to the creation of new terminology: No matter how congruent with the scientific evidence, any belief that homosexuality is not a normal and positive variant of human sexuality is a manifestation of 'homophobia' and 'heterosexism', a symptom of destructive "master narratives of normativity" (of which 'heteronormativity' is a part).

Is homosexuality biologically determined at birth? A pervasive understanding is settling into Western culture that homosexual orientation, indeed any and all sexual orientations, has been proven by science to be a given of the human person and rooted in biology. Why does this falsehood – that homosexuality has been proven to have an exclusively biological cause – matter? It is the basis for asserting that sexual orientation is the same sort of characteristic as race or skin color, which has become, for instance, the foundational metaphor in the push for the right to marry someone of the same sex.

One reason it is generally believed that homosexuality is conclusively caused by biological factors is the supposed lack of a credible alternative. Two astonishing examples: The 2009 APA task force report on Sexual Orientation Change Efforts (SOCE), Appropriate Therapeutic Responses to Sexual Orientation, presents over and over as established 'scientific fact' that "no empirical studies or peer-reviewed research supports theories attributing same sex sexual orientation to family dysfunction or trauma." Neuroscientist Simon LeVay, author of a major book on the science of same sex attraction, in considering environmental and psychological factors influencing sexual orientation concludes that "there is no actual evidence to support any of those ideas."

There are, in fact, many such studies and a lot of actual evidence. Recent studies show that familial, cultural, and other environmental factors contribute to same sex attraction. Broken families, absent fathers, older mothers, and being born and living in urban settings all are associated with homosexual experience or attraction. Even that most despised of hypothesized causal contributors, childhood sexual abuse, has recently received significant empirical validation as a partial contributor from a sophisticated thirty-year longitudinal study published in the Archives of Sexual Behaviour. Of course, these variables at most partially determine later homosexual experience, and most children who experienced any or all of these still grow up heterosexual, but the effects are nonetheless real.

To say that psychological and environmental variables play a part in causation does not mean that biology does not, rather just not to the extent that many gay-affirming scholars claim. The two most influential contemporary theories of biological causation focus respectively on fraternal birth order and genetics; each has some level of support, but for modest-sized causal effects at best.

The fraternal birth order theory hypothesizes that some mothers develop something akin to an allergic reaction to their body's encounter with the male hormones generated by their male fetus, and hence manifest a hormonal resistance against the masculinization process in the developing male fetus. Males who were the product of such wombs are incompletely masculinized. And it is posited that the more male children such mothers bear, the more profound their reactions and the greater the likelihood that the later-born sons will be homosexual. In short, the more older brothers, the more likely the younger brothers are to be homosexual. The actual evidence such an immunological reaction exists is minimal apart from the raw claim that gay men tend to have disproportionate numbers of older brothers. But do they?

Early studies claiming to demonstrate a disproportionate presence of older brothers among homosexual men were based upon advertisement-recruited, volunteer samples vulnerable to volunteer bias. As Anthony Bogaert and Ray Blanchard, the major proponents of this theory, multiplied their reports of this phenomenon, their larger and larger samples were created by folding new volunteer samples into a common pool with their original samples, thus creating larger and larger non-representative samples.

Recently, Bogaert analyzed two nationally representative samples and found only an exceptionally weak older-brother effect, but only for same sex attraction, not for same sex behaviour. Then he analyzed an independent and truly representative sample eight times the size of his previous studies, finding no older-brother effect. At roughly the same time, a study of two million Danes and another of 10,000 American teenagers both failed to find the effect. It is thus mystifying why many gay-affirming researchers still confidently assert, like Simon LeVay, "that gay men do have significantly more older brothers, on average, than straight men."

If there is a genetic component to sexual orientation, then the more two people share their genetic endowment, the more likely they are to share the same sexual orientation. The then-moribund genetic theory received a huge boost from J. Michael Bailey's famous 1991 study that recruited subjects through advertisements and posted announcements throughout Chicago's gay community. Bailey examined three groups in descending order of genetic similarity: genetically identical twins, fraternal twins and non-twin brothers who are essentially 50 percent identical, and adopted siblings who have no particular genetic similarity. Bailey reported a widely misinterpreted 52 percent 'concordance' for identical male twins, compared with 22 percent for fraternal twins, 9 percent for non-twin brothers, and 11 percent for adopted brothers. The results generated wide and simplistic media coverage. It had been settled, the media suggested: sexual orientation was determined by one's genes. What was not widely understood was that only in 14 of the 41 identical-twin pairs did the two twin brothers match for sexual orientation; in the remaining 27 sets the identical twin brothers did not match.

But the deeper problem with the study was again one of sample representativeness. What if individuals were more likely to volunteer for the study if they shared same sex attraction with a sibling, and less likely to do so if they didn't? Using a more representative sample from the Australian Twin Registry, Bailey in 2000 saw the concordance for identical male twins fall from 52 to a mere 20 percent, and the matching for homosexual orientation between each pair of identical male twins fell to a mere 3 out of 27 pairs (11.1 percent). The findings of Bailey's new study failed to reach statistical significance. The ballyhooed genetic effect had shrunk considerably, a fact that failed, of course, to capture any media attention and is often left out of the textbook treatments of the subject. In 2010, an impressive and much larger study utilizing the Swedish Twin Registry produced almost identical results: Among the 71 pairs of identical male twins of whom at least one twin was gay, in only seven cases (9.8 percent) was the second twin also gay, yet another statistically insignificant result.

But the search for a genetic mechanism continues, using a more statistically powerful calculation, that of heritability, which estimates how much of the variability of sexual orientation may be attributed to genetic influences. The higher this estimate, the greater the suggested genetic contribution. The best recent studies consistently generate heritability estimates for male homosexuality of 30 to 50 percent, a statistically significant finding that sounds quite powerful. Heritability estimates for female homosexuality are slightly less than for males, but still statistically significant. But what do heritability estimates of 30 to 50 percent mean?

Behaviour genetics has established heritability estimates for a vast array of psychological traits. Quite a number of traits demonstrate much higher heritability than does homosexual orientation. Those with roughly similar heritability include social attitudes such as right-wing authoritarianism, inclination to religiosity, and church attendance. One study by a giant of behavioural genetics, Robert Plomin, found that the proclivity to watch television has an average heritability estimate of 45 percent, on par with the typical estimate for the heritability of male homosexuality.

Contrary to the assumptions of many social conservatives, biology does appear to play a modest part in determining sexual orientation. Contrary to the assumptions of many social progressives, psychological and environmental variables also appear to play at least a modest part in determining sexual orientation. In contrast to the hubris of those prone to making emphatic pronouncements, what we do not yet know about the causation of sexual orientation dwarfs the bit that we are beginning to know. And the fact that causation is indubitably a complex and mysterious by-product of the interaction of biological and psychological variables confounds the assertion that sexual orientation is just like skin colour, determined at birth or even conception. And contrary to the suggestions of some, the involvement of some biological influence does not prove that change in sexual orientation is impossible. One of our foremost behaviour genetics experts, Thomas Bouchard, has argued forcefully that "one of the most unfortunate misinterpretations of the heritability coefficient is that it provides an index of trait malleability (i.e., the higher the heritability the less modifiable the trait is through environmental intervention)."

If some measure of heritability does not establish that the trait is not modifiable, what does the direct evidence show about change? Attorney General Eric Holder, explaining the Obama administration's decision not to defend the Defense of Marriage Act, repeatedly cited the 'immutability' of sexual orientation: "A growing scientific consensus accepts that sexual orientation is a characteristic that is immutable." The recent APA *amicus* brief for the Proposition 8 case is also forceful on the issue of change; contrary to claims that change is possible, they say, "research suggests the opposite".

Has science established that sexual orientation cannot change? Dozens of scholarly papers appeared in journals from the 1940s to the early 1970s reporting that a substantial portion of those wanting to change homosexual orientation did change to some degree. But rarely since 1980 has a professional publication reported such results. Did science change direction and prove change impossible? Not quite.

Certainly, there has been lately less research of late studying the possibility of change. The removal in 1973 of homosexuality from the Diagnostic and Statistical Manual of Mental Disorders both changed the political environment in the mental-health professions and undermined grant funding for research on this subject. Many academics no longer had any motivation to study this phenomenon and considerable political reasons not to do so. Further, prior published research is commonly dismissed as inadequate. The APA's website stated for many years that claims that homosexual orientation can change "are poorly documented. For example, treatment outcome is not followed and reported over time as would be the standard to test the validity of any mental health intervention."

Such criticism took its most comprehensive form in the report of the 2009 APA task force studying SOCE (sexual orientation change efforts). These scholars set extraordinary standards of methodological rigour for what they regarded as a reasonable scientific study of the possibility of sexual orientation change, a move that resulted in the classification of only six studies out of dozens as meriting close examination. These studies were, in turn, dismissed for a variety of reasons, leaving the panel with no credible findings, by their standards, documenting the efficacy of SOCE. After dismissing SOCE for its lack of empirical validation, the panel then recommended gay-affirming therapy while explicitly acknowledging that it lacked the very type of empirical validation required of SOCE.

In the absence of evidence, it would be proper scientific procedure to acknowledge one's ignorance. The members of the APA task force claim that their review has established that "enduring change to an individual's sexual orientation is uncommon" and "that it is unlikely that individuals will be able to reduce same sex attractions or increase other-sex sexual attractions through SOCE." But even more forceful claims have been made. The Public Affairs website of the APA for many years stated, "Can therapy change sexual orientation? No" and insisted that homosexuality "is not changeable". But has science proven this? Not at all; rather, skeptical reviewers have dismissed evidence of the possibility of change for some on the basis of such studies being methodologically inadequate by *post hoc* and artificially stringent standards.

Is sexual orientation immutable? With Mark Yarhouse of Regent University, I recently studied people seeking to change their sexual orientation. We assessed the sexual orientations and psychological distress levels of 98 individuals (72 men, 26 women) trying to change their sexual orientation through ministries organized under Exodus International, beginning early in the process and following them over six to seven years with five additional, independent assessments. Our original round of findings was published in a book titled Ex-Gays?; the latest round, in the Journal of Sex and Marital Therapy.

Of the 61 subjects who completed the study, 23 percent reported success in the form of 'conversion' to heterosexual orientation and functioning, while 30 percent reported they were able to live chastely and had disidentified themselves from homosexual orientation. On the other hand, 20 percent reported giving up and fully embracing homosexual identity, and the remaining 27 percent continued the process of attempted change with limited and unsatisfactory success. On average, statistically significant decreases in homosexual orientation were reported across the entire sample, while a smaller but still significant increase of heterosexual attraction was reported. The attempt to change orientation was not found to lead to increases in psychological distress on average; indeed, the study found several small significant improvements in psychological distress associated with the interventions. And lest we fall prey to the same mistakes we have been criticizing in others, we have said repeatedly that because our sample was not demonstrably representative of those seeking change among all religious homosexuals, these are likely optimistic outcome estimates.

I conclude that homosexual orientation is, contrary to the supposed consensus, sometimes mutable. 'Homosexuality' is a multifaceted phenomenon; there are likely many homosexualities, with some perhaps more malleable than others. Not all interventions are the same; not all practitioners are equally skilled. Perhaps most important, those seeking change vary considerably in their intensity of motivation, in their resourcefulness, and in the context in which they try to change. Most of those seeking change and most of those who actually attain some level of change are highly religiously committed, and these individuals who believe in a God who intervenes in their lives are embedded in communities of care and are motivated by their core understanding of who they are as a person before God. It is a wonder that anyone without such resources successfully obtains sexual orientation change.

Are homosexual relationships equivalent to heterosexual ones? In his ruling overturning Proposition 8, Judge Vaughn Walker cited UCLA psychologist Letitia Peplau's testimony that "despite stereotypes suggesting gays and lesbians are unable to form stable relationships, same sex couples are in fact indistinguishable from opposite-sex couples in terms of relationship quality and stability." The APA's brief for this case similarly claimed that "empirical research demonstrates that the psychological and social aspects of committed relationships between same sex partners closely resemble those of heterosexual partnerships." That brief relies upon the 2007 overview of research on same sex relationships by Peplau and A.W. Fingerhut.

Here again we return to the issue of sample representativeness, which Peplau and Fingerhut handle with unfortunate evasiveness. They typically launch into discussions about various characteristics of homosexual couples without ever clearly stating that the studies they cite do not examine representative samples. They offer only intriguing hints that the studies on which they rely may be unrepresentative and hence potentially biased. They also raise in passing the provocative possibility that homosexual couples may bias their self-reports to look good.

Even so, intriguing hints of differences, of 'non-equivalency' between heterosexual and homosexual couples, emerge from Peplau and Fingerhut's survey. They mention one large study that found that 28 percent of lesbians had had sex outside their primary relationship – comparable to the 21 percent of women in relationships with men and 26 percent of men in relationships with women. By contrast, 82 percent of gay men had had sex with someone other than their main partner. However one construes such a striking difference in sexual monogamy, whether as a trivial stylistic difference or as indicative of something fundamental and pervasive, such a finding seriously challenges the equivalency hypothesis.

Stability is a relational characteristic of direct relevance to the types of functional concerns intrinsic, for instance, to evaluation for adoption fitness. How does equivalence look in this area? Peplau and Fingerhut cite one study that found that over a five-year period, 7 percent of married heterosexual couples broke up, compared with 14 percent of cohabiting male couples and 16 percent of cohabiting lesbian couples. They also summarize, without mentioning specific numbers, a more representative study from Norway and Sweden, which have sanctioned same sex partnerships since the 1990s, reporting "that the rate of dissolution within five years of entering a legal union is higher among same sex partnerships than among heterosexual marriages, with lesbian couples having the highest rates of dissolution." Their rendering underplays the magnitude of the actual findings, which was that gay male relationships are 50 percent more likely to break up than heterosexual marriages, while lesbian relationships are 167 percent more likely to break up than heterosexual marriages. Odd that they would not mention these actual numbers.

One common obfuscation of such matters can be illustrated through the sensitive issue of rates of homosexual attraction among children raised in homosexual households. Summarizing this research, Gregory Herek, a psychologist who specializes in the study of homosexuality, wrote that "the vast majority of those children eventually grow up to be heterosexual." It appears he is right, technically. Terms such as "a vast majority" are often used in this literature to obscure probabilistic trends in the data. The small bit of research that exists suggests increased rates of same sex orientation among the children of such couples; my informal synthesis would be that gay parenting approximately triples or quadruples the rate of same sex attraction. It may be technically true that "the vast majority of these children eventually grow up to be heterosexual", but only because if being raised by same sex parents increases the occurrence of same sex attraction from 2 percent to 8 percent, 92 percent are still heterosexual. But a fourfold increase is still a sizable effect statistically.

Has empirical science established homosexual identity as positive and legitimate? Some would claim so. University of California psychologists Phillip Hammack and Eric Windell argue that a dramatic shift has "repositioned the scientific narrative of homosexuality from sickness to species" and homosexuality is to be affirmed as "a legitimate minority identity akin to race and ethnicity". The APA task force on SOCE declared in 2009, "Same sex sexual attractions, behaviour, and orientations per se are normal and positive variants of human sexuality."

Declarations that homosexuality is "normal," "positive," and "legitimate" would seem be the product of value judgments rather than objective science. The APA's Proposition 8 brief argues that sexual orientation "encompasses an individual's sense of personal and social identity based on those attractions, behaviours expressing them, and membership in a community of others who share them." There indeed are persons who organize their lives around their sexual orientation. But to claim for all human persons that "sexual orientation encompasses an individual's sense of personal and social identity" is remarkable both conceptually and scientifically. I cannot conceive of data comprehensive enough to support this claim. And how does science establish that such a grounding of human identity is "positive"?

Science may be able to contribute valuable evidence about the association of such identities with certain measurable functional realities of life, such as whether such individuals experience heightened levels of emotional distress, report levels of self-esteem comparable to those of others, and so forth. But how did science become the arbiter of what is positive? Such a thing can happen, precisely as Hammack and Windell suggest, through a paradigm shift within the discipline, a decision of practising psychologists to embrace the "minority narrative of homosexuality". But can empirical science establish homosexual orientation as "a legitimate minority identity" or sexual orientation as a fundamental for constituting the self? I hardly see how.

The APA SOCE task force, and the gay-affirming psychological mainstream it represents, describes gay-affirming therapy as pursuing 'congruence' between identity and sexual orientation. It seems to take this as a self-evident good. But the task force also seems to recognize that an affirmation of same sex attraction goes beyond the traditional competence of science. Reflecting on the clash of scientific and religious perspectives on this point, they note that "some religions give priority to telic congruence" while, in contrast, "affirmative and multicultural models of LGB psychology give priority to organismic congruence." In a moment of exceptional clarity, the task force put its finger on a core issue: Gay-affirming psychologies necessarily embody extra-scientific moral and ethical deliberations that raise the potential of conflict with religious beliefs, precisely because the very act of giving priority to organismic congruence is a religious and ethical choice.

As the late theologian Don Browning noted, psychology "cannot avoid a metaphysical and ethical horizon". Meaningful consideration of the nature of personhood always involves moving beyond the analysis of human life to the broader valuation of this or that characteristic, this or that phenomenon, this or that outcome. The social sciences do not contain within themselves adequate resources to adjudicate among conflicting ways of understanding the good. Individual scientists, stepping beyond their professional bounds, may declare homosexual orientation positive, normal, and legitimate, but such science cannot make this judgment. Such judgments are the domain of religion, theology, and philosophy. The twin claims that science conclusively establishes that sexual orientation grounds human identity and that psychology as a science establishes the legitimacy of such a claim are too far a reach.

So where does this leave us? We know much more now than we did ten and thirty years ago about the emotional well-being of homosexual persons, the complicated interaction of nature and nurture in the causation of sexual orientation, of the complicated and difficult possibilities of sexual-orientation malleability, of the functional and descriptive characteristics manifest in same sex partnerships, and of the contours of the psychological identities of homosexual persons. The contributions of science to this area, however, remain sketchy, limited, and puzzling. It is remarkable how little scientific humility is in evidence given the primitive nature of our knowledge.

Nevertheless, our culture is polarized between those relentlessly advancing the full acceptance and normalization of homosexuality, indeed of all sexual variations, and those resisting those moves. As religious believers, we must confess our own culpability in creating the mess we are in.

We were complicit, even if ignorantly and passively so, in the cultural embrace of the disease conceptualization of homosexuality. We off-loaded responsibility for the articulation of a thoughtful, caring, theologically rich, and pastorally sensitive understanding of sexual brokenness grounded in our various religious traditions by conceptualizing homosexuality as a disease, and so we were unprepared for the vacuum created by that explanation's timely demise. The best ecclesiastical, professional, legal, and social policy will be founded not on falsehoods or grotesque and indefensible simplifications but on a clearheaded grasp of reality in all its complexities, as well as on a humble recognition of all that we do not know.

Chapter 3

Facts and figures

David J Randall

David Randall was parish minister in Macduff from 1971–2010, and convened the Church of Scotland Apologetics Committee from 1993–97, producing the 'What Can I Say' leaflet which has just been re-published by the Mission and Discipleship Council.

This chapter will be mainly concerned with the statistical evidence regarding the stability (or instability) of non-marital sexual relationships – mainly homosexual although this chapter will refer to unmarried heterosexual partnerships also.

A suitable starting-point comes from an article in the Gay Times in the year 2000:

> The fundamental advantage gay relationships have over marriage is that we can tailor them precisely to our requirements. We can make them up as we go along, change with the circumstances and go with the flow. We don't have to promise sexual exclusivity or to share our worldly goods if we don't want to.[1]

Many cohabiting couples, however, would reject such a casual attitude and current debate centres around the issue of committed relationships. Some are not content with civil partnership, and particularly in the case of people in active homosexual relationships (in society and now also within the church) strongly emphasise their desire for recognition of the permanent commitment of two same-gender people to each other and their right to 'marry' if they so choose.

Yet another writer – who has been described as "one of the leading gay intellectuals in the West" and whose book *Virtually Normal* has been described as "the most articulate case for gay marriage" – argues

---

1   Terry Sanderson; quoted in The Guardian, 2 September 2000.

that homosexual partnerships have many advantages over heterosexual marriage. He claims, "There is more likely to be greater understanding of the need for extramarital outlets between two men than between a man and a woman . . . Their failures entail fewer consequences for others".[2] It was researchers sympathetic to homosexual rights who reported that most homosexual men have several partners – on average seven per year[3] – and against this background we will consider the evidence regarding the duration of such relationships.

Our thesis will be that such relationships are intrinsically insecure and that marriage between one man and one woman is not only the divine design for human relationships but also the proven foundation for the good of individuals, the protection of children and societal well-being. It accords with what God has revealed and it has stood the test of time. Other chapters in this volume will deal specifically with the first (what God has revealed); this chapter is concerned with the evidence for the second – that marriage is God's plan "for the welfare of human society, which can be strong and happy only where the marriage bond is held in honour".[4] The Bible gives us the Maker's instructions for our lives and it is folly to ignore them. Just as a railway track is extremely restrictive and yet it is that track that enables a train to be a train, so running along God's guidelines is the way to human fulfilment.[5]

The meaning of marriage

Most people marry and most marriages last for life. A government survey found that 80% of young people expect to marry sooner or later[6] and it seems that the answer to Groucho Marx's famous quip about marriage being a-wonderful-institution-but-who-wants-to-live-in-an-institution is that most people do!

---

2   Andrew Sullivan, *Virtually Normal* (Picador, 1996), 202; quoted in *'Gay Marriage' in all but name,* The Christian Institute, 2004, 23.

3   *The Sexual Lifestyles of Gay and Bisexual Men in England and Wales* (HMSO, 1992), 19

4   From the marriage service in the *Book of Common Order* of the Church of Scotland (OUP, 1965), 155.

5   Cf. John 8:32.

6   *Supporting Families – A Consultation Document* (Home Office Stationery Office, 1998), 4. A survey, Young People's Lives in Britain Today (London: The Opinion Research Business, 2000), found that only 4% agreed with the statement, "Marriage is old-fashioned and no longer relevant" and 89% said that they would like to get married at some time in the future.

But there are enormous pressures to undermine or re-define marriage in our contemporary world. At the time of writing, the Scottish Government has issued a consultation document on the subject, asking for people's view on whether marriage should be re-defined. The implication that marriage is open for such redefinition is a striking instance of human arrogance. Governments can do many things, but they cannot change the meaning of words. The real world is not the world of Humpty Dumpty, with his assertion that when he used a word it meant whatever he chose it to mean, neither more nor less.[7] When Alice says, "The question is whether you can make words mean so many different things", Humpty Dumpty's answer is, "The question is, which is to be master – that's all"![8]

Again, a government might argue till it is blue in the face that objects dropped from a height should no longer fall to the ground. It might initiate a consultation on the matter and even pass legislation that 'redefined' the law of gravity, but everybody knows that such action would make no difference to anything.

Marriage – as the committed relationship of two people of opposite gender in a permanent and exclusive relationship – is an objective reality which exists independently of what any government may make of it. The state did not invent marriage and it is not in the state's provenance to alter or 'redefine' it. Common sense tells us that 'same sex marriage' is as meaningful as 'square circle'. Such common sense, along with a bit of basic biology, confirms what both nature and Scripture teach: that from the beginning[9] God's plan is that marriage is about a man and a woman leaving their own families to become a new family. The fact that many marriages fail, even with all the heart-ache and distress caused thereby, does not negate this basic pattern any more than the fact that some people are tone-deaf calls in question the possibility and beauty of music.

Statistics

Exaggerated figures are sometimes quoted about the percentage of people who are homosexuals. It is sometimes claimed that up to 10% of people have a homosexual orientation. For example, in October 2011, Education Scotland (formerly Learning and Teaching Scotland) withdrew a teaching resource from its website following representations made by

---

7   L.Carroll, *Through the Looking Glass* (Puffin, 1984), 100.

8   *Ibid.*

9   Cf. Matthew 19:4.

CARE for Scotland.[10] The resource, *Dealing with Homophobia*, which was funded by the Scottish Government's Education Department with support from the Equality and Human Rights Commission, claimed that there could be up to 100 lesbian, homosexual, bisexual or transgender pupils at the average 1000-pupil Scottish secondary school. It asserted that the views of any parents who raised objections to the (pro-homosexual) material should be disregarded. The material was withdrawn after organisations including CARE protested about its implication that people who disapprove of homosexual practice are 'homophobes'.

Unfortunately the results of the 2011 Census are not likely to be available until the latter part of 2012, but the Office of National Statistics conducted a Household Survey in 2011 for which the base was 420,000 people. In terms of size, this is second only to the National Census.[11] It found that 1.5% of adults aged 16 and over identified themselves as homosexual or bisexual. This represents a small increase from 2010, but it still indicates that many claims made by the homosexual lobby are vastly exaggerated. An earlier British survey revealed that 1% of men and fewer than 0.5% of women have had any kind of homosexual experience.[12]

Clearly there should be no antipathy (or 'homophobia', although the word is an unfortunate misnomer) toward any person who, for whatever reason, is homosexually inclined, but it may also be stated that these figures lead us to the conclusion that the percentage of homosexual people in public life and the media is unrepresentative and that the prevalence of homosexual themes in broadcast material, especially drama, is unwarranted. One may go further and express concern about the level of opprobrium (not to say intolerance) heaped on Christians today as a result of the belligerence of political correctness. Melanie Phillips has recognised

---

10 http://www.care.org.uk/news/impact-direct/teaching-resource-which-implies-that-christians-are-homophobic-is-withdrawn-following-cares-intervention

11 The extensiveness of this survey may be illustrated by contrast with a survey (on Scottish Independence) which was reported in the Scotsman on 17 October 2011. It was a front-page story and took up two full inside pages, yet it described the poll as a UK-wide one of only 2000 people. A well-publicised report in Science magazine in 1991 claimed to have found physiological differences in the brains of homosexual men and those of heterosexuals. Aside from other factors about the claim, it was based on a sample of 35! (Article by Simon Levay, cited in Alex Tylee, *Walking with Gay Friends*, IVP 2007, 47)

12 Quoted by CARE from: K.Wellings, J.Field, A.M.Johnston & J.Wadsworth, *Sexual Behaviour in Britain: The National Survey of Sexual Attitudes and Lifestyles* (Penguin Books, 1994), 203-21.

this. Before giving examples such as the forced resignation of a registrar who refused to officiate at a same sex civil partnership ceremony and the closure of adoption agencies which refuse to place children with homosexual couples, she writes:

> In Britain, the anti-discrimination orthodoxy has led to a systematic campaign against Christians – particularly over the issue of homosexuality, the key area where Christians run up against social libertarianism in the public square. Freedom of conscience, the cardinal tenet of a liberal society, has been swept aside in the cause of gay rights. While true prejudice against homosexuals or anyone else is reprehensible, 'prejudice' has been redefined to include the expression of normative values.[13]

Civil partnership

The Scottish Government's Consultation Paper on same sex 'marriage' states that in 2010 only 465 civil partnerships (which extend the same legal benefits as marriage does) were registered in Scotland (a 6.6% drop from the previous year). The fact that so few have taken up this option does not speak highly of the much-vaunted degree of commitment to each other of homosexual or lesbian people.

The Office for National Statistics[14] reports that in the UK as a whole 6,385 civil partnerships were registered in 2010 (for the first time the majority were female). The figures are as follows:

	UK	Scotland	England	Wales	N.Ireland
2005 (Dec. only)	1,953	84	1,790	67	12
2006	16,106	1,047	14,383	560	116
2007	8,728	688	7,635	294	111
2008	7,169	525	6,276	282	86
2009	6,281	498	5,443	244	96
2010	6,385	465	5,536	268	116

The table below gives the statistics about the dissolution of civil partnerships. To obtain such, a couple (who may already have been cohabiting for some time) must have been in a registered civil partnership for at least

---

13 Melanie Phillips, *The World Turned Upside Down* (Encounter, 2010), 101.

14 The following statistics from: Office for National Statistics, Statistics Bulletin: Civil Partnerships in the United Kingdom 2010, 7 July 2011.

twelve months). It shows that in 2010 there were 509 such dissolutions in the UK, representing an increase of 44% over the previous year. In the period since civil partnership was introduced in 1995, 1.6% of male and 3.3% of female partnerships have been dissolved.

	UK	Scotland	England & Wales	N.Ireland
2007	41	1	40	0
2008	180	14	166	0
2009	353	24	329	0
2010	509	34	472	3

Duration of homosexual relationships

When we go on to consider homosexual relationships more widely, there is little doubt that, even allowing for those relationships in which two males or two females commit exclusively to each other, there is generally a high degree of promiscuity among homosexual people.

After recognising that Scripture regards homosexual activity as sinful in itself, Dennis Wrigley and Linda Stalley go on to say, "The problem confronting society today is the phenomenal degree of promiscuity which is associated with homosexuality".[15] Thomas Schmidt, in his thoroughly-researched study (with a massive degree of citation), describes "fidelity even in the short term" as "foreign to the experience of most male homosexuals".[16]

An article in the Canadian Catholic Insight,[17] in a discussion of whether the ban there on homosexual people being blood donors should be lifted, gives the results of several surveys which reveal high rates of promiscuity among homosexual people and short duration of even committed relationships. It found that more than 75% of homosexual men admitted to having multiple partners. The article cites a study in Holland (where same sex 'marriage' was instituted in 2001) which revealed high rates of promiscuity even within 'committed' gay relationships which last, on average, a year and a half. Homosexual men had an average of eight partners a year outside of their supposedly 'committed'

---

15 In Healing and Wholeness: chapter 12 of *God, Family & Sexuality*, ed. D.W. Torrance (Handsel, 1997), 194.

16 Thomas E.Schmidt, *Straight & Narrow?* (IVP, 1995), 58.

17 Information in this section from: http://catholicinsight.com/online/political/homosexuality/article_1000.shtml

relationships.[18] 'Gay' men had sex with someone other than their primary partner in 66% of relationships within the first year, rising to 90% of relationships after five years.[19] The article includes a quotation which matches the words with which we introduced this chapter – the recognition of many homosexual writers that "gay liberation was founded . . . on a sexual brotherhood of promiscuity."[20]

The American Family Research Council[21] quotes the figure given above of 1½ years as the average duration of homosexual relationships and contrasts this with surveys of marital relationships in answer to the claim that high divorce rates indicate that heterosexual couples fare little better than homosexual ones. It refers to a survey of over 2000 people which revealed that 77% of married men and 88% of married women had remained faithful to their spouse.

It may be relevant also to consider the question of life expectancy for people who engage in homosexual practices. The authors of an article which appeared in the International Journal of Epidemiology[22] expressed concern that their findings (from a study in Vancouver in the late 1980s and early 1990s) were being 'used' by so-called homophobic groups in an attempt to restrict "the human rights of gays and bisexuals rather than promoting their health and well-being". Nonetheless, their findings were that life expectancy at age 20 for gay and bisexual men is 8 to 21 years less than for males generally, and that only about half of these 20-year-olds would reach their 65th birthday. The article also suggests that if this analysis were repeated now, life expectancy for homosexual and bisexual men would be greatly improved since deaths from HIV infection have decreased since 1996, but it remains true that there are major health risks for people who engage in homosexual activity (see Appendix 3).

It is surely obvious that no-one should take any kind of pleasure in such facts,[23] but on the other hand neither should such facts be ignored. It

---

18 M.Xiridou, *et al.*, "The contribution of steady and casual partnerships to the incidence of HIV infection among homosexual men in Amsterdam" (AIDScience, 2003); 17: 1029-38.

19 J.Harry, *Gay Couples* (Praeger, 1984).

20 G.Rotello, *Sexual Ecology* (Dutton, 1998).

21 www.frc.org/get.cfm?i=IS04C02&f=WA06L27

22 R.S.Hogg, S.A.Strathdee, K.J.P.Craib, M.V.O'Shaughnessy, J.S.G.Montaner, M.T.Schechter, "Modelling the impact of HIV disease on mortality in gay men", International Journal of Epidemiology 1997; 26(**3**): 657–61. *See* ije.oxfordjournals.org/content/30/6/1499.full

23 Cf. "The overwhelming evidence that people who engage in homosexual acts are harming themselves and others should cause great sorrow. No one should make it into a

is an interesting anomaly that our government has become unashamedly prescriptive in relation to cigarette smoking, banning it in public places and seeking to dissuade people from smoking (for their own good and for the good of society, while also presumably saving the NHS money) while at the same time making greater and greater concessions to those who engage in homosexual practices despite their obvious risks. Homosexual activists have disputed some of the statistics but, even making allowances for some variation, and while abjuring all pleasure in grim figures, it remains true that the practice of homosexuality is dangerous and life-shortening. It may be said to be another indication of why our Creator has proscribed homosexual practice and calls for faithful heterosexual relationships.

Duration of cohabiting heterosexual relationships

The instability which characterises homosexual relationships also characterises cohabiting heterosexual relationships. CARE's *For Better Or For Worse* is sub-titled, "Marriage and Cohabitation Compared". It highlights the fact that the trend toward cohabitation has been both rapid and extensive. Its rapidity is shown by the fact that in the early 1970s one in ten first marriages were preceded by cohabitation whereas in the early 1990s the figure was seven in ten.[24] A newspaper article in 1997 told of a prospective bride who was arranging her gift-list at a department store, and "the assistant filling out the form assumed bride and groom were at the same address. She was startled when I corrected her".[25]

Although 60% of cohabiting relationships go on to become marriages, the other 40% break down within ten years, and the average length of cohabitation in Scotland is three years.[26] And, although some cohabiting couples have exclusive and lasting relationships, cohabitation is, at root, an arrangement in which one or both parties are unwilling to make the publicly recognised commitment of marriage. A survey based on the 2001 census shows that one in three unmarried couples with children separate before the child's fifth birthday; this is four times the rate for married

---

bludgeon for culture-war speeches or public policy debates"; Thomas E.Schmidt, *[over]* *op. cit.,* 101 (Schmidt also makes the point that his devastating analysis of the health risks of homosexual behaviour is based not on anti-gay writings; "I document every point of fact only from scholarly, secular medical and social scientific publications").

24 Philippa Taylor, *For Better Or For Worse* (CARE, 1998), 6.

25 Victoria Coombe, *Daily Telegraph*, 14 August 1997.

26 Figures from *Scottish Social Attitudes Survey, 2000*; quoted in *Marriage: Worth Fighting For* (Christian Institute, 2005), 6.

parents. Of the 60% of families which remain whole until the children reach the age of 16, 97% are married and only 3% unmarried.[27]

Other figures suggest that at least half of couples who cohabit before marriage are likely to divorce within eight years of marriage.[28] This degree of what might be called uncommitment is illustrated in a survey which found that 41% of unmarried but cohabiting fathers were not opposed to marriage "if the 'right' woman came along"![29] A report in the Daily Mirror on 17th April 1989 quoted one young woman as saying, "It's a bit like membership of a club or gym. You try it out for a bit and, if it's a hit, you become a life member".[30]

The sub-title of *Marriage-Lite* is, "The Rise of Cohabitation and its Consequences", and the author's assertion is that "the most striking – and most often unappreciated – fact about cohabitation (apart from its growth) is that it tends to be short-lived".[31] It may be useful to list some of the points made by the author, Patricia Morgan, in her thorough and well documented study (it has 404 footnotes in its 90 pages):

> Overall, the median duration of a childless cohabitation is 19 months, before it leads to a birth, a marriage or terminates. By three years, three-quarters of women in the British Household Panel Study either (sic) had a birth, got married or dissolved the union. The median duration of all cohabitations involving never-married women is just under two years, and less than four per cent of cohabiting unions last ten years or more.[32]

> If we look only at cohabitations that do not convert to marriage, it seems that they are about four times more likely to break down than marriages.[33]

Only 8.7% of British women having their first child in cohabitation are still cohabiting ten years on.[34]

Cohabitations with children tend to break up at four- to five-fold the rate of marriages.[35]

27 From Bristol Community Family Trust: Daily Mail, 21 January 2010.
28 *Social Trends 24* (HMSO, 1994), 38.
29 Patricia Morgan, *Marriage-Lite* (Institute for the Study of Civil Society, 2000), 55.
30 G.Jenkins, *Cohabitation: a Biblical Perspective* (Grove Ethical Studies 84; 1993), 3.
31 Patricia Morgan, *op cit,,* 13.
32 *Ibid.*
33 *Ibid.*, 14.
34 *Ibid.*, 15.
35 *Ibid.*, 21.

In Britain 92% of marriages survive to five years after the birth of a child; those who cohabit and then marry show a 75% survival rate; those who only cohabit have a 48% survival rate.[36]

Other research, conducted in 1992, found that UK couples marrying in 1970-74 were 30% more likely to divorce after five years if they had cohabited; those marrying in 1975-79 were 40% more likely, and those marrying in 1980-84 were 50% more likely.[37] Another study says that 43% of cohabiting men in the UK reported being faithful to their partners in a five-year period, compared with nearly 90% of married men.[38]

Recent research by the Jubilee Centre gives much detailed information about the changes that have occurred in recent decades. Among the key findings listed at the outset of *Cohabitation: An Alternative to Marriage?*[39] are:

> Since the early 1980s cohabitation has been the most common form of first live-in relationship, although the proportion is levelling out at around the 85 per cent mark. However, marriage remains by far the most common family form of choice overall.

> More couples are cohabiting for longer, with the median duration rising from 2½ years to 3½ years between the 1980s and early 2000s. Mean lengths of cohabitation have roughly doubled over 40 years. However, fewer than 1-in-4 couples cohabit for more than 6½ years and even fewer couples now cohabit for very long periods of time before they separate or get married.

> Overall, the changing dynamic since the 1980s appears to be that more couples used to decide to marry and then moved in together, albeit before the wedding. Now, a greater proportion tend to postpone the decision to marry until after first living together.

> Those cohabitations that lead to marriage are associated with a significantly greater risk of divorce than for couples who have not first lived together. Those couples who have lived with each

---

36 *Ibid.*, 28.

37 J.Haskey, "Premarital Cohabitation and the probability of Subsequent Divorce", Office of Population Censuses and Surveys, Population Trends, Vol. 68, Summer 1992; quoted in Marriage-Lite, op. cit., 27.

38 K.Wellings *et al., op. cit.*, 116; source: P.Morgan, *op. cit.*, 40.

39 Dr John Hayward & Dr Guy Brandon, published by Jubilee Centre (Cambridge, 2011); freely available to download from www.jubilee-centre.org/uploaded/files/resource_417. pdf.

other are noticeably (around 15 per cent) more likely to divorce; couples who have previously lived with a different partner before getting married are around 45 per cent more likely to divorce.

Lessons from the past

So far we have been considering the present situation, but it is pertinent to think also about the past and the future? Are there lessons to be learned from the past and are there legitimate concerns for the future? So far as the past is concerned, the Christian Institute has pointed out that there are no precedents in recorded history where advanced civilisations have endured based on homosexual or temporary relationships.[40]

They cite the famous and exhaustive (with its 715 footnotes!) *Sex and Culture* by J.D. Unwin, who ". . . concluded, after studying eighty primitive and sixteen advanced societies, that cultural achievement and sexual licence were incompatible for more than one generation. Societies flourished where absolute monogamy had been practised".[41] Unwin came to the conclusion that it is sexual restraint rather than sexually promiscuous behaviour that holds the key to the healthiest development of a society. He described monogamous marriage as ". . . the institution under which alone in the past sexual opportunity has been reduced to a minimum, and which alone, therefore, has produced the greatest social energy and the highest human culture".[42]

In the records of history there is no example of a society displaying great energy for any appreciable period unless it has been absolutely monogamous. Moreover, I do not know of a case in which an absolutely monogamous society has failed to display great energy. In the past different societies have risen up in different parts of the earth, flourished greatly, and then declined. In every case the society started its historical career in a state of austere regulations, and relaxed after a less rigorous tradition had been inherited by a complete new generation.[43]

Unwin's conclusions are all the more remarkable when considered against the background of his own declared neutrality. In his preface he wrote,

---

40 *'Gay Marriage' in all but name, op. cit.*, 24.
41 *Ibid.*, 24.
42 Unwin, *Sex and Culture* (OUP, 1934), 379.
43 *Ibid.*, 369.

> I have not tried to prove a thesis, and have none to prove; I have merely conducted an inquiry. . . When I started these researches I sought to establish nothing, and had no idea of what the result would be . . . I was so far from desiring to illustrate a personal conviction that I always struggled against arriving at the conclusions which the evidence appeared to force upon me; and I continued to work, resisting every temptation to speak, until I was satisfied that I could find no exception to the apparent rules.[44]

This approach makes it all the more significant when he asserts that ". . . no change in the sexual opportunity of a society produces its full effect until the third generation. Thus when a society appears in the pages of history it is displaying an energy produced in the two previous generations".[45] If this be so, it raises grave concerns for the future of our society, but, before proceeding to that concern for the future, we may recall two particular previous attempts to alter social life in terms of a rejection of marriage and family.

Both the French revolutionaries and the Russian communists tried to abolish the concept of marriage, only to find that the destruction of family life destroyed society. "In short, the State's rejection of marriage as an absolute resulted in social harm to such an extent that the Russian revolutionary practice in creating 'new families' had to be completely reversed . . . and in 1794 the leaders of France set out '. . . to affirm the family as the bedrock of society'."[46] If people will not learn from the Bible, perhaps they need to learn from history.

Concern for the future

Turning now to the future, we should consider the potential of present trends to set the scene for disastrous developments in the future, and the implications of present-day deliberations for our children, grandchildren and generations to come.

In the year 2000, Home Secretary Jack Straw was quoted as describing marriage as "a union for the procreation of children, which by definition can only happen between a heterosexual couple. So I see no circumstances in which we would ever bring forward proposals for so-called gay marriages".[47]

---

44 *Ibid.*, vii.

45 *Ibid.*, 429.

46 *'Gay Marriage' in all but name, op. cit.*, 26, quoting L.Hunt, *The Family Romance of the French Revolution* (University of California Press, 1992) 160f.

47 The Times, 2 October 2000.

Yet, within a few years, we find that politicians of practically all political persuasions (including Mr Straw) are arguing in favour of just such a change. The present Deputy Prime Minister, Nick Clegg, said in February 2010, "I support gay marriage. Love is the same, straight or gay, so the civil institution should be the same, too".[48] The present Prime Minister, shortly before the last General Election, said publicly that he was "not planning" to change the law,[49] but at his party conference in October 2011 he publicly spoke in favour of same sex 'marriage', and has even pledged to slash aid to countries which are seen to have poor records on homosexual rights.[50] The leader of the Scottish National Party, First Minister Alex Salmond, has also expressed support for same sex 'marriage'.[51]

It is, however, a slippery slope, as we should recognise by now. Before the introduction of civil partnership, it was predicted that the legislation, far from satisfying gay rights groups, would lead to increased pressure for gay 'marriage'. An article in the Pink Paper on 19 March 2004[52] admitted that their agenda was to campaign for legislation to allow same sex couples to 'marry' and that civil partnership was a huge step towards achieving that. It was a Trojan Horse and other things are waiting to emerge from it.

We have referred to Mr Cameron's speech at the recent (2011) Conservative Party Conference. It was reported that he reminded conference that

> they had clapped him five years ago when he had said that 'it shouldn't matter whether commitment was between a man and a woman, a woman and a woman, or a man and a man'. So, he effectively commanded them, they should clap him now when he announced that he favoured legalising gay marriage. They clapped, obediently if not enthusiastically . . . Suppose that Mr Cameron had got up and told his conference, "it shouldn't matter whether the commitment is between a man and a woman, or a

---

48 Pink News, 16 February 2010, quoted in Christian Institute Update 13, Summer 2010, 23.

49 Pink News, 4 May 2010, quoted in Christian Institute Update 13, Summer 2010, 23.

50 http://www.dailymail.co.uk/news/article-2047254/David-Cameron-Foreign-aid-cut-anti-gay-countries.html The article mentions that the Government has already cut aid to Malawi by £19,000,000 after two homosexual men there were sentenced to 14 years hard labour. Protest may be appropriate about the way in which homosexual people are treated in some countries, but cutting aid to one of the world's poorest countries will presumably only result in greater hardship for many poor people.

51 Sunday Herald, 24 April 2011.

52 Quoted in 'Gay Marriage' in all but name, op. cit., 38.

man and four women", would he have been able to make his audience clap?[53]

That this is no extreme or absurd thought is shown by the fact that in Canada, where homosexual marriage has been legalised, there is a legal battle in one province where a man is pushing for the legalisation of polygamy. Once on the moral slippery slope it is difficult to stop. Such a recognition of polygamy (loving, committed, consensual relationships) may be further down the slippery slope, as also could be temporary marriages.

We are already on this slippery slope. We live in an unprecedentedly fast-changing society and even just ten or fifteen years ago it would have seemed outrageously alarmist to suggest that a time would come

- when a British government would effectively close adoption agencies rather than allow them to place children only with heterosexual couples,
- when television soap-operas would become vehicles of vigorous campaigning for the homosexual cause,
- when a former leader of a political party would be dismissed from a Citizens' Advice Bureau position because he called for a referendum on proposals for same sex 'marriage'.

This rapid social change has been illustrated in a recent book review which refers to ". . . the impact and progress of the homosexual lobby over 40 years, from the Stonewall riots in 1969 to President Obama's reception for 300 gay activists at the White House in 2009. It (the book being reviewed) tells the story of how the radical activism of the 1970s has become the reigning orthodoxy today".[54]

It probably seemed ridiculous to many when Aldous Huxley, in his *Brave New World* (1946) wrote, "In a few years, no doubt, marriage licences will be sold like dog licences, good for a period of twelve months, with no law against changing dogs or keeping more than one animal at a time".[55] Now we are told that in Mexico, two years after homosexual marriage

---

53 Charles Moore in The Telegraph, 7 October 2011.

54 Review of *A Queer Thing Happened to America* (EqualTime Books, 2011) in Family Education Trust Bulletin 146 (March 2012). The book by Michael L Brown is described as measured, well-reasoned, thoroughly-referenced and compassionate in tone, but the author had to launch his own imprint for it. Other publishers raised no objections to the accuracy or quality of the book; it was simply too hot to handle.

55 A.Huxley, Foreword (pages unnumbered) to 1946 edition of *Brave New World* (HarperCollins, London).

was legalised, it is being proposed that couples should have the option of obtaining a two-year marriage licence which would allow them to test married life and then either renew the licence or split without having to go through divorce proceedings.[56]

Again, why shouldn't the law be changed to allow loving sexual relationships with children? Such a possibility would presumably be viewed with horror by most people regardless of sexual orientation, but – once on the slippery slope, who knows where it will end? After all, liberalisers say, aren't love and tolerance the only things that count, and so long as the adult can give an assurance that the child is happy with the relationship, why should such a thing be prevented by law?

The well-being of children and of future generations is one of the major concerns in the consideration of the acceptability or otherwise of same sex 'marriage' (and of cohabiting heterosexual relationships). Children need a father and a mother, and the fact that this is sometimes unattainable (as a result of death, divorce or separation) does not negate the basic fact. Much discussion around these subjects gives insufficient attention to the children who suffer as a result of the widespread rejection of marriage according to God's design. One study showed that when parents separated, "children whose parents had not married were twice as likely to lose touch with their fathers as those with divorced fathers".[57]

Lord Sacks, the Chief Rabbi, has written forthrightly on the subject:

> Children have been the victims of our self-serving beliefs that you can have partnerships without the responsibility of marriage, children without the responsibility of parenthood, social order without the responsibility of citizenship, liberty without the responsibility of morality and self-esteem without the responsibility of hard work and achievement.[58]

And, as Rob Parsons points out, these children are not merely statistics; they are people. He tells the moving story of a grown woman who could recall her childhood conversation with her father in the hallway as he was leaving. He had another woman waiting for him and when the daughter asked, "Dad, will I ever see you again?" he tried to reassure her – "We'll work something out". "But what?" the daughter asked, "You'll be living away and I'll be here". She said, "Daddy, I don't want you to go" and he answered, "I

---

56 The Telegraph, 30 September 2011.

57 Philippa Taylor, *op. cit.*, 24.

58 The Times, 12 August 2011, cited in Family Education Trust Bulletin 145, Autumn 2011.

know, but I have to". In the end she remembers saying, "Well, daddy, I guess that's the way life goes sometimes", and the sad ending of the story is: "After her father walked out of the door, she never saw him again".[59]

Of course many single people make a wonderful job of bringing up their children, but at the same time there can be little doubt that children are the often-silent sufferers because of our society's rejection of God's family plan. In relation to adoption, it is regrettable, to say the least, that legislation now allows homosexual adoption, not only because so many homosexual relationships are short-lived but also because the lack of a male or a female role model is undesirable in itself.

In the present debates about whether marriage should be re-defined to allow same-sex "marriage", one of the concerns felt by many is that, if such a re-definition were to be enacted, it would mean that the new definition of marriage would be the one that schools would be expected to teach. It is well-known that some homosexual campaigning groups are promoting books (e.g. *Daddy's Roommate, King & King, Hello, Sailor*) which tell stories about men 'marrying' men, etc., and a head teacher has been quoted as saying, "We can't guarantee that when they leave that nurturing environment that their parents, their grandparents, their neighbours, are going to hold the same values as we do and that's why we need to make sure our children are resilient and proud and assertive so that their generation will actually change".[60] Such implications of the changes in marital law are extremely worrying in relation to future generations; they will also create a crisis of conscience for many present and future teachers who would be simply unwilling on conscientious grounds to propagate the same sex message.

Conclusions

Such alarming statistics as have been drawn out in this chapter led Gavin Poole, the Executive Director of the Centre for Social Justice, to say:

> Current high levels of cohabitation are a key factor in the rise of family breakdown in our country and this paper shows that we have not been here before. The CSJ has consistently argued, from the evidence, that marriage and commitment tend to stabilise and strengthen families and cannot be ignored.[61]

---

59 Rob Parsons, *Loving Against the Odds* (Hodder & Stoughton, 1994), 144f.

60 Quoted in Christian Institute leaflet, *Do you want primary school children to be taught that two men can marry each other?* (October 2011)

61 Quoted in http://conservativehome.blogs.com/thinktankcentral/2011/04/csjfamily-breakdown.html

Similarly, Robert Rowthorne, Professor of Economics at Cambridge University, summarising the statistical evidence, has said, "A massive social experiment has been carried out in Britain and America during the last 30-odd years. The values of the 1960s generation have dominated the evolution of family structures. Personal fulfilment has been elevated over old-fashioned concepts of duty and commitment. Divorce rates have soared and lone-parents households have proliferated". He goes on to say, "Everyone can point to lone parents or cohabiting couples who have charming and successful children", but:

> It is now clear that children brought up in a stable, two-parent family as a rule do better than in other family types. This is true for almost every indicator used to measure their personal development . . . Both physical and sexual abuse are much less frequent for children who live with their married, biological parents than in other kinds of family set-up. By far the riskiest situation for a child is to live in is a step-family. And marriages are on average more stable than cohabiting unions. This applies whether or not children are present. The instability of cohabiting unions is to be expected since many of them involve no lifelong commitment and the option of breaking up is consciously preserved.[62]

Research consistently shows that marriage is the best context for the healthy development of children. Not all married couples are able to, or choose to, have children, but, as the Christian Institute says in summary, "Social science confirms that lifelong and loving marriage is the ideal context in which to raise children".[63] Then follows a quotation from Professor A.H. Halsey, Emeritus Professor at Nuffield College, Oxford:

> . . . what should be universally acknowledged is that the children of parents who do not follow the traditional norm (i.e. taking on personal, active and long-term responsibility for the social upbringing of the children they generate) are thereby disadvantaged in many major aspects of their chances of living a successful life. On the evidence available such children tend to die earlier, to have more illness, to do less well at school, to exist at a lower level of nutrition, comfort and conviviality, to suffer

---

62 Robert Rowthorne, "Happy Ever After," quoted from newsletter of Family & Youth Concern (now Family Education Trust), Issue 104 (summer 2001).
63 'Gay marriage' in all but name, op. cit., 20.

more unemployment, to be more prone to deviance and crime, and finally to repeat the cycle of unstable parenting from which they themselves have suffered . . . The evidence all points in the same direction, is formidable, and tallies with common sense.[64]

It also tallies with the teaching of Scripture in which, as expounded elsewhere in this volume, we have the Maker's instructions for the well-being[65] of human beings, families and society.

Appendix 1: Why marriage matters

Article: "Why Marriage Matters", Institute for American Values and National Marriage project (2011), pp 12-13 – published in Bulletin 145 (Autumn 2011) of the Family Education Trust. Based on a survey of over 250 peer-reviewed journal articles on marriage and family life from around the world, a team of 18 leading American family scholars chaired by Professor W. Bradford Wilcox of the University of Virginia has drawn 30 conclusions about the positive benefits associated with marriage under five headings. Each of the conclusions is substantiated in the report and 20 pages of supporting references can be downloaded from http://www.americanvalues.org/wmm/

Family

- Marriage increases the likelihood that fathers and mothers have good relationships with their children.
- Children are most likely to enjoy family stability when they are born into a married family.
- Children are less likely to thrive in complex households.
- Cohabitation is not the functional equivalent of marriage.
- Growing up outside an intact marriage increases the likelihood that children will themselves divorce or become unwed parents.
- Marriage is a virtually universal human institution.
- Marriage, and a normative commitment to marriage, foster high-quality relationships between adults, as well as between parents and children.
- Marriage has important biosocial consequences for adults and children.

Economics

- Divorce and unmarried childbearing increase poverty for both children and mothers; cohabitation is less likely to alleviate poverty than is marriage.

---

64 *Ibid.,* 20f., acknowledging quotation from: N.Dennis & G.Ernos, *Families Without Fatherhood* (IEA, 1993), xii.

65 John 10:10; Proverbs 3:6; Psalm 1:1.

- Married couples seem to build more wealth on average than singles or cohabiting couples.
- Marriage reduces poverty and material hardship for disadvantaged women and their children.
- Minorities benefit economically from marriage also.
- Married men earn more money than do single men with similar education and job histories.
- Parental divorce (or failure to marry) appears to increase children's risk of school failure.
- Parental divorce reduces the likelihood that children will graduate from college and achieve high-status jobs.

Physical health and longevity

- Children who live with their own two married parents enjoy better physical health, on average, than do children in other family forms.
- Parental marriage is associated with a sharply lower risk of infant mortality.
- Marriage is associated with reduced rates of alcohol and substance abuse for both adults and teens.
- Married people, especially married men, have longer life expectancies than do otherwise similar singles.
- Marriage is associated with better health and lower rates of injury, illness and disability for both men and woman.
- Marriage seems to be associated with better health among minorities and the poor.

Mental health and emotional wellbeing

- Children whose parents divorce have higher rates of psychological distress and mental illness.
- Cohabitation is associated with higher levels of psychological problems among children.
- Family breakdown appears to increase significantly the risk of suicide.
- Married mothers have lower rates of depression than do single or cohabiting.

Crime and domestic violence

- Boys raised in non-intact families are more likely to engage in delinquent and criminal behaviour.
- Marriage appears to reduce the risk that adults will be either perpetrators or victims of crime.
- Married women appear to have a lower risk of experiencing domestic violence than do cohabiting or dating women.
- A child who is not living with his or her own two married parents is at greater risk of child abuse
- There is a growing marriage gap between college-educated Americans and less-educated Americans.

Appendix 2: Sexual identity in Britain

Figures from the Office for National Statistics survey of 238,206 people across Britain (as reported in: www.guardian.co.uk/news/datablog/2010/sep/23/gay-britain-ons#data)

Category	Hetero–sexual	Gay/lesbian/bi-sexual	Don't know/refused	No response
Totals, %	94.8	1.5	2.8	0.5
Est. members of British public	46,922 thousand	726 thousand		
% of group who are aged 16-24	14.5	18.4	20.6	35.2
% of group who are aged 25-44	34.1	46.5	29	34.7
% of group who are aged 45-64	31.8	26.9	25.9	25.6
% of group who are aged 65+	19.6	8.2	24.5	4.5
Male	48.7	54.6	47.8	59.1
Female	51.3	45.4	52.2	40.9
Single (never married)	32.5	61.7	41.1	52.3
Married, living with spouse	48.2	19.1	35.9	40.9
Married, separated from spouse	3	1.3	3.2	1.3
Divorced	9.1	5.4	7.5	4.3
Cohabiting	34.6	45.8	17.2	20.2
Not cohabiting	65.4	54.2	82.8	79.8
Scotland	**95.7**	**1.3**		**0.6**

Appendix 3: Dangers of alternative sexual practices (by the editors)

HIV infection, originally thought to arise as a result of homosexual activity, is now known to affect heterosexual activity as well. The risks of transmission during the normal sex act are slightly reduced if the tissues of the penis and vagina are not damaged. The transmission of the virus is greatly enhanced when the integrity of the skin or lining of the penis and vagina is damaged, allowing blood and other body fluids to come into direct contact with the recipient's exposed vascular sub-epithelial tissues.

Because of the recent focus on AIDS, the danger from STIs[66] generally has receded in public awareness (but is actually on the increase). Such infections include chlamydia, gonorrhaea, syphilis and genital warts, as well as links to other health problems.[67]

The sexual revolution of the 1960s has meant that 'alternative sex' is now practised by heterosexuals as well as homosexual men, and that promiscuity is no longer confined largely to the latter. Such promiscuity greatly increases the risk of infection, especially HIV or hepatitis B. Such alternative practices include:

- Oral sex or fellatio (penis to mouth) – risk of STIs to mouth, pharynx and through the blood stream (bacterial & viral, the latter transmitted through abrasions in mouth, gums).
- Cunnilingus, oral stimulation of the female genitalia, sometimes using tongue (instead of penis) for penetration – risk of STI and oral infection.
- Oro-anal 'rimming', using the tongue to stimulate / lick around the anus, using tongue instead of penis for penetration – risk of STIs and bowel infections.
- Anal sex – penetration of the back passage instead of the vagina by the penis.

The most dangerous of these practices, anal sex, is a particular danger to homosexual men, though with heterosexual anal intercourse there is a risk of both HIV and STIs being transmitted to the female partner (or children in a situation of abuse). The act of anal intercourse is hazardous, physically damaging, the trauma allowing easy transfer of the AIDS virus.

The function of the vagina is for sexual intercourse and childbirth, and it has in-built defence mechanisms against infection, unless traumatised.

The function of the lower bowel (rectum) and anus (back passage) is the elimination of body waste (faeces). The lower bowel has in-built mechanisms to prevent infectious organisms, including bacteria and viruses, found in faeces, from entering the body tissues. The lower bowel also removes water from body waste so that faeces are semi-solid rather than fluid. The anus has a strong band of

---

66 Sexually Transmitted Infections.

67 Such as hepatitis B, or bowel pathogens like entamoeba histolytica, giardia, salmonella, shigella, cryptosporidia.

muscle (sphincter) which ensures continence and the ability to control passage of wind (flatus), waste (faeces) and water (fluid faeces), as occurs with diarrhoea or enema –so we can get to the toilet without soiling ourselves.

In receptive anal intercourse the anus and rectum are often traumatised with tearing of the skin and mucous membrane lining of these organs, in spite of lubrication which is often used. The rectum is lined with mucous membrane, which is very easily torn during intercourse. In addition the anal sphincter may be damaged or completely torn (even more so if 'fisting'[68] occurs). Infectious agents from the recipient's own bowel, enteric pathogens or sexually transmitted organisms (bacterial, viral, including HIV) carried on the penetrating penis can infect the recipient. At the same time, the same organisms present in the rectum can enter the urethra, or the space under the foreskin of the partner practising penetrative anal intercourse, causing acute infection.

Some men who regularly engage in receptive anal intercourse suffer from dysfunction of the anal sphincter so that they may have to use incontinence pads or pants.

Anal intercourse, however practised, is hugely risky for the transmission of HIV/AIDS, far more so than straight intercourse (which also carries this risk, if the tissues are damaged by trauma).

Following anal intercourse, the female is especially at risk, if the penis is then introduced into the vagina as bowel infections are deposited at the cervix, the neck of the womb and may cause very severe infections including peritonitis.

In short the bowel because of its anatomy and physiology was neither designed nor intended for sexual intercourse. While the use of condoms may reduce some risks, such use does not eliminate them.

Appendix 4: Response to "The Christian Case for Gay Marriage"

Since this chapter was written, my attention has been drawn to the above significant statement of the case for approval of same sex marriage. In a lecture delivered to the Conference of the Presbyterian Covenant Network in November 2010,[69] David Myers, Professor of Psychology at Hope College, Michigan, argues that homosexual orientation is not a choice and that same sex couples should not be denied the opportunity of 'marrying'.

---

68 Using the hand to stimulate anus, insertion of whole hand or arm into rectum and lower bowel.

69 Full text found at http://covnetpres.org/2011/01/the-christian-case-for-gay-marriage/. For other books by David Myers, see www.davidmyers.org. For further debate, google e.g. 'Gagnon and Myers'.

Despite Myers' argument, it seems that more widespread social (and media-driven) acceptance of homosexual practice has in fact encouraged some people to 'come out', but it will be argued that this is a matter of openly declaring that which was true but previously undeclared. In that sense Myers' argument might seem to have some validity, even in the face of a common perception that an increasing number of people (especially in politics and the media) identify themselves as homosexual. But, as Myers admits in his lecture, such factors do not in fact impinge at all on the question of values or morality: "(T)his evidence, if it persuades you, as it does me – that sexual orientation is a natural and enduring disposition – does not answer questions of values."

The same principle – that descriptive information does not determine moral values – applies to some of the other points raised by Myers in his lecture:

(a) He asserts that marriage has changed (for example from arranged marriages to romantic choice). But clearly we cannot argue from what 'is' to what 'ought' to be.

(b) Against the argument that marriage implies procreation and therefore cannot be homosexual, he points out that society recognises the right of post-menopausal women to marry. Therefore, he argues, same sex couples should not be denied marriage. This by-passes all the issues of simple definition that have been mentioned earlier in this chapter.

(c) In relation to the argument that same-sex 'marriage' might lead on to such arrangements as polygamous marriage, Myers simply states, as if it were obvious beyond any possibility of contradiction, that marriage would continue to be monogamous. One may admire such optimism but question its basis.

(d) Much is made of statistical trends – more and more people, especially young people, see no problem with same sex relationships. Is Myers suggesting that such matters of morality be settled by a vote? One is reminded of Kipling's reference to a village which, in a time of controversy, voted that the earth is flat.[70]

(e) He makes the point that people's attitudes are affected by the friends they have – which may well be true. Indeed it has often seemed to me that the level of argument with some people is: homosexual practice is unnatural and wrong – but we know A and B and they're awfully nice guys (or gals) – therefore it's right after all.

(f) And Myers suggests that a continued resistance to homosexual practice is the biggest factor alienating young people from the Church. This relates to a real issue, but can it really be the case that the Church is to alter its position on various issues in order to avoid putting certain groups off?

This chapter has emphasised the promiscuous nature and often short duration of homosexual relationships. Myers' argument is that same sex marriage would help to counter such trends and introduce faithfulness into such relationships. This

70 Quoted in G.B.Caird, *The Truth of the Gospel* (Oxford University Press, 1950), 8.

is not at all obvious in an age when we observe increasing levels of heterosexual marital breakdown, and one may wonder what grounds there are for such a hope as Myers expresses. He would have us conduct a social experiment, with all the dangers described above in relation to the slippery slope, without having any idea of whether such a result is at all likely. While that experiment would be proceeding, all manner of other undesirable and unhealthy outcomes would be very likely.

In fact it is interesting that, near the beginning of the lecture, Myers seeks to demonstrate the greater stability of children when they live with both natural parents and then towards the end shifts the goalposts by saying, "I showed you a glimpse of it at the beginning of this talk. Children thrive better when co-parented by two adults who love each other and love that child". That transition from male and female to "two adults" begs the whole question.

When Myers refers to the biblical texts on the subject (having made the assertion that he was not offering any biblical expertise), he makes the tendentious claim that, since the word 'homosexual' is not found in computer searches of the RSV or NIV, this means that Scripture has nothing to say on the subject! Then he refers to what he calls the seven 'clobber passages', and his argument seems to be that we ought not to pay much attention to such a small amount of material (0.0002 % of Biblical texts, he claims). One might observe in passing that by such an argument we probably should not observe communion, but more significantly it is difficult to see the rationale for ignoring some texts merely because they are not found in many places. A whole section of this book examines the various passages; rather than overlooking them, we need to take them seriously.

Christian belief

Chapter 4

The authority of Scripture: is the Bible the Word of God or does it only contain the Word of God?

David W. Torrance

The Revd David W. Torrance is a retired parish minister, and was chairman and later honorary president of the Scottish Order of Christian Unity.

Part 1   Introduction

Issues concerning marriage, morality, same sex relationships and education concern both Church and society and raise many questions. Can and should the Church speak authoritatively on these issues? If so, what is the Church's authority? What is the authority of Scripture? What is meant by those who say that the Bible is the Word of God? What is the relation between Jesus Christ as the eternal Word of God and the Bible as the written Word of God? If Jesus is the one eternal Word of God become man for us, and if his Word remains identical with his Person become flesh, in what sense is the Bible the Word of God? Was the Bible authoritative only for the days in which it was written or is it authoritative for us today? "The subject of the Bible is of lasting importance for Christians of all types and denominations . . . It is of the utmost importance that these questions should be answered rightly."[1]

The Church's statement of faith

The confession of the "One Holy Catholic or Universal Church" of which the Church of Scotland according to its Declaratory Articles is part, is that the Bible, embracing Old and New Testaments, is the Word of God.

Christian faith is dependent on the Bible, on the word of holy Scripture. Without the Bible, the written word of God, we would have no knowledge of Jesus Christ, no knowledge of God and no faith in God, no knowledge of the resurrection, salvation and eternal life. The Church would have disappeared long ago. On the other hand, without the Church and the witness of prophets

---

1   John K.S. Reid, *The Authority of Scripture (Methuen 1957),* 7-8.

and apostles to the Word of God, to Jesus Christ, there would be no Bible. The Church and the Bible belong together in the Church's faith.

It is important to recognise that we can never prove that the Bible is the Word of God. just as we cannot prove the presence and existence of God. Just as God alone can and does reveal God through his Holy Spirit, so the Word of God, the divine-human Word, to whom the written word of Scripture testifies, is self-authenticating through the testimony of the Holy Spirit in our hearts. It is in the God-given assurance of the Holy Spirit that the Church believes and confesses that we encounter God and hear him speak through Scripture. "The Bible is the Christ book; not just a book which speaks of him, but a book through which he speaks to us."[2] That the Bible is objectively the word of God is a confession of faith on the part of the universal Church.

The Church accordingly stands under the Bible as the Word of God. She submits to it as God's Word. She listens to it and seeks to obey it and affirms that it is objectively God's Word. It is worth noting here that if the Church in her confession were to follow the order in which God reveals himself, then the statement that the Bible is the word of God would follow God's revelation of himself through Scripture. It would therefore come toward the end of the Church's confession and not as the first article as in the Westminster Confession of Faith.

If we were able to prove the presence and existence of God, as theologians and philosophers in the past often tried to do, we would be positing between ourselves in the world and God a logical continuity in terms of which we could argue from the one necessarily to the other. That would mean that we were exalting ourselves to a position equal or even superior to God and we were able with human reason to prove that the Bible is God's Word. That would mean that we were actually above the Word of God, that we were superior to the Word of God and in a position to submit judgment concerning it. In that case it would not be the Word of God.[3]

The Bible and the nature of its contents and authority

The Bible embraces the Scriptures of both the Old and New Testament. The Old Testament is the Jewish Bible, long embraced by the rabbis as God's word to Israel and the nations. The canon of the Old Testament and its acceptance by the rabbis reach back to antiquity. The canon of the New Testament was finally accepted in the fourth century. Together, the Old

2   Heinrich Vogel, *The Iron Ration of a Christian* (SCM 1941), 29.
3   See C.E.B. Cranfield, *The Bible and Christian Life* (T & T Clark, Edinburgh 1985), 4.

and New Testaments constitute the Bible which in the confession of the Church, is the word of God. Regarded in itself, the Bible is the written word of God, but regarded in conjunction with the living Word of God who speaks through it, the Bible is the Word of God.

The authority of the Bible is thus the authority of the Word of God to whom the written word bears witness. The Word is Jesus Christ the Son of God. As the apostle John tells us in the beginning of his Gospel, the Word was in the beginning with God, is God and became flesh and blood in Jesus Christ.[4] The written word has no authority in itself. Its authority lies in the Word of God to whom it bears witness. The Word of God, Jesus Christ who is God, is the one through whom alone God reveals himself to the world. His revelation of himself in Christ, through the Word, is confirmed and sealed by the Holy Spirit. There is no other confirmation and none is required. In that sense, as we have said, God's revelation of himself through his Word and the Holy Spirit is self-authenticating. Nothing other than God can prove God. As John Calvin said, "God is the only fit witness to himself".

As the primary and unique witness to Jesus Christ and to God's revelation to the world, the Bible is the written Word of God.

God speaks to us through the Bible as we read or hear it preached. It is the place where we meet and encounter God and hear him speaking to us today in Jesus Christ through his Holy Spirit. The Lord is always with his Church. He is present in her midst speaking to his people. The risen Lord said to his disciples, in Matthew 28 verses 19 and 20, "Go . . . and make disciples of all nations . . . teaching them to observe every thing I have commanded you. And surely, I am with you always to the very end of the age." With the presence of the Bible as God's Word in the Church we have in large part the fulfilment of Christ's promise that he will always be with his Church through his Holy Spirit.

The humanity of the Bible and the humanity of Christ

Although it witnesses to the Word of God and is written under the inspiration of the Holy Spirit, the Bible is a human book. When God reveals himself he comes down to us, to our level, as Calvin repeatedly emphasised. He makes himself known to us in human terms, clothing himself in human language. In doing so, he adapts and moulds human language and thought to make it a fit vehicle of his revelation but he does not override the humanity of those he speaks to. Through the Holy Spirit he speaks to

---

4 John 1:1f.

us in and through the human mind and thought forms of prophets and apostles. The Bible is written by men. How then do we understand the humanity of the Bible?

Before considering that question, we need to consider the humanity of Jesus Christ, the divine-human Word to whom the Bible as the written word testifies.

Jesus is none other than God, the Son of God, who came to redeem the world and us. In order to redeem us he the eternal God, our mighty Creator, came down into his creation and took our flesh and blood and became a creature. Without his becoming human and coming down to our level, becoming a man, drawing alongside us and identifying himself with us, we would not, could not know him or enter into fellowship with him or be redeemed. We with our human, finite minds cannot understand and grasp what is in itself eternal, far less in our sinfulness be united with God in his holiness. In Jesus we have the complete fulfilment of God's revelation of himself to and in humanity.

In becoming man, Jesus remained God. As the Bible says,

> God reconciled the world to himself in Christ, not counting their sins against them. (2 Cor 5:19)

> Salvation is found in no-one else, for there is no other name under heaven given to men by which we must be saved. (Acts 4:12)

> He is the image of the invisible God, the first born over all creation. For by him all things were created . . . And he is the head of the body, the church; he is the beginning and the firstborn from among the dead, so that in everything he might have the supremacy. For God was pleased to have all his fullness dwell in him . . . (Col 1:11-21)

In Jesus, in all the fullness of his humanity we have at the same time the fullness of God in all his deity.

The early Fathers at the Council of Chalcedon (451 AD) emphasised the biblical teaching that Jesus is both fully God and fully man and yet one Person. The fact that he is God and man in one indivisible person means that we cannot identify nor yet separate his divinity and his humanity. As one Person, there is a hypostatic union between Jesus as God and Jesus as man and human minds cannot fully grasp that. We accept it in faith. It is the foundation of our faith. It is where all our understanding of God and all our theology begins. Jesus said, "I and the Father are one" (John 10:30).

"Anyone who has seen me has seen the Father" (John 14:9). As God and yet man, as man and yet God Jesus accomplished our salvation through his incarnation, life, death, resurrection and ascension and through his coming in the Holy Spirit at Pentecost to live within his Church and within all who receive him in faith.

As God and as man, Jesus gathered up and fulfilled in his humanity all that went before him in the law and the prophets. They pointed to him and ultimately can only truly be understood and have meaning in him. Throughout his ministry, Jesus by what he said and did was very conscious that he had come to fulfil the law and the prophets. In the synagogue in Nazareth he read from the prophet Isaiah 61:5,

> The Spirit of the Lord is on me, because he has anointed me to preach good news to the poor. He has sent me to proclaim freedom for the prisoners and recovery of sight for the blind, to release the oppressed, to proclaim the year of the Lord's favour. He then said, "Today this scripture is fulfilled in your hearing".[6]

> Jesus was the Servant about whom the Old Testament spoke and on the walk to Emmaus; "Beginning with Moses and all the prophets, he explained to them what was said in all the Scriptures concerning himself" (Luke 24:27). It is still only in and through the witness of the Old Testament that we can rightly appreciate and understand his Person and his saving work. Through the Old Testament Scriptures we are brought to hear and understand God speaking to us in Christ.

In the Prophets and Psalms, Israel was likened to a vine planted by God (Psalm 80:8, Isa 5:1-7, Jer 2:21, Hos 10:1). Jesus said, "I am the true vine" (John 15:1). From these words, it is clear that Jesus was identifying himself with Israel and came to fulfil in himself and in his atoning work God's covenant with and promises to Israel. As the Holy God in love bound sinful Israel to himself in an everlasting covenant, so the Holy God binds us along with Israel to himself in Christ. The humanity of Israel and the humanity of the Prophets are integral to God's revelation of himself to us in the humanity of Christ and in his redemption of us in him.

Likewise in the New Testament, God in revealing himself through Jesus Christ, chose disciples who had accompanied him in his ministry and been eyewitnesses of his resurrection, in order to reveal himself through them.

---

5   Isa 61:1-2.

6   Luke 4:21.

Through their witness to him they would continue his self-revelation and his saving work. He so united himself with them in the Spirit that they were his personal representatives as they went with his gospel to the world. The risen Lord spoke and acted in and through them. The Acts of the Apostles is a record of what the risen Christ continued to say and do through the Apostles. As they preached they slipped into the background. "In the foreground there was the living, acting Word of God, the Person of Jesus Christ".[7] When they proclaimed the Word of God, Jesus was proclaiming the Word and the Word went forth with power accomplishing what was spoken, creating the church.

When Jesus breathed upon them, he said (in John 20:22-23): "Receive the Holy Spirit. If you forgive anyone his sins, they are forgiven; if you do not forgive them, they are not forgiven". After Pentecost when the risen Christ came clothed with his saving work to live in the apostles and to identify himself with them, their ministry was Jesus' ministry. When they preached they were not simply speaking about Christ. They were not reinterpreting what Jesus said. They were not reinterpreting Jesus' life and ministry and what they said did not need to be demythologised as many scholars have mistakenly said. When they spoke as his apostles, Jesus himself spoke. He was speaking in and through their human witness. The signs and wonders which accompanied their preaching were a sign that the risen Christ was speaking and acting in a powerful way through their ministry.

Human though they are, the apostles, like the Old Testament prophets, occupy a unique place. As people listened to them, they met with God. They knew that Jesus was alive and they heard him speaking to them. Their ministry is the foundation of the Church.

The inspiration and humanity of the Bible

Under the hand of God and through the inspiration of the Holy Spirit, the proclamation of the Word of God by prophets and apostles was written down. Had it not been written down and all we had was the living voice of the Church, the Church would never have continued. The voice of the Church would soon have become corrupted. In time, all sorts of stories and myths would have emerged and the Church would soon have died. God's Word is a living Word and always a present Word, which we can hear any time and anywhere. That has been made possible by the written word, the Bible.

That the word of God was written down is a unique historical event. The Old Testament and the New Testament are a library of books, 39 in the

---

7   T.F. Torrance, *Atonement*, 319.

OT and 27 in the NT, written over a considerable period of time, stretching over 1,000 years. They were written under the hand of God and together manifest a marvellous unity in their witness to the divine-human Word that is Christ. Jesus Christ is the unifying factor.

In saying that "all Scripture is God breathed"[8] the Bible does not say or suggest that God over-ruled the humanity of those he chose to write it. God used the humanity of the prophets and apostles. He spoke and acted through them, while each continued to have and manifest his own humanity. Their humanity and individual characteristics are manifested in what they wrote and in the way that they wrote. In speaking through their humanity God is speaking to us in our humanity. The Bible although different from any other book is a human book, written by people like ourselves, although they were writing under the inspiration of the Holy Spjrit.

How then do we understand the humanity of the Bible and its relation to the Word of God? Here we can only be guided by the relation of the humanity and divinity of Christ in his one Person. There is a certain parallel. As the humanity and divinity of Christ are not identical and not separate, so the humanity of the Bible and the Word of God to which it testifies are not identical and yet not separate. That is to say, the relationship between the humanity of the Bible and the Word of God is analogous to the primary, unique relationship between the divine and human nature in the one Person of Christ.

The relationship however is only analogous. It is not identical. In Jesus there is a hypostatic, personal union between his humanity and divinity.[9] Jesus in what he said and did was one Person. There is no such personal unity between what God says through his living Word, who is personal, and the human agency, the written word, which God sanctifies and uses.

At the same time Jesus as fully man was at the same time without sin or imperfection. We cannot make such a claim about the written word of prophets and apostles, no matter how sanctified they were and inspired by the Holy Spirit in their writing. The relationship between the written word of the Bible and the incarnate Word in Holy Scripture is sacramental. This is what the early Church came to recognise when it came to accept the canon of Scripture.

Commenting on what Paul says in 2 Timothy 3:16, that "all Scripture is God breathed", Calvin writes;

---

8   2 Tim 3:16.

9   T.F. Torrance, *Atonement*, 337.

To show its authority, the writer declares that it is divinely inspired. … And this is the principle that distinguishes our religion from all others, namely that we know that God speaks to us, and are certainly assured that the Prophets did not speak on their own, but as organs and instruments of the Holy Spirit, so that they announced only what they had received from on high.[10]

From his *Sermons on Deuteronomy* Calvin says, "Moses wrote what he received from God, and not what he fabricated in his own head". In the Institutes Calvin says that the Scriptures are "God's own voice" (1.7.1). They are "dictated by the Holy Spirit" (4.8.6).[11]

Despite the fact that Calvin uses the word dictate several times and says that Scripture is "dictated by the Holy Spirit", he still believed strongly that the Bible is a human book written by men. God did not over-ride their humanity. He used their minds, their understanding, their humanity and their human style of writing. He acted in and through them. The writers and what they wrote were sanctified. What they wrote was under the inspiration of the Holy Spirit.

The Church's proclamation

The Reformers stressed that when the Church today and its pastors go in obedience in prayer and faith and proclaim God's message from Scripture so "God himself speaks about himself"[12] challenging people to faith and repentance. Barth,[13] in regard to the function of Church proclamation, quotes Luther;

Now I and any man who speaketh Christ's Word may freely boast that his mouth is Christ's mouth. I am certain that my word is not mine but Christ's Word, therefore my mouth must also be his whose Word it speaketh.

'Tis a right excellent thing, that every honest pastor's and preacher's mouth is Christ's mouth, and his word and forgiveness is Christ's word and forgiveness . . . For the office is not pastor's or preacher's, but God's; and the Word which he preacheth, God's Word . . .

---

10 Quoted by John K.S. Reid, *The Authority of Scripture*, 34.

11 *Idem*, 35.

12 Barth, *Church Dogmatics*, Vol. 1, Part 1, 106.

13 Barth, *idem*, 107-108.

THE AUTHORITY OF SCRIPTURE

On the last day God will say to me, "Hast thou also preached that?" I shall say, "Yea exactly." Then God will say to thee, "Hast thou also heard that?" and thou shalt answer, "Yea." And he saith further, "Wherefore hast thou not believed?" And then thou sayest, "Oh, I held it for a word of man, since a poor chaplain or village parson uttered it." So shall the same word, which sticketh in thine heart accuse thee and be thine accuser and judge at the last day. For it is God's Word, 'tis God himself thou hast heard, as Christ saith, "He that heareth you heareth me."

The nature of verbal inspiration

Although Calvin takes, I believe rightly, a very literal interpretation of Scripture, he did not believe, as many later evangelicals have believed, that in its human side the Bible is infallible. He believed that it is infallible in its witness to the Word of God. It is not verbally infallible.

If we claim that the Bible is verbally infallible[14] and seek to identify the Word who is God with the written word then we are not treating the Word as personal. We are regarding it (him) as a set of propositions and flattening the Word into the written word. We are, as it were, seeking to possess and even to control God's Word, which is utterly wrong. God does not give himself to us in that way.[15] God is personal. He is sovereignly free. He is Lord. We are sinful creatures to whom in love he chooses to reveal himself and to redeem. When he does make himself known, he always reveals himself in Person. He does not reveal truths about himself, which we can separate from his Person and possess. His truth is identical with himself and can never be separated from his living Person.

The Bible then, the written word, does not give us a set of propositions. Our faith is neither in statements about God, nor in a creed. It is in the living Person of Jesus Christ together with what he has done and is doing for us and to which the written word testifies.

Calvin and the other Reformers together with "the Holy Catholic or Universal Church" all believed that the Bible is completely reliable. It is not in the least unreliable. It is an infallible witness to the Word of God. We are able to hear God speak in all parts of the Bible despite the fact that the Word speaks to us through a human and therefore frail instrument. Martin Luther famously

---

14 That is, Scripture is verbally inerrant as originally given. What the writers originally wrote down on the dictation of the Holy Spirit is accurate in every detail.

15 C.E.B. Cranfield, *The Bible and Christian Life*, 8.

said, "Christ is the King and Lord of Scripture" and subordinated Scripture to Christ in the well-known utterance, "The Scriptures are the crib, wherein Christ is laid" and "Poor and mean are the swaddling clothes, but precious is the treasure, Christ that lies therein".[16]

Although affirming the inspiration of all Scripture, Calvin denied verbal infallibility. In commenting on Matthew 27:10 he says, "I confess I do not know how the 'Jeremiah' came in here, and I do not worry much. Certainly it is an obvious mistake to put Jeremiah for Zechariah, for we do not find this saying or anything like it in Jeremiah".[17] In Mark 2:26, Mark records Jesus saying, "In the days of Abiathar the high priest". Yet it seems clear that the event to which Jesus alluded was in the days when Abiathar's father was high priest. There are other such passages. None of these issues should trouble us nor lessen our acceptance of the Bible as the Word of God. Emil Brunner when writing about the Christian faith likened the Bible to a gramophone record. He said only a fool would listen or pay attention to the scratching of the needle instead of listening to 'his Master's voice' or the music that is recorded. What is important is that we have the Bible, the whole Bible, as God wants us to have it. It is unerring in enabling us to know the Lord, to hear him speak, to receive his salvation and to live a life of love and service in the way in which God wants.

All Scripture is inspired

> The Reformers accepted all parts of canonical Scripture as inspired and authoritative, although they did not accord an equal degree of importance and relevance to every part. The insistence that all canonical Scripture is inspired was directed against some of the Anabaptist groups who could not agree to the full inspiration of the Old Testament."[18]

Today the Reformers if alive would wish to resist those who believe that the Bible only "contains" the Word of God, and that some parts are not inspired and therefore not the Word of God.

When, with the "Holy Catholic and Apostolic Church", we affirm the authority of the Bible, we are affirming the Bible as a whole not just a part or parts. The theme of the entire Bible is the eternal Word of God who became flesh and blood in Jesus Christ. He is the focus of all Scripture. The

---

16 *Idem*, 6-7. Also Emil Brunner, *The Word and the World*, 84.

17 *Idem*, 7.

18 G.W. Bromiley, "The Authority of Scripture" in *The New Bible Commentary*, 18.

Bible despite being written by many writers over a long period is united in its witness to him. The Bible is a unity. When we recognise its unity and how all Scripture points to Jesus Christ, the Word made flesh, then we begin to understand how all parts of the Bible, even those which at first seem less important or even offensive have a part to play in the total testimony. When we view the Bible as a whole as God intends, then we readily recognise that whereas all Scripture is inspired, "no part is to be regarded as the Word of God in isolation from the rest. It is only in its relation to all the rest of Scripture that each particular part is the true and authentic Word of God".[19]

All Scripture is the Word of God

The early Church and the Reformers, as part of the "Holy Catholic Church", accepted all Scripture, the whole Bible, as the Word of God. They affirmed its unique character as the authoritative Word of God and distinct from every other book or literature. In the Bible we encounter God. We meet him and hear him speak for our salvation and the salvation of the world.

In the Westminster Confession of Faith, the Church of Scotland's subordinate standard of faith, the word "contain" is used. In chapter 1, paragraph 2, we read; "Under the name of Holy Scripture, or the Word of God written, are now contained all the Books of the Old and New Testaments". In the Shorter Catechism, Answer 2 reads; "The Word of God, which is contained in the Scriptures of the Old and New Testaments, is the only rule to direct us how we may glorify and enjoy him".

In the Larger Catechism the word "contain" is not mentioned. Answer 3 reads; "The holy scriptures of the Old and New Testaments are the word of God, the only rule of faith and obedience". Answer 4 reads; "The scriptures manifest themselves to be the word of God, by their majesty and purity; by the consent of all the parts, and the scope of the whole, which is to give all glory to God; by their light and power to convince, to comfort and build up believers unto salvation: but the Spirit of God bearing witness by and with the scriptures in the heart of man, is alone able to persuade it that they are the very word of God."

These particular words of the Westminster Confession and the Shorter Catechism are echoed in Article 1 of the Declaratory Articles of the Church. There we read that the Church of Scotland "receives the Word of God which is contained in the Scriptures of the Old and New Testaments

---

19   C.E.B. Cranfield, *The Bible and Christian Life*, 10.

as its supreme rule of faith and life". From the Westminster Confession, the Shorter and especially Larger Catechism it is clear that those who drew up these documents wished to affirm that the whole Bible is the Word of God.

Part 2 How do we read the Bible?

Prayer

Prayer is paramount in our reading of the Bible, in our understanding of it and in our preaching it. In Acts chapter 6, after it was agreed that the Church appoint six deacons to look after the distribution of food, the Apostles said, "We will turn this responsibility over to them, and will give our attention to prayer and the ministry of the Word".[20] The Reformed Churches have laid a great emphasis on the preaching of the Word. We need to ask, "What about the emphasis on prayer?" The Apostles put prayer before the preaching of the Word.

Prayer and the understanding and preaching of the Word must always go together. The Bible is the place of encounter where we meet with God. God is a Person and we can only meet him in prayer. If the Bible was only concerned with propositional truths and statements and commandments, it might be different. But the Word, to whom the Bible bears witness, is a Person, Jesus Christ. To meet him and come to know him personally and enjoy his love we must speak to him and listen as he speaks to us. We may come to know a lot about a person without speaking to the person, but we can never actually know and love that person, without both speaking and listening to that person. It is likewise with Jesus Christ.

Jesus emphasised the importance of praying by telling his disciples to pray (Luke 18:1) and by teaching them how to pray. He gave them an example of how to pray (Matt 6:9-13) and taught them to persevere in prayer in the parable of the Friend at Midnight (Luke 11:5f.) and the Parable of the Persistent Widow (Luke 18:1-8). He encouraged them saying "Ask and it will be given to you" (Luke 11:9f.) and assured them that God in response to prayer is both loving and generous (Luke 11:11-13). He said, "If you remain in me and my words remain in you, ask whatever you wish, and it will be given you" (John 15:7); "I will do what ever you ask in my name" (John 14:13); "Until now you have not asked for anything in my name. Ask and you will receive, and your joy will be full" (John 16:24).

---

20 Acts 6:3-4.

Jesus as man, united with us through the Holy Spirit, prayed to the Father on our behalf. As he worked out our salvation, he wanted us to share with him his inner communion with the Father. As we pray in Christ we share in his prayer to the Father on our behalf. Only in prayer, and in praying in and with Christ, can we draw near and know the Father, share in fellowship with the Father and know that we truly belong to him.

The Bible is unlike any other book and therefore its reading and study must be different from that of any other book. It must always involve prayer. As was said earlier, the Bible is a human word, which witnesses to the divine Word, enabling us to encounter God and hear him speak.

Whereas in the Bible the human word is not identical with and yet not separate from the divine Word, we can only rightly read, study and understand the Bible as we continually hold before us its sacramental unity as a divine-human Word. This we can only rightly do as we read, study and seek to understand the divine-human Word in the context of prayer. In prayer we encounter the Lord, hear him speaking and come truly to know him. Our attitude should be that which is summed up in the verse of a well-known hymn:

> Break thou the bread of life, dear Lord to me,
> as thou didst break the bread beside the sea;
> beyond the sacred page I seek thee Lord;
> my spirit longs for thee, thou living Word!

Obedience

The words "obey", "obedience" and their equivalent occur some 148 times in the Bible, 96 times in the OT and 54 in the NT. Only as we obey the Lord will we truly come to know him and enjoy his blessings. Obedience to God lies at the heart of the Christian life.

Without obedience, we cannot know the Lord as he wants to be known. Jesus said, "If anyone chooses to do God's will, he will find out whether my teaching comes from God" (John 7:17). Knowledge of the Lord involves humility and repentance on our part.

Repentance in Greek is *meta-noia*, change of mind, a radical change of our whole way of thinking. It involves the willingness on our part, to allow ourselves through the Holy Spirit in Christ to be transformed by the renewing of our minds (Rom 12:2). It is only by this positive renewal of our minds in Christ that we can let go of our human, sinful thoughts and ideas of God and that can only happen as we obey the Lord.

When we approach Scripture therefore and seek to read it and try to understand it, we need to ask God through his Holy Spirit to make us obedient so that willingly, by God's grace, we will do all that God is asking us to do. The Bible is a place of encounter, where we meet with the Lord. It is also a book, not to argue about but to live by. As we obey him we come to understand what we read and to understand and know the Lord.

In that light we cannot seek to stand over the Bible and seek to judge whether what we read is or is not the Word of God. We cannot come in that spirit of criticism and judgement and at the same time come humbly, with the listening ear ready to obey all that God lovingly commands. This, in the present debate in the churches concerning same sex relationships, cannot be emphasised enough.

The Bible however, as emphasised already, retains its full humanity. How can we be faithful to it in its humanity while obedient to God who speaks in and through it? How can we be obedient to the Word of God in his authority over us and hear him speaking to us in the humanity of the Bible and of Christ, for in them God does not bypass our humanity and reason but engages them? The answer is only through new birth in Christ and the conversion of our reason in him.

New birth

Jesus said to the Jews listening to his teaching, "Why is my language not clear to you? Because you are unable to hear what I say" (John 8:43). As the KJV reads, "Why do ye not understand my speech? Even because ye cannot hear my Word." Jesus' "teaching" or as the KJV says, "speech" is his human conversation. The Greek word is *lalia*. He said, you do not understand my human speech, *lalia*, because you are unable able to hear my Word, *logos*, that is, you do not hear God speaking.

Earlier, in conversation with Nicodemus Jesus said, "No one can see the kingdom of God unless he is born of God" (John 3:3) and again, "No one can enter the kingdom of God unless he is born of water and the Spirit. Flesh gives birth to flesh, but the Spirit gives birth to spirit . . . You must be born again" (John 3:5-7).

The natural man could see the man Jesus. They could hear him speak his *lalia*, but there was a veil over their minds and hearts, so that they could not in the Spirit see Jesus, the Son of God. They could not hear nor understand when he spoke to them as God, words of life and salvation. To hear, their ears required to be opened, the veil required to be drawn aside. They required to be born again and become a new creation (2 Cor 5:17).

They required to be renewed in their minds (Rom 12:2) so that they could hear and understand his Word and be saved.

The Bible in its humanity, as written by prophets and apostles, is the human conversation, the *lalia*, of Jesus. We like the Jews who listened to Jesus in the Gospel story, need to be reborn and have our minds and understanding transformed by the Holy Spirit, if we would truly recognise and accept the Bible as the Word of God, understand what we read and hear God speaking.

If the veil is not lifted from our hearts and minds by the Holy Spirit, if we do not hear God himself speaking to us, then we cannot truly understand the words of Scripture no matter how great our scholarship and how hard we try, as scholars have done. The Revd Howard Taylor has given us a helpful illustration of the futility of trying to understand the written word without listening to, or hearing the Word of God speaking in conjunction with it. He says:

> The world's great telescopes are amazing instruments full of all kinds of gadgets to enable the astronomer to come to a knowledge of the particular part of the heavens he is viewing. Let us imagine a team of technicians coming to examine this instrument and make sense of it, without realising that its purpose is to view distant objects in the sky beyond it. They will try to work out what this and that gadget is for, and write many learned papers about them ... What is certain is that they will never be able to make sense of it as a whole until they discover what it is for, and they won't find that until they actually look through it. Once they have made this fundamental discovery then they will gradually be able to make sense of the whole. As they actually use the telescope for its purpose of viewing reality beyond it in the heavens then it will, as it were, be able to unfold its many and varied recourses to them and they will see it as a wonderful inter-related unity. If they refuse to take into account the purpose of the telescope in their investigations, we would have to say that the whole basis of their work is irrational even though it has the appearance of being scientific. Similarly our understanding of the Bible can only come when we use it for its purpose namely to lead us to personal knowledge of God. If we resist such life changing knowledge we will never be able to assess the truth of the Bible. We cannot be detached observers or listeners.[21]

---

21 Howard Taylor, "The Nature and Origin of the Bible", an unpublished address given to the Scottish Evangelical Theological Society in Edinburgh, September 2009.

A similar illustration can be drawn from the use of a telephone. If we had never seen or heard of telephones or knew of their use and walked into a room where a person was speaking on a telephone, we would only hear what is to us, a number of disjointed and unconnected phrases. If the person is receiving bad news we might see him or her weep. On receiving good news we might see him or her laughing. If we tried to understand the situation and make sense of what seemed to us, the person's disjointed phrases and mixed emotions, our conclusions no matter how clever would be wrong. The only way that we could come rightly to understand everything is by our putting our ear to the telephone and hearing the person at the other end speak. It is likewise when we turn to the Bible.

When our ears and minds are opened by the Holy Spirit, when we are born again, we enter what Barth has called "the strange new world within the Bible".[22] God speaks to us. "The Word he speaks to us is himself. His dealings with us are so inexpressibly godly and gracious that he comes to us himself as the Word he is speaking"; "He Jesus Christ is the one Word of God we are to trust and obey in life and in death"; "He comes to you, he speaks to you, he gives himself to you, he steps forth from his concealment and reveals himself as your Saviour and Redeemer".[23]

Converted reason[24]

In our natural, sinful state we cannot understand God when in his holiness he speaks to us. We cannot even "see the Kingdom of God". In Christ, through his birth from above, his growth in wisdom and knowledge of God, his putting to death our sin on the cross and his renewal of our humanity in his resurrection, we are born again and transformed. In union with him through the Spirit, our minds begin to be transformed, renewed and subject to what we seek to understand. We begin to share in "the mind of Christ". We must still use our minds, for mind and reason are the gift of God. It is only in prayer, through the continual transformation of our minds in Christ through the Holy Spirit, that we can we truly understand God's Word, as Paul emphasise in Romans.[25]

We must use our minds in Christ to do the hard work of faithful exegesis of the Bible. Likewise, we must use converted human reason, listening to

---

22 Barth, *The Word of God and the Word of man*, 28f.
23 Heinrich Vogel, *The Iron Ration of a Christian*, 26-28.
24 For further reading on this subject, see T.F. Torrance, *Atonement* (Epilogue, "The Reconciliation of Mind"). Also John Macmurray, *Reason and Emotion*.
25 Rom 12:2.

scholars and scientists and listening to the Word of God in prayer and obedience. As Peter said, "Gird up your minds...";[26] "In your hearts set apart Christ as Lord. Always be prepared to give an answer to everyone who asks you to give the reason for the hope that you have".[27]

Part 3 The words "contained in"

In more recent years, many of a liberal persuasion have laid great emphasis on the word "contain". They say that the Bible only "contains" the Word of God, meaning that some parts of the Bible are the Word of God and other parts are not truly the Word of God. Successive principal clerks to the General Assembly of the Church of Scotland have said this. Others in the General Assembly have also said it, seeking to argue, I believe wrongly, that this is the historic position of the Church of Scotland. In *The Constitution and Laws of the Church of Scotland*, which he edited in 1997, James L. Weatherhead, a former principal clerk and moderator writes under the heading, "4. Key Words: 'contained in'":

> Both in relation to the Scriptures and in relation to the Westminster Confession, the Declaratory Articles use the phrase "contained in". This is quite explicitly to recognise that the Scriptures are not *per se* the Word of God, but that the Word of God is contained in them, and that the fundamental doctrines are not the whole of the Westminster Confession, but are contained in it. The constitutional history of the Church leading to the Declaratory Articles is evidence of the importance of this understanding.[28]

So worded, this is an attack on the Word of God from within the church. Although some within the committees of the churches have held these liberal views, this was never the historic view of the Church of Scotland which according to the First Declaratory Article "adheres to the Scottish Reformation". It also is not the view of the "Holy Catholic or Universal Church" of which the Church of Scotland is part.[29] It would seem that some people of a liberal persuasion are attempting to impose upon the present Church a wrong and liberal interpretation of the Bible, which is alien

---

26 1 Pet 1:13.

27 1 Pet 3:15.

28 Page 26.

29 Articles Declaratory of the Constitution of the Church of Scotland in Matters Spiritual, Article 1.

to the apostolic faith. An unbiased interpretation of Church history should make this clear. The Westminster Fathers used the word "contain" because they wished to affirm that as the Word of God the Bible embraces both the Old and New Testaments and they were wishing to exclude from the Bible as God's Word, the books of the Apocrypha. They were also wishing to distinguish the Bible from every other book and affirm its uniqueness. They did not wish to affirm or suggest that parts of the Bible are not the Word of God. The fact that the Larger Catechism does not use the word "contain" is significant and helps to emphasise that the Reformers wished to affirm, and affirm strongly, that all Scripture is an authoritative witness to the Word of God.

The position that people within the church take in regard to same sex relationships and the ministry is determined by their view of the Bible as the Word of God, and its relevance for today. Those who adopt a progressive position and wish to accept same sex relationships, are generally willing to accept that the Bible is against same sex relationships, but seek to insist that the Bible only "contains" the Word of God. Hence they argue that some things in the Bible, such as the prohibition of same sex relationships, are not the Word of God.

Some of a liberal persuasion wish to say also that the Bible was the Word of God and authoritative for the day in which it was written, but it is not always and necessarily authoritative for us today. They say modern science has enabled us to understand much about creation of which the Biblical writers were unaware. They say it can guide us in our understanding of Scripture and help us to determine what is the Word of God and authoritative. Is this not to adopt the same position as those who say that the Bible only "contains" the Word of God?

If we argue that the Bible only "contains" the Word so that some things in the Bible are not the Word of God, then are we not seeking to place ourselves (as we said previously) above the Word of God so that we can make judgements upon it? In judging are we not, whether we know it or not, claiming to be superior to what we are judging, namely the Word of God and in fact, unwittingly seeking to place ourselves in the position of God? If we seek to argue that it is with the help of the Holy Spirit that we are judging what is and what is not the Word of God, then we are still claiming to be superior to the Word. We are still claiming to be in control. We are judging and the Holy Spirit is simply our helper in judging what is and is not the Word of God! As Christians, this is an impossible position to hold. How can we at one and the same time listen to, and seek to obey God's Word and stand in a position of judgement over it?

While we must use our minds to the full with all their faculties of reason we must at one and the same time listen to the Word of God addressing us in the Bible and acknowledge its authority. Through the Bible, God in Christ engages us to the full in body, mind and reason and we are not to bypass our reason but to allow it to be reborn and converted to him. Converted reason is reason restored, with its eyes opened from above to recognise the truth of Christ as true wisdom and true authority.

The Church owes her authority to the Word of God as witnessed to in Scripture. The Church's authority is the authority of a servant, commissioned to proclaim the Word of God. It has no independent authority of her own. "The church is called, empowered, and guided to her proclamation by Holy Scripture, and that involves the assertion that holy Scripture is the Word of God".[30] If and when the Church questions the authority of the Bible and seeks to elevate herself to a position where she can determine what is and what is not the Word of God, she loses her empowerment. The Church loses her authority to speak to the world. She will inevitably speak with a divided voice, being uncertain about what is truly the Word of God. The Church will lose her identity in Christ. Society and the world will not be generally attracted to the Church or wish to listen to the Church. For the most part the Church will simply say what the rest of the world already thinks and says. The Church in these circumstances ceases to be "the salt of the earth", proclaiming to the world the mind of Christ.

While, in the Old Testament there is a gradual revelation of God, nonetheless God is always true, unchanging and faithful to himself. In Christ, in the New Testament, we have a full and final revelation of God for all generations. God's Word as witnessed to in the written word of the Bible, is authoritative for every generation. This was and is the confession of the one holy Catholic Church. To depart from that is to dissent from the faith of the historic Church. If the Church seeks to accept parts of the Bible and to reject other parts, as authoritative for every generation, then she is in a sea of trouble. This, sadly, is to a great extent the position in which the Church of Scotland and the churches of the West find themselves today in discussing, marriage, morality, samesex relationships and education. As a result, the Church, in the eyes of many, has become irrelevant!

---

30 Barth, *Church Dogmatics*, Vol. 1, Part 1, 122.

Conclusion

In the Epistle to the Hebrews we read that "when Moses had proclaimed every commandment of the law to all the people, he took the blood of calves, together with water, scarlet wool and branches of hyssop, and sprinkled the scroll [KJV the book] and all the people. He said, 'This is the blood of the covenant, which God commanded you to keep'".[31] As Calvin said in his commentary on this passage, "By this ceremony the people were taught that God could only be sought or looked for for salvation or rightly worshipped if in every case faith looked to the mediation of blood" . . . "All worship is faulty and impure unless Christ cleanses it by the sprinkling of his blood".[32] The blood foreshadowed the blood of Jesus Christ. We can only draw near to God and receive the joy of his salvation and blessing through continually sharing with Christ in his death, resurrection and ascension. The sprinkling of the blood was not on the Word. It was on the scroll, which witnessed to the Word, and indicated that the people, and therefore we today, must in our hearts and minds, be continually cleansed, purified and renewed in order to hear and understand what God is saying.

Whether, therefore, we are of a liberal or evangelical persuasion, we all require to think humbly, carefully and prayerfully how we should understand the Bible and God's Word so that we can rightly and courageously proclaim his Word with authority.

If there is a conflict between our natural ideas or our natural wisdom and the wisdom of God in the Bible as we understand it, we must wrestle with the problem in prayer, prepared as we study the scriptures, to have our minds continually renewed that we might move beyond our often entrenched positions on the left and right to a deeper understanding of the Word of God.

Paul's Appeal: "Do not be conformed to this world but be transformed by the renewal of your mind, that you may prove what is the will of God, what is good and acceptable and perfect."[33]

Prayer: "Lord, open my eyes that I may see wonderful things in your law (Word)."[34]

---

31 Heb 9:10.

32 Calvin's Commentaries, *The Epistle of Paul to the Hebrews*, 125.

33 Rom 12:2.

34 Ps 119:18.

Chapter 5

The biblical affirmation of sex

Tom Smail

Canon Tom Smail was a minister of both the Church of Scotland and the Church of England, and formerly principal of St John's College, Nottingham. He died on 15th February 2012.

One thing I learnt in my Glasgow philosophy studies long ago is that a negative depends upon a prior positive; you can say No to something only because you have already said Yes to something else. You reject a false God on the basis of your ideas about the true God; you denounce something as wrong because it contradicts what you, perhaps only half consciously, already affirm to be right. Thus the positive always has priority over the negative, you are against something because you are for something else that is inconsistent with it.

The right relating of positive and negative is important in our present context of the biblical teaching about human sexuality in general and same-sex relationships in particular.

Here it is the negative that is most immediately obvious. The sexual aspect of human life is dealt with in the Decalogue by the seventh commandment's curt prohibition of adultery. In the teaching of Jesus the remarriages of those who have been divorced are also adjudged to be adulterous, and there is evidence that in the New Testament church, as even more in our own day, that hit hard.

When it comes to same sex relationships, the biblical references to the subject are few and brief and without exception negative. One thinks of such texts as Leviticus 18:22, 1 Corinthians 6:9 and 1 Timothy 1:9–10 in which the same sex condemnations are included in a list of other disqualifying vices without any precise definition of the meaning of the terms and where it is simply taken for granted that what is being described is unacceptable to God and so completely forbidden to Christians. It is the brevity and lack of context of these passages that have very much limited their usefulness in the current debates.

Much more substantial although equally negative is the passage in Romans 1:24-27 in which Paul sees homosexual acts as compelling evidence of the corruption of original sin in the intended expression of our sexuality. All who are complicit in the human rebellion against God that we call sin suffer without exemption or exception the consequences of that rebellion in one way or another. Paul mentions idolatry, envy, strife, deceit as typically afflictions of sinners, but for some their sin manifests itself rather in the diverting of their sexual passions and desires away from the opposite sex and on to their own.

To understand this important passage we have to look at the positive of which the homosexual activity it condemns is the contradiction and corruption, namely God's positive and creative will for his human creatures and how that is to be expressed in their sexuality which is their Creator's good gift to them.

God's positive affirmation of and purpose for men and women in their relating to one another is contained in one pivotal verse in Genesis which is the point from which all the central New Testament treatments of the subject start. Genesis 2:24 follows immediately on the story of the creation of Eve and tells us for what purpose the man and the woman were made the way they are and how they are meant to relate, the one to the other, "Therefore a man leaves his father and mother and clings to his wife and they become one flesh." The fact that Adam had neither father or mother to leave underlines the fact that we are dealing not with a historical account of what happened to the first couple but rather an authoritative statement about the Creator's intention in making human beings in the sexual differentiation of male and female.

That is in fact how Jesus deals with it in his teaching about marriage and divorce in Matthew 19 where he appeals past the Mosaic provisions for divorce to this verse. "Have you not read that the one who made them at the beginning made them male and female and said, 'For this reason a man shall leave his father and mother and be joined to his wife and they shall become one flesh." (19:4-5) Everything that Jesus goes on to say is presented as the implications of this one verse and, when we turn to Paul, it immediately becomes clear that all that he has to say about human sexuality and marriage in 1 Corinthians 7 and Ephesians 5 has this same verse as its normative source. In view of its centrality, it is worth looking at it rather more closely.

The first creation story in Genesis 1 is important because it affirms quite unambiguously that both men and women share a humanity that in both of them bears the image of God. The Eden story in Genesis 2 by contrast is more interested in the different but complementary ways in which that image is reflected in the two sexes. The main point is this: in that complementarity both the man and the woman become fully human; he cannot be authentically human without her and she cannot be authentically human without him.

It is not that the man has a set of typically masculine qualities and the woman a set of typically feminine ones; it is not a difference of nature – more like a difference of vocation. The distinctive calling of the man is the care of the garden: the distinctive calling of the woman is the care of the relationships that make life together possible and creative.

The man images God in the way he orders, cherishes, develops and ultimately perfects the created world that God has entrusted to him. That is his distinctive work, but working does not by itself fulfil his humanity. However engrossed or skilled in his work he may be, his life still lacks that which will make it a valid reflection and image of God. God does not only do mighty works, he exhibits self-giving love. In his triune being he does not only create and recreate the world, but he lives in a mutuality of relationships that constitute his very being. According to Genesis 2, it is the vocation of the woman to provide for the man the mutually loving relationships that in himself he both lacks and longs for and that none of the animals that he names can satisfactorily offer. Only when God brings Eve to him can he say, "This at last is bone of my bones and flesh of my flesh, this one shall be called Woman, for out of man was she taken." (2:23)

Because the woman is of the same humanity as the man, and he is less than human without her and she less than human without him, it is at the heart of their created reality that they long for each other and turn towards each other, to find their unrealised completeness. The fact that in the Genesis story she was made from him indicates that he knows he cannot be fully himself without her, and she knows that she cannot be herself in her isolation from him. They belong together; their distinct masculine and feminine vocations are not to be pursued in independence of each other, still less by domination of each other, but rather in sharing with each other. In all his inter-relating to the woman, most of all in his dependence on her as mother and his union with her as wife, the man has the opportunity to acquire the sensitivity and tenderness that make his life open and joyful.

In her relationship with the man first as father and then as husband, the woman, far from being confined to kids and kitchen, has the challenge of finding her place in the work of the world. The patriarchal domination that has for long tried to exclude her from that world sins against her, and also sins against the creative purposes of the God of Genesis 1 who commits the stewardship of his creation to both the man and the woman. She is to learn from him how to work better and he has to learn from her how to love better.

The female emancipation that has rightly become a central contemporary social concern in recent decades is, according to the biblical paradigm, to be seen not only as freedom from the man but freedom through the man by following and bringing her own distinctive contribution to the well trodden paths in which he has for too long walked alone.

This has all sorts of implications for man-woman relationships that we cannot explore here, but it has its archetypical expression in the mutual and unique commitment of marriage, so that the husband and wife relationship has priority over all other relationships – for this reason a man leaves his father and mother and cleaves to his wife. It is within this unique relationship that physical sex has its appointed place, "And they become one flesh". The sexual act is intended to be the bodily expression of the self-giving complementarity of husband and wife to each other. It expresses but also increases and deepens the love that is between them – in their physical union they quite literally fit into each other and make love. Furthermore it is through this sexual self-giving that the unique relationship of husband and wife demonstrates its inherent creativity. It takes both an ovum and a sperm to make a baby, and ideally at least it takes both a father and a mother to bring up a child. Children are born into a context in which what is distinctively male and what is distinctively female are present in a complementarity which, within all its limitations, at least goes some way towards modelling the complete humanity which is the image of God.

Seen in the light of the whole biblical revelation, the vocation of the man and the vocation of the woman are so intimately entwined that neither can be itself without the other, and neither has priority over the other. The God of the Bible is both the worker and the lover, so that the human worker and the human lover are both required if human life is to be an authentic mirror of divine life. The God of Genesis is the working creator of the whole universe, but also the one who comes walking in Eden in order to enjoy fellowship with his human creatures. He does many mighty works to liberate his chosen people from Egypt but he does them in order that he and they may enter into covenantal relationships in which he will be their God and they will be his people in a union that is often compared to a marriage.

The wedding services with which in our different denominations we are familiar all distinguish between the unitive and the procreative purposes of marriage and of sex within marriage. The tone and the quality of the marriage depend on the interaction of both. When the love that binds the spouses together fails, the children suffer. Where the marriage is childless, the spouses suffer, and both kinds of suffering are in evidence with their unhappy effects on family life and wider society around us every day.

Because in God's own life and activity love and creativity belong together, so in the human life that is made to mirror God, things are in good order when they go together as well. Faithful spouses make for happy families. Where a relationship lacks that publicly registered commitment of a man and a woman to stay together for richer or poorer, for better or worse, its future is uncertain and unstable. Because God is love, his purposes for his creation are reliable and unchanging and the married relationship mirrors both that divine love and that stability and reliability when a man and a woman reach the point of ultimate commitment when they are able to say to each other, "All that I am I give to you and all that I have I share with you, within the love of God, Father, Son and Holy Spirit."

It is important to see that the coming together of a man and a woman in the one flesh of lifelong marriage is not a matter of arbitrary divine inter-ference with what would otherwise be sexual autonomy where everybody was free to make their own erotic arrangements. As we have already seen the covenant commitment that constitutes marriage reflects the inmost essence of the life of the Creator that characterises all his dealings with us. In New Testament perspective Paul in Ephesians 5 can see the relationship between husband and wife as mirroring the relationship of Christ and his Church. Furthermore the fact that marriage is introduced in the context of the creation stories of Genesis is an indication that this relationship, far from being an alien and external imposition, is in fact an essential and necessary component that enables the creation to run as it was meant to in a loving environment from which, from generation to generation, the human creation has its continuity and its possibility of fulfilment. In other words, when marriage is honoured and works well, society also works well and where marriage is relativised and replaced, society begins to disintegrate and its future stability and advance comes under serious threat. The negative evidence for that is around us on every side and the current proposals to count same sex pairing as equivalent to marriage, a relationship that the biblical norm clearly shows to be incompatible with it, only make confusion worse confounded and future dangers even more threatening.

But here also we have to accentuate the positive; marriage works and those of us who have lived together as husband and wife over a whole long lifetime can appeal to an experience that confirms the biblical claims. We have not had perfect marriages but amidst faults and failings we have loved each other faithfully enough to see how being together has fulfilled us and opened doors to us that could not have come in any other way and enabled us to make homes in which our children could get at least a glimpse of what it was like for the love of God to be reflected and made credible in the love of their parents.

As I have been writing these last paragraphs, I have been hearing in the background a rising chorus of protests that what I have been saying may be exegetically justified but is hopelessly idealistic and out of touch with things as they are. It is not hard to produce example after example of marriages that have brought to those involved in them frustration rather than fulfilment, oppression rather than liberation, heartbreaking misery rather than exhilarating joy, where the experience of their own homes have made children wary of becoming involved in an institution which has brought such confusion into their lives. Even within the biblical record itself such central figures as Abraham, David and Solomon had dealings with women that were a thousand miles away from what is recommended in Genesis 2, and nevertheless God continued, while rebuking them, to love them and work through them. Even Jesus in the very act of confirming and indeed reinforcing the total claim that marriage imposes on husbands and wives nevertheless concedes that in the world as it is Moses had to make provisions for divorce as the far from ideal but the only available remedy for marriages that have become so destructive that the spouses need to be separated and their relationship dissolved.

All of which exposes within the particularities of sexual relationships the gap between things as God made them to be and things as they actually are with which we have to cope in very area of theological thinking and practice. After the story of the creation comes the story of the fall. The man and the woman have lapsed into a fundamental disobedience to the created purposes of God which has detrimental repercussions in the way they relate to each other and they are expelled from Eden into a far less congenial world which makes things hard for them both in the man's area of work and the woman's area of the birth and rearing of children. We are now in a world in which people are exposed to external influences and internal desires that urge them into relationships that challenge and contradict the purposes of God in the sexual realm as in every other. It is a world of casual sexual relationships, single parent families, oppressive and collapsed marriages and same sex partnerships. Nature and nurture in different combinations give people urges and orientations that, in the light of Genesis 2:24, expose them to sinful pressures not of their own choosing for which they nevertheless have to accept responsibility and make decisions about whether to resist or yield to them.

It is here that it becomes clear that the biblical positive does imply the biblical negatives. In a fallen world people are tempted to sin in ways which are against God's purposes for men and women – against the fidelity of marriage in adultery, against the loving relationship that God intends for husbands and wives in the selfish exploitation and oppression of one partner by the other, against the vocation to parenthood in their failure to give to the needs of children the priority that they require. It should be clear that homosexual activity is neither the only nor indeed the typical form of our falling short in this whole area. But it is equally clear that, in the light of the biblical positive we have been expounding, it is a fundamental deviation from what God requires from and offers to his people. In it sexual bonding is torn out of its ordained context in the rich and complementary relationship of husbands and wives; it can no longer have its intended outcome in the generation and nurture of children and in very many cases it proves itself an insufficient foundation for the faithful relationship of the partners to each other so that when desire fades, the relationship founded upon it often breaks with it. With some honourable exceptions of long faithful and caring same sex friendships that deserve appropriate respect, gay and lesbian relationships tend to be brief, unstable and constantly changing.

That is why in Romans 1 Paul lists erotic homosexual relationships as one of many areas in which our human condition shows itself to be fallen from the purposes of God and therefore under his judgement and, like the rest of us, in sore need of his redeeming grace.

From all this it is clear that Christians for whom the biblical revelation is normative find the redefinition of marriage to include same sex relationships an unacceptable option both for themselves and for a society that is to be built on solid and enduring foundations. Equally they should be concerned to see that children are as far as possible nurtured in families in which the creative loving complementarity of men and women is present to shape and enrich them.

The question remains of how we are to help pastorally, in a way that is consonant with the revealed and unchanging purposes of God, those who through no fault of their own have to cope with a homosexual orientation and relationships in which as a result they have become involved.

To demand instant allegiance to the marital norm without a sympathetic and nuanced response to the complicated changes which this would involve is at best unrealistic and at worst cruel and compassionless. At the other extreme, simply to surrender to urgent desires that are unaccountable to and undisciplined by the marital norm is to sin against the revealed divine purpose and to give free course to the social chaos that then ensues.

I suspect that the mature wisdom that such counsel would involve is still to be sought and is unlikely to be found in the current atmosphere of polemical confrontation in which this whole matter is currently being addressed. There is need for prayer that the Holy Spirit would enable us ultimately to hear amidst the clashing voices, the authentic word of the gospel.

Whatever in pastoral detail that word turns out to be, we can be sure that it will be one that affirms and honours the purposes of God for men and women as Genesis discloses them and as Jesus endorses them. In the meantime we may rejoice in the free grace of Jesus Christ that says to us all in all our sexual sinning, whether straight or gay, "Let him who is without sin among you cast the first stone", and then, "I do not condemn you, but go and sin no more."

Chapter 6

The Church's traditional view

Angus Morrison

Dr Morrison is a parish minister, and a former convener of the Church of Scotland Mission and Discipleship Council.

Proponents of both main positions in the debate on the question of the ordination of practising homosexuals recognize that this is essentially a theological issue, requiring theological justification for the position adopted. This is apparent in the 2007 General Assembly Report, 'A Challenge to Unity', in which many of the key arguments of a biblical and theological nature, in support of these positions, are presented. This paper is a summary of the various 'traditionalist'[1] arguments set out in that document.

The question of whether the Church of Scotland should ordain practising homosexuals is one of the utmost gravity, since apart from questions of how this relates to past understanding, and to other Churches today, such a move from the historic and catholic position entails an overturning of the understanding of Christian marriage held by the universal church from its inception. On any reckoning, this is a matter of deep seriousness. This paper proceeds by first looking at the question of biblical authority and interpretation, before considering important aspects of biblical evidence. The question of ordination in this context is then addressed, before a conclusion attempts to draw the threads together.

Part 1 Scripture in the traditionalist position

A The authority of Scripture

The Church of Scotland "receives the Word of God which is contained in the Scriptures of the Old and New Testaments as its supreme rule of

---

1 In this book, 'traditionalist' is sometimes used for a person who wishes to hold the Church's traditional understanding of marriage and same sex relationships, and 'revisionist' for a person who wishes to revise that understanding.

faith and life . . ." (Article I of the Articles Declaratory). It follows that in all matters of 'faith and life', the authority of Scripture is the fundamental issue.

It is important at this point to recollect that the Church of Scotland is a confessional church. Our confessional position is articulated in the Westminster Confession of Faith. Various attempts over the years to demote the Westminster Confession of Faith, in this regard, have been voted down at the General Assembly. The Articles Declaratory serve to define the confines and scope of the fellowship of the Church. When it comes, however, to the issue of the doctrine of the Church, we are necessarily referred to the Confession of Faith, as "containing the sum and substance of the Faith of the Reformed Church" (Articles Declaratory II). This is the case regarding the Church of Scotland's doctrine of marriage.

Some have sought to argue that the expression, "The Word of God, which is contained in the Scriptures of the Old and New Testaments," implies a disjunction between the 'Word of God' and the 'Scriptures'. This, however, is a very recent attempt to re-interpret theological language which has been used in the Church of Scotland for almost 400 years.

The language here used is that of the Westminster standards themselves. It is taken from the Answer to Q.2 of the Shorter Catechism: "The word of God, which is contained in the scriptures of the Old and New Testaments, is the only rule to direct us how we may glorify God and enjoy him." The meaning attached by the Westminster divines to the phrase "contained in" is clarified both in the Confession of Faith, the Church of Scotland's "principal subordinate standard" (Article II), and in the Larger Catechism. The former states, "Under the name of Holy Scripture, or the Word of God written, are now contained all the Books of the Old and New Testaments" (Westminster Confession of Faith 1/2). The answer to Q.3 ("What is the word of God?") of the Larger Catechism is, "The holy scriptures of the Old and New Testament are the word of God, the only rule of faith and obedience."

From this identification of Scripture and the Word of God, it is clear that the framers of the Westminster documents understood there to be no disjunction between the two. Indeed, a moment's reflection makes obvious that the expression "contained in" is nothing other than a delimitation of what is Scripture (the books of the Old and New Testaments), as distinct from a canon that would include various other books; in particular, as accepted by the Roman Catholic Church, those of the Apocrypha.

In the light of the Church's long-established practice, it would be, at least, highly idiosyncratic to take a set of words with a definite and widely recognized theological history, and suddenly to begin to use them in an entirely different way, without a clear, prior process. Whatever may have been in the minds of the framers of the Articles (and a particular understanding of that has certainly been influential over the years), the consistent testimony of the whole history of theology demands that we interpret the words in accordance with their proper meaning, which is that of the original authors from whom they were taken, more or less verbatim. On this understanding, the Church of Scotland holds to a view of the Bible that does not posit a disjunction between Word and Scripture. The authority of the Word of God is the authority of Scripture.

In the current controversy regarding the ordaining of practising homo-sexuals, most traditionalists would identify the Word of God and Scripture, while most revisionists – certainly those among them who are concerned to show some basis in the Bible for their stance – find it essential to hold a (characteristically strong) view of the disjunction between the two. It seems clear, however, that while the revisionist position certainly demands such a disjunction, the distinction itself does not entail an endorsement of the revisionist position. For it to do so, it would be essential to establish that the Word of God contradicts Scripture. It is highly questionable whether any, on either side of the issue, have reached that particular place.

B Interpreting Scripture: in the company of the church catholic

It is sometimes said that the issue before us is not a question of the authority of Scripture, but of the right interpretation of Scripture. This is a false distinction. The authority of any document (legal, philosophical, educational, etc) is found precisely in its correct interpretation. It is our recognition of the supreme authority of Scripture for 'faith and life' that makes the issue of its correct interpretation of such importance. The authority of Scripture is just Scripture properly interpreted.

The Bible is the Church's book. At an early stage, the Church recognized the imperative of reading Scripture in an ecclesial context in order to attain its authentic Christian interpretation. Our Lord's promise of the Holy Spirit to lead into the fullness of truth has always been understood within this context. In the early Church, with the rise of the Gnostic movement, the Church found itself having to deal with some very strange interpretations of Scripture. Irenaeus of Lyons (c.130 – c.200), widely regarded as one of the church's greatest theologians, took note of the fact that heretics tended to interpret the Bible according to their personal wishes. The maintenance of orthodoxy, on the other hand, required that the Bible be interpreted in ways that their apostolic authors would have approved. Irenaeus recognized that a certain way of reading and understanding biblical texts had developed since apostolic times. This meant that the Church was thereby able to identify those who had kept faith with apostolic teaching, a capacity understood to be of crucial importance.

Since at least the time of Irenaeus, the Church has recognized the necessity, for its health and stability, of attending closely to the Church's 'great tradition' in its reading of Scripture. Failure to do so makes it a prey to the ever shifting currents of the particular culture it inhabits; in our own time of what has aptly been termed a "culture dominated by the ideology of the ephemeral". A major weakness of the revisionist approach is its deep reluctance to handle Scripture in the way the Church has always seen as essential to the 'communion of saints', to its continuity with its past, and to its stability in the present.

Compare Scripture with Scripture

Within this context, it is appropriate to recall that, as a Church, we stand within the Reformed tradition, and the basic hermeneutical approach of that tradition is the grammatico-historical method. The purpose of this method is to establish the intention of the original author of the text, through a careful study of the text in its original language and context, together with an understanding of its genre and canonical setting. One key element within this process is the principle of 'comparing scripture with scripture'. The Reformers believed in the fundamental unity of Scripture as the Word of God, and argued that by comparing scripture with scripture, the fullest depth of the meaning, and of our understanding, of Scripture is attained.

Coherent, not arbitrary

Any valid method of interpreting Scripture must be coherent and must be used consistently. There are approaches to interpreting Scripture that appear to proceed in a manner that lacks such coherence, giving preference to texts that are 'liked', while ignoring or rejecting texts that are 'not liked', with no coherent basis offered for the acceptance of some and the rejection of others. A 'pick and mix' hermeneutic of this sort cannot be acceptable in a Reformed Church which advocates an educated ministry and a serious academic approach to God's Word. Another way to express this would be to say that a hermeneutic must be honest. It cannot be acceptable to claim to adhere to a coherent, Reformed hermeneutic, but then to undermine every text which does not fit in with a worldview which appears to have been otherwise determined.

It is also vital that an arbitrary method of interpreting Scripture be avoided. For example, to privilege one theme of Scripture (say, 'the love of God'), while rejecting any passage of Scripture that appears to conflict with a pre-determined understanding of what that theme means, can hardly be acceptable.

The preaching of the Church

We must also seek to develop a method of interpreting Scripture which enables and sustains the preaching of the church. The example of Karl Barth is instructive. When the young Barth had completed his studies he went to be pastor at Safenwil in Switzerland. Before long he began to encounter difficulties. He found that the liberal theology in which he had been schooled left him with very little to say from the pulpit. More and more, he turned to what he called "the strange, new world of the Bible", and increasingly he recognized what he came to see as the emptiness and the essentially destructive nature of the liberal theology of his teachers. He began his own explorations in theology and these studies eventually led to his publishing a commentary on Paul's letter to the Romans. It was said that this commentary "fell like a bomb on the playground of the theologians". In many ways it could be said that this book spelled the end of classical liberal theology as the dominant force in Christian theology. Barth recognized that some previous scholars, particularly those influenced by the liberal school, had become so preoccupied with technical issues that they no longer allowed the Bible to speak. They treated it as the word of man, and in no meaningful sense as the Word of God. Barth went on to develop the most significant theological project of the 20th century. In some important respects the Church is still catching up with his biblically founded theological insights.

Part 2   Biblical themes and texts

It follows from this view of the authority and interpretation of Scripture that our view of human sexual relationships must be based on Scripture. A summary of that Scripture teaching is provided by our Church's Confession.

The Westminster Confession offers the principal doctrinal standard for the Church's understanding of marriage. This doctrine is set out in chapter

24: "Of Marriage and Divorce". Thus, marriage is to be between one man and one woman (24:1). Further, it 'ought not to be within the degrees of consanguinity or affinity forbidden by the word' (24:4).If marriage is to be between "one man and one woman", then clearly homosexual partnerships must be regarded as 'forbidden by the word'. Thus, the doctrinal norm of the Church, with respect to those partnerships sanctioned in Scripture and the Reformed tradition, is understood exclusively in terms of the partnership between a man and a woman expressed in marriage. This position entails no discrimination against homosexual people, as such, for it recognizes that outwith this context heterosexual and homosexual practice are equally off-limits. Traditionalists take no issue with people of homosexual orientation, who are as welcome into the membership and ordained ministry of the Church as are those of heterosexual orientation. The Christian doctrine of marriage, however, is the proper context for the discussion of the matters before the Church.

The importance of Scripture for determining the Church's position on same sex relationships cannot be sufficiently stressed. In the 1973 Report of the Panel on Doctrine, following some rather speculative material on how we may discern the 'Word of God' for today, the Report states:

> The Reformation Doctrine made preaching subordinate to the Word of God in Scripture, the soundness of preaching being tested by Scripture. And when the Westminster Confession, true to the Reformation, made Scripture "the supreme rule of faith and life", Scripture became the test of the integrity of a man's Christian life . . . If we need such a test in our day, where do we have to go but where the Reformers went in theirs – to Scripture, for it is still the authoritative witness to the living Christ? And the Church does need a criterion – especially in view of our Report's apparent *carte blanche* to recognition and use of all manner non-verbal and seemingly non-theological modes as potential channels of the "Word of God". The Panel has not regarded it as its function to adjudicate in this Report on the relative merits and dangers of those modes we have cited in illustration . . . It is sufficient, but necessary, that we should simply state our awareness that problems could arise for the Church locally and nationally, in practical exercise of the latitude we commend (as theologically just) in understanding what may be and convey the Word of God, and that in such eventualities, as traditionally, the Scripture has an indispensable function (through

the complete clarity with which Paul in Romans 1 "includes homosexual behaviour among the consequences of turning away from God" (Rom 1:27); places in 1 Corinthians 6 homosexual practice alongside "fornication, adultery, idolatry, greed, drunkenness, theft and robbery, as the kinds of behaviour which preclude participation in the Kingdom of God" (1 Cor 6:9f.), and affirms that "through baptism Christians have become free from their entanglement in all such practices" (1 Cor 6:11). He adds, "The New Testament contains not a single passage that might indicate a more positive assessment of homosexual activity to counterbalance these Pauline statements. Thus, the entire biblical witness puts practised homosexuality, without exception, among the kinds of behaviour which give particularly striking expression to humanity's turning away from God."[6]

One particular matter requires brief treatment. It is sometimes argued that the difference between our contemporary situation and that addressed in Scripture, is that the biblical texts do not deal with long-term same sex partnerships, that the Bible condemns only exploitative, pederastic forms of homosexuality. The response to this is two-fold. First, "the biblical texts themselves nowhere limit their rejection of homosexual conduct to exploitative forms."[7] For example, the prohibitions in Leviticus 18:22 and 20:13 are entirely unqualified: "any man who lies with another male in the manner that men lie with women (i.e. engaging in sexual intercourse) has committed an abomination. There are no exceptions . . . Neither is there any mention of the exploitative character of the relationship. If homosexual actions were wrong primarily because they were exploitative, why would Leviticus 20:13 specify a penalty of death for both participants, the exploited as well as the exploiter?"[8] The same absoluteness of wording is found in Romans 1:26-27. The reference there to lesbianism is also significant, for the available evidence indicates that most lesbian practise took place between mutually consenting women of roughly equal age.[9] Paul's linking of male and female homosexual behaviour "suggests that he reject both forms of homosexual behaviour for the same reason; that is, on grounds other than their exploitative or oppressive character."[10] Paul, like other Jews, understood the creation story of Genesis 1–3 "as endorsing

---

6 From the same article.

7 Gagnon, *op cit.*, 347.

8 *Op. cit.*, 347.

9 *Op. cit.*, 348, fn. 6.

10 *Op. cit.*, 348.

only heterosexual unions. Contrary to nature is a reference to erasing the stamp of gender placed on male and female by the Creator."[11]

Further, "it is misleading to argue as if Jewish Christian writers had nothing but negative images from which to base their judgement of homosexuality."[12] The fact is that the Greco-Roman world was very familiar with homosexual relationships that were stable, non-exploitative and not pederastic. Gagnon provides conclusive evidence of this.[13] Dr Richard Corbett, minister in Kilmallie, has a booklet which provides even more evidence.[14] From Plato's Symposium in the 4th century BC to the Pseudo-Lucianic Affairs of the Heart, ca. 300AD (with the literature including accounts of gay weddings in Imperial Rome), incontrovertible evidence establishes that knowledge of faithful same sex relationships was widespread in the ancient world, as well as exploitative homosexual relationships and pederasty.

It is simply not credible that "Jews and Christians could not make the distinction between exploitative and non-exploitative forms. Victimization simply did not factor significantly in the arguments that Jews and Christians made in the ancient world. All forms of homosexual and lesbian conduct were wrong simply because of what it was not: natural sexual intercourse with the opposite."[15] In this respect, there is adequate similarity between the ancient and modern cultural contexts, "because the fundamental aspect of homosexuality and lesbianism that accounts for their rejection remains the same: the lack of gender complementarity in same sex couples. Two thousand years of history have not changed that basic fact of human existence."[16] For a similar view, from arguably the 20th century's greatest theologian, see Karl Barth, *Church Dogmatics* III.4, 166.

If the 1973 Panel on Doctrine Report is right (as it surely is) to state that, in respect of resolving such problematic issues as the one before us, the testimony of Scripture holds an "indispensable function", there can be little doubt as to the conclusion to which we are constrained. The universal and unequivocal testimony of Scripture is that same sex sexual relations are invariably sinful.

---

11 *Op. cit.*, 350.
12 *Op. cit.*, 350.
13 *Op. cit.*, 350-361.
14 Richard Corbett, *Is The Very Concept of a Same Sex Faithful Relationship in the Context of Love, or indeed the Idea of Sexual Orientation an Anachronism for Paul?*
15 *Op. cit.*, 360.
16 *Op. cit.*, 360–61.

Part 3 Ordaining practising homosexuals

The question of the ordination of practising homosexuals introduces a further range of theological issues. Their discussion, of course, becomes redundant if the understanding of Scripture expressed in the previous section is accepted. A number of points, however, may usefully be made, with particular reference to the Form of Presbyterial Church Government (1645), and the 2000 and 2001 Reports to the General Assembly of the Panel on Doctrine. It is clear that nothing essential has changed in our understanding of the place of life, doctrine and gifts, in the context of ordination, since production of the 1645 document.

A *The practice of ordination within the Church of Scotland is inherently theological in its nature.*

"What is required is a doctrine of ordination soundly based on a theological understanding of the Church and its ministry."[17]

For the church this has clear implications for its assessment of scientific and legal perspectives, for example in respect of 'rights conferred by civil law'. Ordination, as an extension of baptism (in its turn an extension of the biblical doctrine of election), can acknowledge talk of 'rights' only within the context of the doctrine of grace. It is in fact doubtful whether the current secular debate can have any particular interest in the church's doctrine of ordination or induction.

B *Ordination within the Church of Scotland has an essentially catholic character.*

The 2000 Panel on Doctrine Report produced a set of 'Criteria for Ordained Ministries' which may be regarded as the conclusion of that Report and as providing the foundation of the Panel's further report in 2001 (13.4). Integral to the Criteria is the relationship between the ordained ministries and the "Holy, Catholic, or Universal, Church", that is, the church in the full depth and breadth of its universality as expressed in the particularity and richness of the communion of the Roman Catholic, Orthodox, Free, Lutheran, Anglican and Reformed Churches. The Church of Scotland affirms that it "is part of the Holy, Catholic, or Universal, Church" (Article I of Articles Declaratory of the Constitution of the Church of Scotland). Any decision taken by the Church of Scotland on this

---

17 2000 Report, 1.4.

issue impacts upon the sense in which this Church is and continues to be "part of the Holy Catholic, or Universal, Church". How do we understand what it means to be "part of the Holy Catholic, or Universal, Church"? One influential understanding is that offered by Vincent of Lerins (c. 434 AD), who expresses that participation in terms of the universality of the belief of the Holy Catholic Church. In his Commitorium 4.3.4, Vincent expresses this in terms of the 'canon': *quod ubique, quod semper, quod ab omnibus creditum est.* Thus, he writes:

> Now in the Catholic Church itself we take the greatest care to hold that which has been believed everywhere, always and by all. That is truly and properly 'Catholic,' as is shown by the very force and meaning of the word, which comprehends everything almost universally. We shall hold to this rule if we follow universality, antiquity, and consent. We shall follow universality if we acknowledge that one Faith to be true which the whole Church throughout the world confesses; antiquity if we in no wise depart from those interpretations which it is clear that our ancestors and fathers proclaimed; consent, if in antiquity itself we keep following the definitions and opinions of all, or certainly nearly all, bishops and doctors alike. What then will the Catholic Christian do, if a small part of the Church has cut itself off from the communion of the universal Faith? The answer is sure. He will prefer the healthiness of the whole body to the morbid and corrupt limb. But what if some novel contagion try to infect the whole Church, and not merely a tiny part of it? Then he will take care to cleave to antiquity, which cannot now be led astray by any deceit of novelty. What if in antiquity itself two or three men, or it may be a city, or even a whole province, be detected in error? Then he will take the greatest care to prefer the decrees of the ancient General Councils, if there are such, to the irresponsible ignorance of a few men. But what if some error arises regarding which nothing of this sort is to be found? Then he must do his best to compare the opinions of the Fathers and enquire their meaning, provided always that, though they belonged to diverse times and places, they yet continued in the faith and communion of the one Catholic Church; and let them be teachers approved and outstanding. And whatever he shall find to have been held, approved and taught, not by one or two

only but by all equally and with one consent, openly, frequently, and persistently, let him take this as to be held by him without the slightest hesitation.

Thus, the reception of the Christian faith within the communion of the Holy Catholic Church is understood in terms of a holding to that which has been believed everywhere, always and by all. According to this understanding, one of the concerns that ought to motivate the Church of Scotland is the sense in which any decision made with respect to the ordination of a minister of Word and Sacrament is consonant with the understanding of Ordination within the Holy Catholic Church. It is within this context that the "Criteria for Ordained Ministries" are to be understood:

1) Ordained ministries should be those which are concerned not just for one part of the Church's life and activity, but for the Church as such, for its character as the Church. They are ministries whose concern is to keep the church faithful to its nature and calling.

2) The fact that such ministries are concerned with the Church's fidelity to its nature and calling means that they are answerable to the Church – the whole Church. They are therefore considered to be ministries of Christ's Church, the Church Catholic, not simply the local church. Such ministries, being answerable to the wider Church, are recognized and authorised by the wider Church.

If the Church of Scotland were to depart from the teaching of the "Holy, Catholic, or Universal Church" in relation to the ordination to the ministry of Word and Sacrament, it would thereby distance itself from the reality of what it means to be part of the One, Holy, Catholic and Apostolic Church, and place in question the extent to which the Church of Scotland could affirm that it "adheres to the Scottish Reformation; receives the Word of God which is contained in the Scriptures of the Old and New Testaments as its supreme rule of faith and life; and avows the fundamental doctrines of the Catholic faith founded thereupon" (Articles Declaratory I)

Fidelity to the teaching of the "Holy Catholic, or Universal, Church", as it continues to be held by the great majority of communions, is the issue before the Church of Scotland in its consideration of ordination to the Ministry of Word and Sacrament. Any departure from this teaching imperils the claim of the Church of Scotland to maintain an ordained ministry which stands in the Apostolic Succession.

C The Reformed tradition recognizes an important distinction between the 'inner' and 'outward' call to the ordained ministry.

While an 'inner' call from God is necessary, such an 'inner' call does not have "the church as witness" (Calvin, Institutes 4.3.11). A person is called to ministry because the Church discerns that they evidence learning, piety and gifting, not because they can offer evidence of an 'inner' call.

Indeed, a congregation can object to a nominee on the basis of "life or doctrine". The former has always been taken to mean a moral life lived in conformity with the teaching of Scripture.

D In that discernment, within the Reformed tradition, the recognition of gifts has been recognized as important.

Of far greater importance in this tradition, however, has been the issue of sound doctrine and holiness of life. In this context, for example, when Calvin, in the Institutes, speaks of gifts, his stress even there is on the gift of being able to instruct the people in godliness and the gift of exercising discipline (4.3.6). Calvin concludes his thoughts on this matter by saying: "To sum up, only those are to be chosen who are of sound doctrine and of holy life, not notorious in any fault which might both deprive them of authority and disgrace the ministry." (4.3.12)

The subsequent Reformed tradition has consistently echoed that emphasis. For example, the Form of Presbyterial Church Government (1645) instructs that the Presbytery, in considering whether or not to ordain a man to the ministry, should "proceed to enquire touching the grace of God in him, and whether he be of such holiness of life as is requisite in a minister of the gospel . . ."

Part 4 Conclusion

In the article already referred to, Wolfhart Pannenberg makes the important point that "homophile inclinations . . . need not be denied and must not be condemned". There must be a welcome place in the ordained ministry of the church of people, otherwise suitably qualified, of homosexual orientation. There can be no debate on that matter.

The significant, and difficult, matter for us however is to "deal with the conclusion that homosexual activity constitutes a departure from the norm for sexual behaviour which has been given to men and women as creatures of God."[18] Pannenberg's concluding words are so important that they merit citation in full:

> In the view of the Church, this is the case not only for homo-sexuality but for any sexual activity that does not intend the goal of marriage between man and wife, and hence in particular for adultery. The Church has to live with the fact that, in this area of life as in others, departures from the norm are not exceptional but common.

The Church must encounter all those concerned with tolerance and understanding, but must also call them to repentance. It cannot surrender the distinction between the norm and behaviour which departs from it.

Here lies the boundary of a Christian Church that knows itself to be bound by the authority of Scripture. Those who urge the Church to change the norm of its teaching on this matter must know that they are promoting schism. If a Church were to let itself be pushed to the point where it ceased to treat homosexual activity as a departure from the biblical norm, and recognized homosexual unions as a personal partnership of love equiv-alent to marriage, such a Church would no longer stand on biblical ground but against the unequivocal witness of Scripture.

A Church which took such a step would thereby have ceased to be one, holy, catholic, and apostolic.

It would be difficult to express more succinctly the inescapable conclusion flowing from the theological exposition in this paper than in the following words of Professor N.T. Wright (formerly Bishop of Durham):

> First, the Church cannot sanction or bless same sex unions; second, since the ordained ministry carries a necessarily representative function for the life of the Church, those who order their life in this way cannot be ordained.[19]

---

18 Article cited.
19 Article in Fulcrum, 2009.

Chapter 7

Understanding marriage

David J Torrance

The Revd David J. Torrance is a parish minister of the Church of Scotland.

Questions of marriage and same sex relations cannot be considered in isolation. They carry implications for other, more central matters of Christian understanding and it is because of this inherent interconnectedness of faith that these issues are so divisive. There is an impact on the core recognitions of the Christian faith.

Part One – Theological considerations

We begin with some theological observations which must inform our approach to marriage.

Relational Knowing

Christian thinking about male and female involves a relational way of knowing which denies the possibility of knowing maleness and femaleness 'in themselves', or in relational abstraction from each other. To understand this it is necessary to refer back to how we know God as presented to us in the Scriptural witness and in the historic formulations of the faith.

In the early centuries of the Christian church, the church fathers were forced to articulate key elements of the Christian faith as they grappled with the cultural implications of Greek thought. They had to spell out the boundaries of faith in the context of many challenges which threatened the foundation of the gospel. In particular, they had to focus on questions about the person of Christ and the triune nature of God as Father, Son and Holy Spirit and yet one Person. This helps us in our approach to understanding one another and the importance of marriage as God intended:

It is not given to us to know Jesus in himself as an independent individual. We can only know him as 'Son of the Eternal Father' and as anointed by the Holy Spirit – i.e. within the relational dynamic of triune being. Neither is it given to us to know the Father except as 'Father of the Eternal Son' and by the Holy Spirit.[1] Similarly, we cannot know the Holy Spirit in any independent individuality, except as the Spirit who proceeds from the Father and the Son and imparts to us the reality and presence of the Son and in him, the Father.

We cannot extract any of the three from the matrix of their eternal divine relations and consider them independently. Challenging as it is, we must learn to try and think all three together, as three-in-one. Any attempt to do otherwise necessarily brings about a distortion in our understanding and daily walk with God. Practically, we may begin speaking of one before we speak of the others, yet to be faithful to the revelation of the gospel, we imme-diately find ourselves compelled to speak of the other two. To pursue truly Christian theology, we must commence with a proper recognition of Trinity and continually refer back to it – allowing this to influence our conversations at every stage. Despite the practical and experiential reality of how we may have personally come to faith and understanding, 'Trinity' is our theological starting-point. We must begin with the mystery of divine inter-relations.

Similarly, we cannot understand what it means to be 'man' or 'woman' except in relational terms. Man is the counterpart of woman. Woman is the counterpart of man. Attempts to extract 'man' or 'woman' from the relational dynamic of this inter-relatedness invariably end up ensnared in a morass of stereotypical categorisation – usually, to the detriment of the woman.

When speaking of the creation of humanity, the narratives oscillate freely between God and man in both the singular and the plural. Consider Genesis 1:26ff. and Genesis 5:1 – God is us/our/he. Man is him/them.

Humanity in the image of God must be understood in profoundly relational terms. Humanity is not just male and female, found either as an individual man or as an individual woman. Challenging as it may be for us in the cultural context of Western individualism, we must also think of 'both together'; humanity (singular) as male-female.

We Know by Encounter

We cannot truly know God except as he encounters us in those divine inter-relations – as he comes to us in the humanity of Christ in the physical dynamic of the Incarnation and in the baptism of the Spirit. We can only know him as the Holy Spirit dwells within us and as the Father and the Son

---

1 "No-one has ever seen God; the only begotten God, being in the bosom of the Father, he has declared him." (John 1:18)

make their abode in us,[2] and as we are gathered up to abide in him and dwell within the triune inter-relations of his eternal being. These are the "unfathomable riches of Christ" and the astonishing reality of divine love by which God comes to us in our frailty and takes us to himself. By grace we are caught up, in him and in all our creaturely humanity, to participate in the "fellowship (*koinonia*) of the mystery".[3]

It is only in relationship, as we are related to him in his divine inter-relations and in his relatedness to us, that we can know and speak of him. We cannot know him in abstract or by standing back and observing in detached analysis. We must receive and yield to him and to his cleansing, healing and transforming presence and power.

We are designed for relationship and encounter, so that we can only truly know ourselves as we encounter God. There is an insatiable human longing which can only be satisfied as we know him and are gathered home to him.

Likewise, we can only know each other through encounter. Broadly: in terms of social human encounter with other men and women. Specifically: in terms of our maleness and femaleness. Although we may have a broad sense of being male or female by means of our physical design and through association with others of our own gender etc; nevertheless, each individual can only know their particular sense of maleness or femaleness as they encounter someone of the opposite gender. This does not require sexual encounter, just a healthy and wholesome interaction between the sexes. However, there is a profound sense in which this is particularly true in male-female sexual encounter.

We return again to the creation narratives. When God fashioned woman out of man, He presented her to the man (*adam*). As he recognised her as his counterpart, his response was to exclaim, "'This other' is now (at last) bone of my bones, flesh of my flesh. 'This other' shall be called female (*ish-shah*) for 'this other' was taken out of male (*iysh*). Therefore shall a male (*iysh*) leave his father and mother and cleave (join) to his female (*ish-shah*) and the two shall become one flesh".[4] We note:

- The woman is 'other' to the man.
- He calls her female (*ish-shah*), as opposed to himself, as male (*iysh*). This is a Hebrew play on words. His term for her, *ish-shah*, might be better translated as 'she-male', for she was taken out of male, (*iysh*).

---

2   John 14:23.

3   Eph 3:9.

4   Gen 2:23.

- Up to that point, he has always been called 'man' (*adam*). Now, having encountered his counterpart in the female (*ish-shah*) he calls himself male (*iysh*). It is 'she' who has awakened his sense of maleness.
- His recognition of her as female, plus the awareness of his own maleness, which he only now knows as he encounters her femininity, is prior to any sexual encounter.
- The coming together of the male and female counterparts of humanity is described as a 'joining' to become one flesh.

The words *iysh* and *ish-shah* could also be translated as husband and wife. In a very obvious way, he only becomes 'husband' as she becomes 'wife'. The word 'husband' has no real meaning except as 'her husband'. Similarly 'wife' has no meaning except as 'his wife'. They are relational terms. We cannot, therefore, abstract 'husband' or 'wife' from the context of 'husband-wife' and find meaning in these terms themselves. They only have meaning in relation to 'the other'.

Part two – Image of God

One of the key assertions about humanity is that we are made in the image of God and according to his likeness. Humanity is called uniquely to represent God within creation, to be his agent and viceroy. Genesis 1 presents humanity primarily in vocational terms. God blessed them,[5] as stewards, exercising dominion and authority as his ministers and representatives.

Although not specifically stated, it would not be beyond the sense of this vocation to think of it in prophetic, priestly and kingly terms. These words, especially favoured by the Reformers, describe the ministry of Christ – Prophet, Priest and King – who is himself "the image of the unseen God; firstborn of all creation".[6] From the beginning, humanity was patterned and called according to the likeness of the image of Christ, "the firstborn of all creation". Colossians also communicates an understanding of Christ as visibly manifesting and perfectly revealing God in human form.

It is too simplistic to assume that every Old Testament passage was clearly understood in its own day. There are many things in the Old Testament witness which do not make sense until seen in the light of the New Testament and the incarnation and atonement in Jesus Christ. Christ is the prototype for human imaging of God, as well as the prototypical, visible

---

5   Gen 1:28.

6   Col 1:15.

manifestation and revelation of God in human form,[7] sharing in the same flesh and blood of our creaturely humanity.[8]

Although we must give due weight to the Genesis narratives, we must allow the New Testament witness about Christ to inform and enlarge our understanding. Humanity made in the image of God means, made according to the likeness of the physical humanity of Christ – the image and visible manifestation of God in human form – albeit that his manifestation in our space time continuum was yet to come. He is "the firstborn of all creation, in whom all things were created . . . He is before all things and in him all things consist".[9] Jesus, therefore, is the 'guarantor' of our creaturely humanity, giving significance, meaning, value and worth in this life; and, because of his bodily resurrection and ascension, in all eternity.

We make several observations:

(a) **The image of God is a relational image.** We cannot abstract humanity from relationship with God and then search within for certain god-like characteristics, which we possess intrinsically within ourselves or in contradistinction from the rest of creation. There may well be! But the sense in which the Bible uses the phrase is to describe how, with upturned faces, in loving service and obedience, we are designed to reflect the glory of God and exercise his reign as he indwells us. It is an image we bear in reference to him, not something we now possess in independence from him.

(b) **The image of God is corporate.** Both the blessings and the injunction to have dominion were explicitly given to 'them' – not the man alone but both man and woman together. When thinking of Christ as the image of God, we need seriously to consider the formation of the church, brought forth by the Spirit from his side, as his bride, and raised up in covenant union to reign with him, and share in him in bearing the divine image. Ultimately it is the entire social corpus of humanity which is called to represent God. This is specifically the case with the church. Thus, although all believers, in their singleness or individuality, display something of Christ in the world, yet there is a unique way in which we reflect something together which cannot be displayed by the individual in isolation.

(c) **It is a gendered image.** The basic unit of humanity is male female – man and woman together as one in a corporate unit. It is not man in his

---

7 Heb 1:3.

8 Heb 2:14.

9 Col 1:15-17.

masculine individuality, or woman in her feminine individuality. This does not mean that gender has no meaning or that any person's singleness is in any way deficient. Even within marriage a person still remains the particular man or woman they were created to be. In this sense, they don't become something else. Nevertheless, marriage has meaning. In a very general way it is intended to reflect, model and express the fundamental value of all men and all women made together in the image of God. We are each – all humanity before God – partakers of one flesh. In this broad sense, we must think of our common humanity as a corporate union, rightly understood as analogous to, and mirroring (however inadequately) the relationship of the Father and the Son through the Holy Spirit. In a more particular sense, we must also understand marriage as being reflective of, or analogous to (however inadequately) God in his triune inter-relations.

In a very unique way, marriage – the joining together of one man and one woman to become one flesh – is intended to form the basic unitive foundation of all humanity and society. We are all – gay and straight alike – born of the union of male and female. How we may live the life which has been given to us is necessarily and always secondary to the fact that we have been given it in the first place. Thus, same sex relations do not and never can have the same value and significance as the union of male and female. This is a fact of origins. It is 'without exception' and an unalterable reality.[10]

We can never understand God simply from an understanding of our own humanity. Rather, we understand humanity from our understanding of God and in terms of the Son of God become man in Christ Jesus. Any attempt to do otherwise involves a type of mythological approach to God which self-deifies us. In debates about Christ within the early church, Athanasius, a champion of orthodoxy, told his opponent, Arius: "You are a mythologiser (mythologein), projecting your own images onto God. We do not engage in mythology but in theology (theologein)."[11] We must therefore allow God to manifest his own nature to us – a process which shatters our preconceptions, interrupts our speech and thought processes, and imparts its own categories of language and understanding. It is God himself who is the great iconoclast.

Thankfully, God accommodates himself to our human frailty to reveal and speak to us – while always calling us into a whole new appreciation

---

10 "Honour your father and mother" (Deut. 5:16); "the first command with a promise" (Eph 6:2f.).

11 J B Torrance, *Worship, Community and the Triune God of Grace*, 88.; cf Athanasius, *Contra Gentes*, 19.

of his nature. The appellation, 'Father', is a name which he gives to us, yet it is much more than a name. It depicts something of his eternal nature in relation to the eternal Son. Although God is never called, 'Mother', neverthe-less there are still clear passages where we see 'mothering' in his fatherhood. His fatherhood is utterly unlike our own. In the language of the Nicene Creed; he is eternally Father, eternally begetting, and the Son is eternally the Son, eternally begotten not made. We cannot explain that by reading upwards from our own fallen experience of fatherhood, or motherhood or from our own 'begottenness' and project that back onto God. It is from him that we derive any true sense of these things, not vice versa. Our human experience is simply a corrupted reflection of what we see in God.

In the creation narratives we see God acting creatively, calling forth creation. He does so in and of himself, both in his unity and in his triune inter-relations. Finally he calls forth humanity in his image – both in its unity and duality; an image which requires a duality of gender within humanity to represent him. In this sense we have to say that gender finds its origin in God. Yet, we must stress, this is a very different thing from reflecting our sense of gender back onto God, in a mythological way, and attributing our sense of maleness or femaleness onto him. Gender belongs to our human existence, yet it has its transcendent reference in God. To quote C.S. Lewis: "Gender is a reality, and a more fundamental reality than sex. Sex is, in fact, merely the adaptation to organic life of a fundamental polarity which divides all created beings".[12]

Jesus said that in the resurrection people will neither marry nor be given in marriage.[13] This does not mean a terminus to gender. God has created humanity in two forms, male and female. He does not discard what he has created. There will be men and women in the resurrection – albeit renewed, transformed and glorified.

(d) It is a physical image. God created men and women to bear his image in a material world – not in some nebulous or spiritualised way, but practically and physically. The image of God is not just some inner spiritual quality or likeness. After speaking of Christ as the image of God, Paul stresses that "in him" all things were created, both in heaven and earth (including the physical), whether seen or unseen.[14] Later, in verse 19, he says that God was pleased to have all his fullness dwell in him (in his physical humanity),

---

12 C.S. Lewis, *Perelandra*, ch 16, 200.

13 Matt 22:30.

14 Col 1:15.

and through him (through his physical humanity and suffering) to reconcile all things, whether on earth or in heaven. Later still, Paul spells it out, "In Christ (the image of God) all the fullness of deity dwelt in bodily form".[15]

It has often been said, "the unassumed is the unredeemed". If the Son of God did not assume full, bodily, human existence then there is no bodily or physical redemption. For this reason the early church stressed both the virgin birth and the resurrection of the body, as they are both clearly attested in the New Testament. Paul states, "The body is for the Lord and the Lord for the body . . . Do you not know your bodies are members of Christ himself?"[16] God has made us as physical human beings. Our bodies have value, both here and in the hereafter. As the creeds say, "We believe in the resurrection of the body". As with gender, he does not discard what he has created. Our physical, gendered humanity is not abolished in the resurrection. On the contrary; having suffered death, it is raised up anew, transformed, glorified, and affirmed in Christ.

(e) **It is a marred image.** The question is sometimes asked as to whether humanity continues to bear the image of God when it is turned from him in sin. We must say, 'yes'. The gifts and calling of God are irrevocable.[17] Yet we bear it in corruption and in sin, defaced, sometimes scarcely discernable – a poor reflection of the glory for which we were made, and a poor steward as God's viceroy in the world, frequently causing more harm than good. But, by his grace, as his Spirit strives with us, we bear it still.

Romans 1

The recognition of humanity made in the image of God is important in understanding some of Paul's words to the church in Rome.

In Romans 1:18-2:2, Paul identifies a refusal to acknowledge God as inherent within the sinful condition of humanity. He speaks of the ungodliness and wickedness of men who suppress the truth in unrighteousness, despite knowing about God (God having made it plain to them). Although they knew God, they neither glorified him as God nor were they thankful. Indeed, they changed the glory of God into an image of themselves and other creatures. This precipitates the action of God in giving them up to the desires of their hearts – to uncleanness and the dishonouring of their bodies. He further gives them up to passions of dishonour – to

15 Col 2:9.

16 1 Cor 7:13ff.

17 Rom 11:29.

unnatural relations, including same sex conduct. And he gives them up to a reprobate mind and to improper conduct – which is described by a whole catalogue of unloving human actions.

We may well ask, what is the 'underlying connection of thought' in this passage? For example, why does God not throw thunderbolts or send famine or plague instead? Why this way?

There are several things to say:

(a) This is to be understood as a general statement of humanity. Whilst we might recognise some of our sins in Paul's list, this should not be taken as an indication of God having given us up personally.

Unfortunately, the force of the passage is frequently obscured by translations which insist on translating 'image' in the plural, as if it refers merely to pagan idolatry. The Greek text plainly uses the singular; which suggests Paul is addressing a monotheistic error as well as that of the polytheist.

(b) One of the keys to understanding it is in Romans 2:1ff., where Paul turns the tables on any who might be tempted to sit in judgement on their fellows. "You are without excuse, whoever you are, for at whatever point you judge the other, you condemn yourself, because you . . . do the same thing." However, there is a legitimate question as to how this could be true. When looking at Paul's list, there will be many who simply cannot identify with each and every sinful expression listed there. So how can Paul say, "you do the same thing"? We conclude that the passage only makes sense if we refer back to the original sin of idolatry mentioned in Romans 1:23.

(c) Paul is drawing our attention to the root issue – which is the temptation to read upwards, from ourselves or from what we see, and project that back onto God. That temptation comes to each of us; the temptation to see God as it suits us, rather than to receive him as he is. This is as much the sin of the monotheist as it is of those steeped in polytheism. It can be just as much the temptation of the Christian as it is of the pagan idolater.

(d) Paul is making a very simple point. Everything on his list is a relational disruption of the image of God. When we deliberately 'suppress the truth of God's identity' and re-image him according to our desire – rather than appreciating him as he is and allowing him to address us – he surrenders us up to the consequences of worshipping the image we have chosen. He 'gives us over' to our chosen sin. He does so because we are made to reflect his image. If we tamper with God's image, then, because it is imprinted on us, we reap relational disruption of one kind or another. This is the human situation.

Part Three – Marriage as union

Although the Gospels do not record much in the way of Jesus' direct teaching about marriage; that does not imply that he had little to say, or he regarded questions of sexuality as insignificant. There are numerous allusions, relational comments and indirect references in what is given to us – both in his teaching and, more implicitly, in his pastoral encounters. These, taken together, make it very clear that Jesus did not depart from the wisdom, teaching or commands given to the Old Testaments prophets. Indeed, he emphasised and deepened their significance for our lives and applied them in even greater comprehensiveness – yet, with an immense affection and compassion towards people in their individual circumstances.

Throughout the Old Testament, God's giving of himself in loving covenant relationship with Israel was generally likened to a marriage – a covenant union in which he, in holiness, forever bound himself in redeeming love to his sinful people. It is important to recognise that this was not simply a case of taking the human analogy of marriage and applying it to God. It was the other way around. In Jewish thinking, marriage was established, sanctioned and patterned on God's covenant with his people. Indeed; when a marriage was 'of God' and was 'created by God', it actually caused that marriage to be embraced within his covenant. In Orthodox Jewish marriages to this day, the bridegroom takes his marriage vows quoting the words of God's covenant with his people used in Hosea 2:19,20.

The full significance of God's union and 'marriage covenant' with his people was not fully understood until after the marriage in Cana of Galilee[18] – the first of Jesus' miraculous signs – and then, later on, after the gift of the Holy Spirit at Pentecost. Jesus affirmed this way of thinking when describing himself as the bridegroom, either directly or through parable, and in his choice of words when speaking of the new covenant at the last supper or in other places such as John 14 – all of which carry allusion to betrothal. Paul also, in Ephesians 5, patterns Christian marriage on Christ's relationship with the church. As such, part of God's purpose for marriage – including its sexual consummation – is to help us understand something of God's loving, covenant union with his people. Marriage is not simply to be understood in terms of creation, but christologically, from our understanding of headship and union with Christ.

---

18 John 2:1-11.

Those parts of Jesus' direct teaching which have been recorded, generally occur within a broader context of other questions. Nonetheless, what we are given is highly significant.

In Matthew 19:1-12 Jesus is challenged by Pharisees to give an account of his approach to questions of divorce. In the background is a violent dispute between two schools of Rabbinic teaching – one of which greatly limited the circumstances in which divorce was permitted; while the other interpreted the Mosaic enactments in the widest possible way, allowing divorce for "any and every reason". Jesus' initial response is to direct his listeners back to the original plan and purpose of God in his ordering of creation and the structure of human relations. "Have you not read that the one who made them, from the beginning made them male and female? For this reason a man shall leave his father and mother and shall be united (cleave) to his wife and the two shall become one flesh, so no longer are they two, but one flesh. What therefore God has joined together, let no-one put asunder."[19]

When pressed to explain why Moses then allowed divorce, Jesus explained that this was a concession to the reality of human experience – to the "hardness of their hearts" – yet, "from the beginning it was not so", i.e. this never formed part of God's original intention for us.

Without entering into the pastoral questions of divorce, there are certain things we can note:

a) In quoting from the creation narratives Jesus affirms their value and relevance for our understanding of God's intention and what it means to be human. We cannot ignore the affirmations of the Genesis passages or pass over them as if they are only of secondary importance in our understanding of God and humanity, or in our approach to marriage and sexual relations.

b) Jesus affirms an inherent structural pattern for human existence. Sexual difference is basic to the plan and purpose of God. Male and female belong to the fundamental ordering of humanity. They are not simply transient morphological phenomena, incidental to human life before God, or with only biological relevance for the propagation of humanity. Gender has meaning.

c) God's creative purpose here on earth is that the two should be joined together to become 'one flesh'. Men and women belong together. And it takes male and female to form 'one flesh'. Gender has purpose.

---

19 See also Mark10:9.

d) There is nothing in Jesus' words which imply that the union of male and female is simply for the sake of providing for children or family. It has value, meaning and purpose in itself.

e) The ultimate union of male and female is God's doing and it is his intention that this should come about by the creative 'joining' of God himself. Furthermore, it belongs to God's will and purpose that the two should not be separated.

There is a separate question about whether God always joins a man and a woman in every legal and socially recognised marriage. Quite clearly there are weddings to which God has not been invited. This passage should not be taken to suggest that our human decisions can somehow compel God to sanction what we have previously determined without recourse to him. Jesus is speaking in a Jewish religious context in which it would have been unthinkable to pursue marriage except in relation to God. From a Jewish perspective, therefore, marriages are quite literally 'made in heaven'. Hence the joyful significance of Jesus changing water into wine for the happy couple in Cana of Galilee – the wine being a crucial symbol of God's blessing and his sealing of their union. No wine, no wedding!

Nevertheless, this does not imply that a couple who marry without referring to God as he is revealed in Christ, are anything less than married. He has given us a freedom to act without reference to him, even contrary to his will, and he will still honour it. People who marry in this way are still 'married in God's eyes' and should be honoured as such by all. Our point is that their marriages are not 'made in heaven'.

Paul, in 1 Corinthians 6, when speaking of the sexual union of a man with a prostitute, also quotes from Genesis 2:24, "the two shall become one flesh." In addition to the phrase, "one flesh" (sarx), Paul immediately precedes it with the unusual designation, "one body" (soma). "Don't you know that he who is joined to a prostitute is one body with her? For it is said, the two shall become one flesh," (v. 16). The context of the passage contains a clear emphasis on the use of the body in a way that is incompatible with our relationship with Christ. The implication is that such encounters do in fact still forge a union of some kind – a union which can exist quite outside the will of God – a union which may be forged without love, without any sense of personal commitment and without even knowing the other person's name. These are not of the same order as the marital union created by God's action in uniting a couple. Yet they are still unions of a sort – enacted despite God and 'from below', rather than 'from above'; unions formed by bodily action through physical consummation, and with attendant personal and spiritual implications for the people involved.

The passage also implies that one may become 'united' in some 'soulish' way to a multiplicity of people. Pastorally, it has frequently been observed that some of the most fragmented personalities are people with a history of numerous sexual partners. Yet, when these 'unions' are broken by the grace of God, a new level of freedom is experienced and a profound healing begins to take place. Similar observations can be made with people who have been the victims of rape and sexual abuse. When these 'soul ties' are broken in Christ's name, the resultant sense of freedom can be dramatic. Those proponents in the church, who advocate a so-called 'freedom' of sexual expression and experimentation, as if it has no effect on a person, are the naïve and unwitting agents of immense pastoral devastation. They have a lot to answer for.

We should mark well: the wisdom of God's gracious and loving commands is given to us for our protection and for the health and well-being of family, individuals and society. Despite the Jewish hesitation over Jesus as Messiah, their general adherence to the moral precepts of Old Testament teaching through many centuries of dispersion has spared their families and communities from many of the ills which afflict our contemporary Western cultures. There is much less divorce, less child abuse, less pregnancy outwith marriage, less incidence of homosexuality and a significantly greater marital and family stability among their more-orthodox communities than can be found in our society, or even within the church. There could be few greater testimonies to the practical wisdom of Scriptural injunction than that. We ignore it at our peril.

This understanding of the possibility of multiple unions is also of relevance for polygamous marriages. It is notable that monogamy was not an automatic insight in ancient Israel but was a recognition which people came to under the progressive revelation of the Holy Spirit – and one which was only fully received by the early Christians. Although polygamy is not part of God's intention for us, this does not mean that parties to a polygamous marriage should be regarded as anything less than married.

Arguments from silence must always be pursued with great care. Nevertheless, it is also useful to recognise some things Jesus did not say:

Perhaps most surprisingly, Jesus makes no appeal to covenant when speaking of marriage, adultery or divorce. Neither did Jesus speak of adultery or divorce as a breach of loving, faithful and committed relation-ships. These are implicit, yet the fact that he makes no appeal to them suggests that he does not regard them as the primary terms in which to understand the meaning of marriage. His focus is upon the one flesh union of male and female, which God effects. This does not imply any denigration of covenant or love. Quite the opposite! It suggests that when we use the terminology of covenant, we must understand it as 'covenant union' - and when we talk of love in relation to God's purposes in marriage, we must understand it as 'loving union'.

In Matthew 19:9, Jesus says that anyone who divorces a wife, except for fornication, and marries another commits adultery. Some texts have included a further sentence, similar to the second half of Matthew 5:32, where Jesus says that anyone who divorces a wife, apart from a matter of fornication, causes her to commit adultery. The second half of this saying states that anyone who marries such a divorced woman also commits adultery.[20]

It is not our purpose to consider here how this should guide us in the pastoral and practical matters of divorce and remarriage. That would be appropriate as a study in its own right. Yet a couple of questions very naturally arise. In the culture of the day, a wife could be divorced with or without her consent but a husband could be divorced only with his consent. There were a few circumstances in which a wife could compel a husband to divorce her but otherwise she had very limited legal entitlements. So, how can a wife, divorced without justifiable reason, in a culture where the right of divorce rested predominantly with the man, and she had virtually no power to stop him, be caused to commit adultery? Furthermore, how can another, single man, who chooses to marry such a mistreated woman, also be understood to commit adultery?

This only makes sense if we recognise that the focus of Jesus' teaching is upon the one flesh union of man and woman which God effects, rather than on the outward covenant which accompanies it – a union which continues despite the legal dissolution of that covenant. The statement that "anyone who marries her also commits adultery", does not make sense if the meaning of marriage is foremost to be found in our understanding of outward covenant. How could a man, who was not party to that covenant, be guilty of adultery – unless adultery is, in the first instance, a description of assault upon the 'one flesh union'?

---

20 See also Luke 16:18.

Neither in Matthew 19, nor in any of its equivalents in Matthew 5, Mark 10 or Luke 16, is Jesus ever reported as saying that divorce should never happen, or that a marriage cannot be put asunder. Neither, does he actually say that the woman should not remarry or that a man should never marry a divorced woman. From this we conclude that he is not so much issuing a new law, as primarily making a descriptive statement about the reality of the human condition. Immediately preceding the Matthew 5 passage, Jesus states that anyone who looks at a woman lustfully has already committed adultery with her in his heart. While we must affirm that this is not how things should be and it calls for a response on our part, it appears that Jesus' chief purpose is to demonstrate, simply and devastatingly, our desperate need of salvation. The human condition is such that we are frequently embroiled in sinful situations in which we may not always have a choice between a right and a wrong but are caught between two wrongs. Jesus does not revoke the Mosaic concession about divorce by issuing a new command. He directs our attention to the original plan and purpose of God in creation, "From the beginning it was not so."[21] This is not a licence to do as we choose, based on a gratuitous claim that 'God understands my weakness' – which was the error into which many of Jesus' listeners had descended – but as an invitation to humility, faith and repentance.

The word 'covenant' can be understood in different ways. In common speech, covenant and contract are often used interchangeably, but from a Biblical perspective it is important to distinguish between them. A contract is a conditional pledge based on both contracting parties fulfilling certain conditions. By contrast, covenant is an unconditional pledge or under-taking – and when used of marriage, it is the giving of one whole person to another. In Scripture, God's covenant is unilateral in that it is God who maintains the covenant. God gives himself in an unconditional and eternal covenant with his people, in which he lovingly takes us to himself, pledging total allegiance and personal self-giving. Rather than being an undertaking between two equal parties, it is an act of grace in which God stoops to lift us and gather us to himself. We can only either reject him or yield to him in thanksgiving, as he acts to effect that covenant.

The marriage covenant, which reflects God's covenant with his people, is intended as a loving commitment and indissoluble bond. Yet it is volun-tarily entered into by equals in the sense that both parties take the other to themselves, in an unconditional pledge of personal allegiance and total

---

21 Matt 19:8.

self-giving. This is reflected in the traditional words "I . . . take you . . . t be my wife/husband, to have and to hold from this day forward, for bette or for worse, for richer, for poorer, in sickness and in health, to love an to cherish, till death do us part". There are, of course, many other forms o wording which may be used. Given the one flesh union which God effects it is appropriate that it be accompanied by a total covenanted self-giving ot this nature.

To date, in civil weddings, the essence of this is reflected in the legal definition of marriage which is read out by Registrars at a Civil Marriage Ceremony. As it is contained in their hand-book, "Marriage according to the law of this country is a union of one man and one woman voluntarily entered into for life to the exclusion of all others".

According to the Marriage Unit of the General Register for Scotland, there is no legally prescribed form of words to be used in relation to 'marriage vows' in Scotland. The detail of the ceremony is decided by the celebrant. But the form of ceremony must include, and must be in no way inconsistent with:

- a declaration by the parties, in the presence of each other, the celebrant and two witnesses, that they accept each other as husband and wife; and

- a declaration by the celebrant, after the foregoing declaration, that the parties are then husband and wife.

Both union and covenant are intended to involve the totality of one's person; spiritually, emotionally and physically. The sexual act is a sign, seal and consummation of that union. The importance of the physical aspect of the union is very clear in the biblical description of marriage as two becoming one flesh – not one soul or one spirit, but one flesh. This is further attested by Paul's use of one body, as well as one flesh, in 1 Corinthians 7.

The totality of this self-giving is further signified by Jesus' words, "They are no longer two but one flesh". By covenant, they have sunk their future and identity into loving union with each other. Biblical covenants are accompanied by, or enacted by means of, a sacrifice. There is a dying to self. This is the marriage union as God intended it.

Chapter 8

Same sex relations: some theological pointers

David J. Torrance

The Revd David J. Torrance is a parish minister in the Church of Scotland.

It is simply not possible to present same sex relations as equivalent to marriage without a radical re-interpretation of the meaning of marriage, covenant, gender, sexual encounter and what it means to be physically human in the image of God.

The following traces through some of the logical consequences:

- Marriage must be re-interpreted primarily in terms of covenant rather than 'covenant union'. Far from elevating same sex relations to the status of marriage, it achieves 'equivalence' by demoting marriage and the marriage covenant to the level of partnership. Thus 'marriage' must be re-understood as a 'partnership of persons', rather than a total self-giving of male and female to each other to form one flesh. Covenant is reduced merely to the level of promise.

- The terminology of 'one flesh' is effectively rendered meaningless in Christian terms. Rather than being descriptive of the uniting of male and female, it denotes an 'alliance of companions' to become a legal and socially-recognised unit.

- Sexual encounter is to be pursed simply for pleasure or for procreation. It may be an expression of the mutual affection or attraction individuals feel for each other, and it may play a role in extending their sense of togetherness. Yet, logically, it cannot be regarded as God's gift to consummate or seal a one-flesh union of male and female. It symbolises nothing beyond what it means to the individuals involved.

- Gender is relationally irrelevant, except in medical and biological terms, and for procreation purposes. Beyond that, it symbolises nothing.

Gender references should ultimately be abolished. Women should not be valued as women but essentially regarded as if they are the same as men, but who happen to be wearing a woman's body. Gender has only temporal value and there will be no men and women in the resurrection.

• Physical difference has little significance except, perhaps, for procreation. People are ultimately 'persons inhabiting a body' and the 'authentic person' should be distinguished from the body they happen to be wearing. Having made this dualistic distinction, all that's important relationally is that these 'persons' should be loving, faithful and committed – if that.

We can only truly promote same sex relations as equivalent to marriage if we abolish any ultimate distinctions between male and female and attribute little theological value to the human body. This entails a significant departure from the Biblical witness and all the historic formulations of the faith in the early centuries.

These attempts at the redefinition of what it means to be human are ultimately disastrous for Christology and the central affirmations of the Christian gospel – in particular, the incarnation and atonement. They promote a 'container view' of the human person, in which the 'authentic individual' somehow inhabits a physical body which has no ultimate relevance. When this is applied to Christ it means that his physical body was of no real importance, or that the Son of God never properly became human. These dualistic and 'docetic' views were solidly condemned by all the early church councils. For this reason the early creeds stressed both the virgin birth and the resurrection of the body.

If the conception of Jesus came about by normal human means then this baby was 'adopted' as the Son of God without God ever properly becoming a physical human being – he was just a 'Christ' which somehow inhabited the body of Jesus. If there's no resurrection of the body – Jesus somehow having discarded it after the cross – then, similarly, his body could not have materially belonged to his incarnation and he should also be seen as a 'Christ' inhabiting a body. In neither case did the Son of God truly take physical human flesh to himself, nor is our physical flesh redeemed.

It is no accident that a significant proportion of those who propound a revisionist view of marriage and human sexuality have also departed from these twin doctrines of the virgin birth and the resurrection of the body – despite both being clearly attested in Scripture. Nor is it any accident that they also have a similar 'container view' of the Scriptures themselves. Thus the actual words of the Bible do not ultimately matter, any more than the body of Jesus ultimately mattered. What counts is the 'Word of God' inside of it/him.

This disconnects the Word of God from the words of Scripture in a similar way that the 'authentic' human person – whether ours or Christ's – is disconnected from the physical body. If the physical human body doesn't matter then the physical human words of Scripture cannot matter either. Instead, one must look for an interior, intuitive 'Word' within the words of Scripture. This, essentially Gnostic approach to the Bible, thus repeatedly makes claim to an interior and esoteric notion of 'love' as its justification for revising the more obvious teaching of Scripture – yet a notion of love which is itself disconnected from how the Bible speaks about love.

Some might protest that they do indeed take the physical body seriously. Yet our point is that a disconnection has occurred and they 'take their readings' independently from any orthodox theological understanding. Almost without exception, every revisionist appeal to what 'science' supposedly says draws upon a completely materialist, anti-supernatural and deterministic interpretation of science and psychology. Instead of beginning with the givenness of the Word of God or of man-woman in the Image of God, such appeals commence their understanding with the supposed 'givenness' of homosexuality – and then revise their approach to humanity, marriage, sexual ethics, Scripture, theology, even God himself, on the basis of it. They 'drink from another well'.

Both Christ and the Scriptures gave dignity, affirmation and value to the whole person, in all its relational and physical aspects, in a way which was lacking in the surrounding cultures of the day. Later on, as the early Church engaged with these cultures and the challenge they presented to the faith, the church was forced to articulate the gospel in relational, dynamic and holistic terms, which avoided the essential dualism underlying those cultures. The church of the 21st century faces the same task. The ideas associated with contemporary questions about marriage, family and same sex relations are merely a modern-day re-presentation of the same old issues as yesteryear – albeit in new guise. 'There is nothing new under the sun'.

Challenges to marriage and family – gay agendas

It has often been said that an acceptance of same sex relations, as the equivalent of marriage, poses no challenge to marriage, family or society.

Yet, from the outset, gay activists have explicitly recognised that this is not the case. They have been very clear in stating that the full acceptance of homosexuality within Church and society requires a radical reinterpretation of gender, marriage, family and sexual morality – and nothing less than a revolution in social terms. It is the thesis of this chapter that it also requires a radical reinterpretation of the church's understanding of God, humanity, Scripture and theology, which carries right to the heart of the Christian faith.

In response to any who might claim this is not the case, it must be stated that it is exactly this agenda which has been behind certain key strategies of gay activism in the last 40 years. It is helpful therefore to consider the published intentions of gay activism from the pioneering days of the Gay Liberation Front (GLF).

The GLF was the name of a number of groups, all working for long-term transformation in social attitudes, which emerged in the USA in 1969 and in the UK in 1970. Although the GLF had disintegrated by the mid 1970s, it was a defining period and from it emerged many other groups and networks of individuals. The campaigning organisations Outrage! and Stonewall also developed from the same root. Peter Tatchell, who was 19 at the time, wrote on its anniversary in the Guardian in 2010, "GLF's strategy for queer emancipation was to change society's values and norms . . . We sought a cultural revolution . . ."

It would be unfair to attribute this agenda to all lesbian, gay, bisexual and transgender (LGBT) individuals or their advocates in church or state. Nevertheless, the essential recognition of gay activism – that marriage, family and sexual morality must be reinterpreted if their cause was to succeed – remains true.

The following are some excerpts from the GLF Manifesto in the UK. It was premised on a disparaging assessment of family, marriage and church.

- "The oppression of gay people starts in the most basic unit of society, the family . . . The very form of the family works against homosexuality."

- "What we are taught about the differences between man and woman is propaganda, not truth."

- "We gay men and women do deny these values of our civilisation."

- "We, along with the women's movement, must fight for something more than reform. We must aim at the abolition of the family . . ."

- "WE CAN DO IT . . . although this struggle will be hard, and our victories not easily won, we are not in fact being idealistic to aim at abolishing the family and the cultural distinctions between men and women. True, these have been with us throughout history, yet humanity is at last in a position where we can progress beyond this."

- "Monogamy . . . Not that sexual fidelity is necessarily wrong; what is wrong is the inturned emotional exclusiveness of the couple . . . People need a variety of relationships in order to develop and grow, and to learn about other human beings."

- "The long-term goal of Gay Liberation . . . is to rid society of the gender-role system which is at the root of our oppression."

- "Formal religious education is still part of everyone's schooling, and our whole legal structure is supposedly based on Christianity whose archaic and irrational teachings support the family and marriage as the only permitted condition for sex."

- "But gay liberation does not just mean [legal] reforms. It means a revolutionary change in our whole society."

- "As we cannot carry out this revolutionary change alone, and as the abolition of gender rotes is also a necessary condition of women's liberation, we will work to form a strategic alliance with the women's liberation movement, aiming to develop our ideas and our practice in close inter-relation."

Produced collectively by the Manifesto Group of GLF, London 1971, revised 1978, and reprinted by the Gay Liberation Information Service.

The complete document is also available for viewing online at www.fordham.edu/halsall/pwh/glf-london.asp.

The Bible and homosexual practice

Chapter 9

The case against homosexual practice according to Robert Gagnon: *The Bible and Homosexual Practice*

Paul Burgess

Paul Burgess taught hermeneutics at Gujranwala Theological Seminary, Pakistan before retirement, and was a former warden of Carberry Tower. He was asked to write this summary and review because Gagnon's book, although published a decade ago, is regarded by many leading biblical scholars as a definitive study of the subject.

Robert Gagnon is associate professor of New Testament in Pittsburgh U.S.A. The full book is available on Amazon in paperback or as a Kindle download.

At the heart of the same sex controversy are different ways of reading the Bible. At issue are two questions:

First, there is the question of Biblical authority: what credence should be given to those parts of the Bible that conflict with conventional wisdom today? Are they to be taken as unquestionable revelation of how God wants us to live today? Or are there areas where we do indeed 'now know better than the Bible'? Granted the latter, then there is no more argument. Any 'hard-line' or 'difficult' text can be set aside and a code of practice be agreed based on a more selective approach to Scriptural passages, such as those expressing nebulous 'core values' in line with a supposed 'spirit of Jesus'. Thus many opposed to the traditionalist position can accept that in the Bible all forms of homosexual practice are condemned, yet will dismiss as culturally conditioned those passages that treat same sex practice negatively. Obviously there is room here for a wide variety of conclusions about what is, and is not, acceptable practice.

But there is also wriggle room for a second category of readers who, while accepting in general the divinely inspirational nature of the Bible, emphasize that there is more than one way to interpret these Scriptures. This is, second, the hermeneutical question. And this is the area of debate that Robert Gagnon seeks to address in his exhaustive apologetic work on

The Bible and Homosexual Practice in the face of revisionist re-reading of key passages in both Old and New Testaments.

Exegesis: the texts examined

Related to this hermeneutical issue is a prior subsidiary question: From where in Scripture should one construct, on the basis of accurate exegesis, an ethic of sexuality that relates to the contemporary issues surrounding same sex relationships? Two-thirds of Gagnon's book is taken up with a close scrutiny of texts from several genres of Old and New Testament writings: the creation narrative of Genesis 1–3, certain historical narratives in Genesis 9 and 19, and Judges 19, legislation (of diverse nature and purpose) recorded in Leviticus 18 and 20, gospel narratives that reflect Jesus' attitude to sexuality, and the epistolary exposition and exhortation of Paul in Romans 1–3, 1 Corinthians 6, and 1 Timothy 1. In addition he explores various background sources such as ancient Near Eastern culture, Canaanite religion and practice, and early Judaism, to ensure a rigorous contextualization of his biblical exegesis.

Hermeneutics: the framework adopted

It may come as a surprise to some traditionalists reading this work that Gagnon opens his exegetical argument by referring to the higher critical sources, J, H and P.[1] For Gagnon works within the framework of the Documentary Hypothesis of Wellhausen to present his case for a traditionalist reading of OT texts relevant to the issue of homosexual practice.

Gagnon has written elsewhere:

> I make full use of historical-critical methodology, see development and significant tensions within the canon, take account of metaphors and the imaginative power of stories, and recognize the necessity of interpreting texts anew in our contemporary context. This last named step of 'translating' the Bible into our own day, of developing principles of interpretation for moving from 'what it meant' to 'what it means', is called hermeneutics. I consider the hermeneutical aspect of the homosexuality debate so important that I devote a third of my book to it.[2]

---

1   J is the 'Jahwist' source, from the use of the Hebrew word JHWH, translated LORD in the King James Version. H is the 'holiness code' source - see page 128. P is the 'priestly' source, for text which was judged to come from a later school of priests.

2   *The Authority of Scripture in the 'Homosex' Debate*, 2002.

He cannot be accused of ignoring the tools of source criticism generally accepted by academia.

Motivation: reasons for writing

Gagnon gives "three generic reasons for speaking out against same sex intercourse." First, he believes that the Bible "speaks unequivocally and forcefully to the issue of homosexuality" and that "God calls us to live holy lives subject to the divine will and not according to our own desires." Second, since "without a moral compass love is mere mush . . . the church has an obligation both to protect the church from the debilitating effect of sanctioned immorality and to protect the homosexual for whom more is at stake than the satisfaction of sensual impulses." Third, Gagnon believes that "the window of opportunity for speaking out against homosexual behaviour is closing," and so there is an urgency to prevent "a potentially irreversible change in the morality of mainline denominations." There is no doubting that Gagnon sees his campaign as both urgent and pressing!

'Gay' sex: not 'fit for purpose'?

A key part of Gagnon's hermeneutic is that:

> The Bible presents the anatomical, sexual, and procreative comple-
> mentarity of male and female as clear and convincing proof of
> God's will for sexual unions. Even those who do not accept the
> revelatory authority of Scripture should be able to perceive the
> divine will through the visible testimony of the structure of
> creation. Thus same sex intercourse constitutes an inexcusable
> rebellion against the intentional design of the created order.[3] (37)

The homosexual act distorts the passive male's sexual identity as created by God. In short homosexual behaviour, in its unnatural use of human anatomy, is not 'fit for purpose'.

In all this it is important to make clear that experiencing homosexual desires is not sinful, only the nurturing of them that culminates in acting upon such desires in homosexual practice. "What matters is not what urges individuals feel but what they do with these urges." To the argument that such urges for some are only 'natural', Gagnon responds that so are many other urges, such as lust, anger, adultery, etc., to which the proper response

---

3 Figures in brackets are page references to *The Bible and Homosexual Practice. Texts and Hermeneutics* (Abingdon Press, Nashville, 2001).

is not indulgence but control. Further, he maintains that proponents of homosexual behaviour cannot take refuge in the notion "that homosexual orientation is primarily due to genetic causation," as "the most that can be claimed is that homosexuality arises from a complex interplay of genes, intra-uterine and post-uterine biological development, environment, and choice."(38) Contrary to popular belief no 'gay gene' has yet been discovered to explain orientation.

Concluding verdict: homosexual intercourse uniquivocally sinful

Does the Old Testament really reject all homosexual behaviour out of hand as an 'abomination', and is there firm evidence to claim that the New Testament endorses this assessment? The assertion that Robert Gagnon seeks to demonstrate beyond all doubt is that indeed "the Bible unequivocally defines same sex intercourse as sin." After examining all the biblical evidence he will conclude:

> The biblical proscription of same sex intercourse, like those against incest, adultery, and bestiality, is absolute (encompassing all cases), pervasive (by both Testaments and within each Testament) and severe (mandating exclusion from God's kingdom). (489)

If we are to understand why Scripture is so absolute in this matter, we must take seriously how we conduct our hermeneutics. Hence the subtitle, "Texts and Hermeneutics", introducing Gagnon's second objective: to demonstrate that:

> There exists no valid hermeneutical argument, derived from either general principles of biblical interpretation or contemporary scientific knowledge and experience, for overriding the Bible's authority on this matter. (37)

The importance of genre in the debate: complementarity deducable in creation narrative

An important tenet of hermeneutics is that the reader must interpret a text according to its genre. Thus narrative material is to be taken as descriptive of events and incidents, not necessarily as normative for forming the reader's consequent behaviour, while passages concerning law must be seen as either prescriptive or proscriptive and must be applied according to the purpose for which they were promulgated and in the time frame for which their enforcement was intended.

This is not to conclude that no principles of behaviour can be deduced from narrative texts. Far from it. Gagnon demonstrates that right from the opening chapters of Genesis the creation narratives (distinct from the historical narratives that follow) reveal to us truths about God's design for human relations, in particular the complementarity of man and woman and its role in human sexuality. In this way "even though the creation accounts are directed toward other purposes, they provide guidance for the interpretation of homosexual intercourse." (43) In a later chapter Gagnon expounds his intriguing 'restorative' understanding of Adam's union with Eve (Gen 2:18-24).

His side is split open in order to provide for him the companionship of a complementary being. Marriage between a man and a woman reunites these representatives of the two genders into "one flesh", and is not simply a union of two individuals. The missing part of man is found in woman and vice versa. Sexual intercourse or marriage between members of the same sex does not restore the disunion because it does not reconnect complementary beings. An alternate pattern of sexuality requires an alternate creation myth. (194)

Further, Gagnon argues, the male and female perfect anatomical fit also point to this divine design for complementary marriage.

In passing Gagnon makes the critical point that "While J[4] views the subordination of women to men as a product of the fall (implying the woman's equal status pre-fall), he unmistakably views the divine authorization for (and only for) heterosexual marriage as a pre-fall phenomenon. Those who argue that the case for validating homosexual behaviour is comparable to the case for validating women's equal status overlook this point." (61)

The Ham-Noah-Canaan conundrum

What significance can be deduced from the various accounts in the Old Testament of apparent homosexual acts? What should we make of the story of Ham's "seeing the nakedness of" his father Noah? (Gen 9:20-27) The serious consequences of this incident ("what his youngest son had done to him", verse 24) would indicate something more culpable than voyeurism or just an unintentional glance (as is implied by the major English Bible translations). Gagnon exegetes the text as referring to homosexual rape undertaken for political reasons.

---

4   See footnote 1.

By raping his father and alerting his brothers to the act, Ham hoped to usurp the authority of his father and elder brothers, establishing his right to succeed his father as patriarch . . . Understanding Ham's action as incestuous, homosexual rape of one's father explains the severity of the curse on Canaan. (67)

The term, "seeing the nakedness of", is ambiguous and is used in Leviticus 20:17 to denote sexual intercourse (compare renderings in KJV with NIV). Gagnon also points out that:

The same Greek term *ten aschemosynen* ("shamefulness") employed by the LXX in the phrase "uncover the nakedness of" throughout Leviticus 18:6-19 and 20:11, 17-21 (referring to incest) . . . is also applied by Paul to homosexual intercourse in Rom 1:27. (68)

Certainly God considers this action so horrible that he later "vomits out" the Canaanites from the land because of their "abominable (immoral) practices". Hereafter the Canaanites are seen as innately evil. This becomes the justification for the dispossession of their land by the Israelites for whom it also later became a cause of cultural temptation. Gagnon concludes:

The etiological thrust of Genesis 9:20-27 lies at the forefront: the Canaanites deserve to be dispossessed of the land and made slaves because they are, and always have been, avid practitioners of immoral activity. In the post-diluvian world, it was their ancestor that committed the most heinous act imaginable – not just rape, but incest: not just incestuous rape, but homosexual intercourse: not just incestuous, homosexual rape, but rape of one's own father, to whom supreme honor and obedience is owed. It is, in effect, in the Canaanites' blood to be unremittingly evil. (67)

Those who have difficulty with Gagnon's thesis at this point have to answer all the questions that are left begging about the severe consequences of a supposedly innocent 'glance' which Ham's brothers studiously avoided copying in the handling of their father's nakedness.

Sodom and Gomorrah (Gen 19:4-11)

Revisionists have often claimed that the story of Sodom and Gomorrah is not about homosexuality, as traditionally it has been regarded, but about inhospitality and rape. Gagnon admits that it has nothing to say directly about consensual homosexual relationships. Yet the narrator plays upon "the inherently degrading quality" he sees in same sex intercourse "to elicit feelings of revulsion on the part of the reader/hearer." Thus for Gagnon "it is likely that the sin of Sodom is not merely inhospitality or even attempted rape of a guest but rather attempted homosexual rape of male guests." (75) For whatever might be said about the immorality of Lot offering his daughters to such men, their demands revealed gross depravity meriting their eventual destruction. Gagnon sees this episode of potential same sex intercourse as an instance of pride, supplanting God's design for sex in favour of men's own. It is the same repugnance at homosexual acts that he sees in the appalling story of an old man offering his daughter and his guest's recently recovered concubine to a gang of scoundrels bent on homosexual rape (Jdg 19:22-25). For Gagnon such episodes illlustrate the extent to which the homosexual impulse will go as it contravenes the natural order of God's creation.

Temple male prostitution and the Holiness Code

Before turning to the Levitical proscriptions on homosexuality, Gagnon examines the cult of temple male prostitutes in Israel during the period of the divided monarchy. In answer to those who say that the accounts of what led to Josiah's reform "only tell us what the author believed about consensual homosexual practice conducted in the context of idolatrous cults and prostitution, not the kind of loving expressions of homosexuality we witness today", Gagnon observes that such argument neglects the ancient Near Eastern context where same sex intercourse in a temple was the most, not the least acceptable form of homosexual practice, other expressions being considered utterly degrading. "When the biblical authors rejected homosexual cult prostitutes . . . they were in effect rejecting the whole phenomenon of homosexual practice. They were repudiating a form of homosexual intercourse that was the most palatable in their cultural context." (108-109)

Taking the injunctions in Leviticus seriously

Two verses in Leviticus, 18:22 and 20:13, provide the Old Testament's strongest indictment of homosexual practice: a male lying with "a male as with a woman". Gagnon introduces his discussion of them thus:

Unlike stories, commands have a definite prescriptive or proscriptive (not just descriptive) function. Both of these commands occur in the context of a larger block of laws (Lev 17–26) that many scholars refer to as the Holiness Code (H), a law code which urged all Israelites (not just the priests) to keep the land (not just the sanctuary) unpolluted through holy obedience to the commands. (111)

Some dismiss the Levitical injunctions against homosexual behaviour on the grounds that the Holiness Code was concerned with ceremonial purity and pollution and thus irrelevant to the contemporary moral discussion. Gagnon's response is to point out that these purity requirements, while formulated to meet the challenges of the times, still reflect the same morality to be seen in the more obviously abiding moral injunctions. God's people should still be seen as 'different' in their moral behaviour from their godless neighbours. He cites six features of these two commandments as "establishing their hermeneutical relevance":

1 The abiding validity of other prohibitions of sexual crimes in the context of Leviticus 18:6-23

2 The degree of revulsion associated with the homosexual act

3 The extremity of the penalty

4 The unqualified and absolute character of the prohibition

5 A reforming, rather than a conforming, intention in an unholy environment

6 The continuity in attitude with the New Testament

What did Jesus think?

Turning to the New Testament, the crucial texts relate to the teaching of Jesus and of Paul. "What would Jesus do?" has become a popular battle-cry in contemporary ethical debates. Arguments from silence can, of course, be made both ways: either it can be argued that Jesus did not care about homosexuality since he never even alluded to it let alone pronounce upon it, or it can be argued, as Gagnon does, that Jesus, as a 1st century Jew, would have accepted the monogamous stance portrayed in Genesis 1 and would have shared his countrymen's repugnance at homosexual practice of any stripe as being 'contrary to nature'. (Gagnon has a whole chapter on early Judaic attitudes to same sex intercourse, demonstrating that early Judaism was unanimous in its rejection of homosexual conduct.)

Some have emphasized Jesus' teaching on tolerance, which has been applied by many to 'responsible' homosexual behaviour. But equally Gagnon points out Jesus' high regard for the fidelity due in the covenant of marriage; in the case of the women caught in adultery, "casting the first stone" implies no suspension of criticism or advocacy of sexual tolerance, but is rather the precursor of "go and sin no more!" All humans, whether 'heterosexual' or 'homosexual', are prone, to some degree or other, to the very sin being brought to Jesus' attention in this dramatic way. Gagnon points out that the standard Jesus upheld on marriage was stricter than that propounded under Moses. It would be unlikely that he would have been more 'tolerant' of homosexual practice than the Levitical compilers.

Paul's condemnation: a violation of nature that exchanges God's truth for a lie

The most explicit statement on homosexuality in the whole Bible is found in the first chapter of Paul's letter to the Romans. The so-called 'clobber verses', 24-27, have rightly been identified as containing the most severe condemnation of homosexual practice in all Scripture. This is partly because of the dark picture Paul paints of sin which forms its immediate context. But more important is the logic Paul employs in his condemnation. The apostle is keen to show the crucial connection between idolatry and all the various sins that emerge from it, including homosexual practice. His thesis is that people have suppressed the truth about God, even after they had formerly known it, which had led to idolatry (a lie concerning who God is), which in turn had encouraged same sex immorality (a lie about what God had created), which in turn had resulted in spiritual death in the form of various 'pay-backs' of decadent behaviours. By exchanging the truth for a lie at each turn, they had violated nature and become unnatural in their behaviour and stood condemned and thus liable ultimately to exclusion from the Kingdom of Heaven.

Common objections to a traditionalist reading

Against this presentation of the Biblical view of homosexual practice, many objections have been raised by revisionists who still want to appeal to a supposedly biblical silence on the issue of 'consensual monogamous homosexual practice'. Gagnon turns, under the heading of "The herme-neutical relevance of the Bible Witness", to some of the more common arguments made against the traditionalist hermeneutic.

Only about exploitative homosexuality?

The first most common objection is that the Bible only condemns exploitative and promiscuous homoeroticism, in the same way as it condemns the abuse of heterosexuality. Because contemporary expressions of homosexuality can be mutual and loving, no-one can say how the biblical authors would have reacted if these had been the prevailing models in their day.

Gagnon describes the notion that "mutually caring same sex relationships first originated in modern times" as "absurd," and rejects the claim that "homosexuality then and now are two fundamentally different phenomena." In fact Paul himself "emphasizes the mutuality of affections ... He is not presuming a situation in which only an allegedly active older partner in the relationship is sexually gratified. But mutuality does not imply moral goodness to Paul." (351) One wonders how far the 'prevailing models' of homosexual behaviour today could truly be described as 'mutual and loving' rather than exploitative. Hardly at all if Gagnon's statistical evidence is to be believed.

Male dominance the real concern?

The objection is sometimes raised that the biblical writers, as people of their time and culture, were really only concerned about male dominance which homosexual acts by their very nature threatened since the act involved one partner assuming a 'soft' or 'passive' role. However, Gagnon argues that it is hardly credible that Paul was so interested in this kind of male dominance. His concern in the context of Romans 1 is far more likely to be about how same sex behaviour is totally contrary to the design for human sexuality inserted into the natural order by the Creator. In the argument about human anatomy, adopting passive roles must rank lower in significance than the issue of complementarity in sexual intercourse. Fit for purpose criteria would indicate that "the anatomical clues [of penis fitting vagina] point to God's intention that human sexuality involves opposite sex pairing as opposed to same sex pairing." (365)

Orientation not understood?

Revisionists often bring into the debate the question of whether the Bible contains an awareness of homosexual orientation, since no category exists for same sex orientation as distinct from same sex practice; therefore we cannot expect biblical authors to show empathy for any who could not experience heterosexual eroticism. The Bible's silence on orientation, however, arises out of its own nature and purpose. Scripture, while containing much that provides insight into human psychology, is not an exhaustive compendium of psychology. Thus Paul is not concerned with the innateness of personal passions but with the moral fitness of the actions they produce.

No awareness of contemporary loving relationships?

It is also misleading to assume that biblical authors were not aware of any loving same sex relationship. David and Jonathan are a case in point. Their love for each other was remarkable, "surpassing the love of women", though with no suggestion of eroticism. (The claim that David and Jonathan exhibited a "committed consensual homosexual relationship" such as 'non-promiscuous' homosexuals advocate today is assuredly an example of eisegesis, as is the suggestion sometimes made that Ruth and Naomi were involved in a lesbian relationship! Earlier Gagnon has a whole chapter on this issue.)

As far as Paul is concerned, there is no evidence to suppose that the range of homosexual relationships he was likely to have encountered or observed in Greek society did not include, as well as dominance and exploitation, relationships of mutuality.

A 'gay gene'?

The media have raised a fourth objection to the traditionalist position, claiming that since some people are 'born gay', it is grossly unfair to condemn a behaviour that is for them innate: and of course the Bible didn't know about genes, so cannot be considered a reliable witness in the debate. However, scientists are still divided over the existence of a so-called 'gay gene'. Until very recently all homosexuals, and even now, most homosexuals have been children of two heterosexual parents. So, one might ask, whence the gay gene? But even if it could be proved that some people are genetically inclined towards a homosexual orientation, there are so many other factors and influences to consider also, not least cultural influence.

Romans chapters 1–8 teach that what is undoubtedly innate in humanity is sin! This is experienced in the internal human mind where a 'law' (or driving force) is experienced which is in conflict with both the demands of God's external Law and the law (another driving power) of the Spirit. While the external Law found in Scripture lays down the behaviour God desires, it is the restraint exercised through the power of the Spirit that can control the drive of innate passions that remain with us till we die. Consequently, restraint for homosexuals is no more 'oppressive' than for heterosexuals who experience their own inner impulses that require being kept in check.

Only a marginal issue in the Bible?

A fifth common objection is that homosexuality, because of the rare occurrence of references to it in Scripture, is only a marginal issue in the Bible and therefore no fuss should be made about it. But this logic confuses frequency with importance. One might compare the infrequency of references to prostitution in the Bible and conclude that it is equally 'of marginal significance!' Indeed, while several prostitutes figure in biblical narratives (most notably an ancestor of Jesus!), no public hero in the Bible indulges in homosexual conduct, while every regulation and all references in wisdom literature assume a man-woman relationship.

Gagnon points out that "the debate on same sex intercourse receives greater stress in the contemporary context than it does in most writings of the Bible because it has now become affirmed by a large minority of Christians, whereas in the first century there was no serious debate about its legitimacy." (434) He concludes:

> To say that there are only a few texts in the Bible that do not condone homosexual conduct is a monumental understatement of the facts. The reverse is a more accurate statement: there is not a single shred of evidence anywhere in the Bible that even remotely suggest that same sex unions are any more acceptable than extra-marital or premarital intercourse, incest, or bestiality. (439)

Why select this issue when many other 'proscribed' behaviours are now ignored?

A sixth common argument brings up the many other biblical injunctions that no-one feels obliged to observe today. These concern issues as diverse as slavery, divorce and women's ordination, not to mention wearing multi-fabric clothing, breeding two different kinds of animals and cutting the edges of one's beard! Civil and ritual reasons can be given for many of their original promulgations, reasons that no longer apply today. But should women still be required to follow Paul's requirement that they wear veils during worship? Gagnon admits that "a host of texts in the Old and New Testaments that would seem to be an impediment to women's ordination have been swept aside or thought to be less a word of God than texts affirming women's equality and involvement in ministry." (441) Why is slavery apparently tolerated in the Bible but vehemently opposed today? Why be so adamant that all homosexual conduct is wrong?

Gagnon's answer is to draw attention to what he sees as "a trajectory within the Bible itself that justifies a critique or moderation of such texts" that seem absolute but are no longer deemed authoritative for today.

> For example, on the question of divorce, there are New Testament authors that moderate Jesus' stance. Jesus' words were so radical that both Matthew and Paul found ways to qualify them (Matt 5:32; Matt 19:9; 1 Cor 7:12-16). These kinds of qualifications at least provide a basis for further exploration of the issue. Some divorce is permissible for some biblical texts so that one cannot say that the Bible has achieved a unanimous position on the subject. Alternatively, one could argue that the church has become too lenient on the issue of temptation in recent years and needs to do what Jesus did: stand against rather than with the culture. (442)

Considerations that cannot be ignored

In an excursus on slavery (a poor parallel for the homosexuality debate as it is never affirmed in Scripture, only tolerated at most), Gagnon concludes that "there is very little that commends the use of changing Christian views on slavery as an analogous basis for disregarding what Scripture has to say about homosexuality." (448) He argues instead:

> What makes the biblical mandate concerning homosexuality so hard for Christians to ignore or downplay are seven considerations:
>
> First, it is proscribed behaviour . . . a sin of commission rather than omission . . .
>
> Second, it is proscribed behaviour, not proscribed thoughts, theories or world views.
>
> Third, it is behaviour proscribed by both testaments . . . When the two testaments are in complete agreement that a given action is morally wrong, the biblical witness is hard to circumvent.
>
> Fourth, it is behavior proscribed pervasively within each Testament. There are no dissenting voices anywhere in either Testa-

ment. The 'big picture' of the Bible [to which some attempt to appeal for general statements that prioritize love, tolerance and inclusiveness] consists not of this misunderstood application of love but rather of the heterosexual model for sexual intercourse provided in Genesis 1–2, consistently affirmed throughout the history of Israel and the church.

Fifth, it is severely proscribed behaviour . . . In Romans 1:24-27, it epitomizes the height of Gentile depravity and folly in the ethical sphere.

Sixth, the proscribed behaviour is proscribed absolutely: that is, the proscription encompasses every and any form of homo-sexual behavior . . .

Seventh, it is proscribed behaviour that makes sense. The complementarity of male and female is a clear indication in the natural order of God's will for sexuality. (449-450)

False analogies

The main point, however, is that the analogies often quoted are not true analogies. Take, for example, the analogy with divorce: divorce was once condemned out of hand but is deemed allowable today, it is argued – so it should be with homosexuality. Few church people would argue that divorce should be celebrated as a positive 'good' or 'grace' as homosexuals will claim for their homosexual acts. Likewise the inclusion of Gentiles in the early Church is not analogous to an 'inclusive' church celebrating contemporary homosexuality.

Gentile ethnicity is a different ball of wax: it has to do with ancestry, not desire . . . In the case of same sex intercourse, the Bible is primarily condemning an activity, not a state of being . . . The mere inclination or the experience of temptation is not sin. The issue is whether one is mastered by the desire . . . Unlike the Bible's stance on same sex intercourse, the Hebrew Bible or Greek Septuagint is not unequivocally and univocally opposed to Gentiles. (461-3)

It was, as a quote from Richard Hays puts it, indeed "the experience of the uncircumcised Gentiles responding in faith to the gospel message" that "led the church back to a new reading of Scripture. Only because the new experience of Gentile converts proved hermeneutically illuminating of

Scripture was the Church, over time, able to accept the decision to embrace Gentiles within the fellowship of God's people."[5]

A similar acceptance of practising homosexuals, based on a revisionist reading of Scripture, is of course exactly what those calling for an 'inclusive church' are wanting. The problem is that Scripture is not, in the view of Gagnon, amenable to such a revisionist hermeneutic. And he has gone to great lengths in his book to prove his point.

Negative effects of the endorsement of same sex behaviour

A final section of Gagnon's book (answering the objection: why single out the sin of same sex for condemnation?) jumps from hermeneutics and biblical arguments to practical considerations for being concerned about homosexual practice. There are, in Gagnon's view, six important negative effects of the current social endorsement of same sex behaviour, the first three being documented by an array of statistics.

1 Medical facts surrounding homosexuality indicate same sex practice as bad for one's health.

2 The promotion of homosexual awareness increases paedophilia.

3 Sexual promiscuity increases.

4 Gender norms are obscured and ultimately destroyed.

5 Those who protest the whole culture of homosexual practice are marginalized and penalized.

6 Practising homosexuals endanger their relationship with their Maker who sees their lifestyle as sin, and risk ultimate exclusion from his Kingdom.

Gagnon concludes that all same sex intercourse is rejected and condemned by Scripture primarily because it ignores the divine design in nature, accelerates immoral behaviour in society and places the homosexual's own relationship with the Creator in jeopardy.

Meticulous scholarship and trenchant argument

What should we make of this impressive assembly of biblical and extra biblical evidence in defence of the traditionalist position? The overall plan of Gagnon's book is clear and well signposted. The scholarship displayed is meticulous, as the copious footnotes on every page bear testimony. Thus, for

---

5   Hays, *The Moral Vision of the New Testament*, 399, quoted by Gagnon, 463.

example, before he tackles the argumentation of Paul in Romans 1:24-27, he provides a note on Translation, and Translation Notes that reference 8 standard lexicons, 13 standard NT translations, and 43 commentaries.

In discussing the Levitical injunctions Gagnon attempts to show a connection between a purity code that relates to Israel's need to be different from the surrounding pagan society, and a morality that relates to today's world. Other scholars, however, have seen in the Old Testament laws three distinct kinds of legislation, fulfilling different purposes for different periods:

1 Moral laws that have abiding application,

2 Cultic or ceremonial laws, that relate to a system of worship instituted to prepare Israel for their Messiah,

3 Civil laws, that were meant to provide a distinct visual identity for God's people in an environment where people behaved contrary to the Creator's design for his creation.

Certainly this exhaustive piece of in-house apologetic, argued robustly, tends more to polemic than to dialogue, producing a clear polarity of view-points that leaves little room for mutual accommodation. Also, though the arguments may remain valid, one wonders whether a book written over a decade ago may require its statistical and medical evidence to be checked.

Complementarity proven?

Two key questions remain. First, how crucial is Gagnon's argument that the exclusive complementarity of the opposite sexes is deducible from the creation account and therefore foundational for a traditionalist reading of Scripture? In other words, is "the anatomical, sexual, and procreative complementarity of male and female as clear and convincing [a] proof of God's will for sexual unions" as Gagnon maintains (37), or is it "an assumption that Gagnon brings to the text and then claims to have established as a biblical concern", as Ted Grimsrod suggests in his extensive Peace Theology blog (Feb 10, 2009)? The most compelling argument for such complementarity being the norm is, of course, its necessary role in procreation.

The challenge of 'positive' gay experience

Second, can a traditionalist conclusion regarding biblical teaching on same sex relationships ever be reconciled with the positive contemporary experiences of sexual intimacy claimed by revisionists for couples in the context of a covenanted, healthy, loving same sex partnership?

Gagnon, in maintaining the traditional position, has made clear his theological answer to such oft repeated arguments: 'gay' sex, in whatever context, is not 'fit for purpose'. However, he gives only passing pastoral consideration[6] to the struggles that gay Christians experience and shows no awareness of any possible qualitative differences between the experiences of gays and those of lesbians. Rather he majors on the negative and self-destructive experiences of promiscuous gays, without admitting any degree of moral distinction within the whole range of homosexual behaviour.

The Indian poet and writer Vikram Seth in a recent BBC radio interview described some of the angst he has experienced and still does experience as a homosexual person. First, the uncertainty about his own identity, about acceptance by society, about ever finding love; then the loneliness as a child perpetuated throughout adulthood as shyness when it comes to expressing oneself in intimate matters. "I do have loneliness now but it doesn't do any good to dwell on it. I have a very loving family, brother, parents, nieces, etc. and a wonderful circle of friends. So these are huge blessings! And I do long for someone to complete my life, so to speak."

One wonders, in the face of such an experience so poignantly and philosophically expressed, what the apostle Paul would have said! Neither Gagnon nor anyone else, of course, can answer that question! Yet it remains the most troubling and perplexing question of the whole debate. Despite the magisterial marshaling of biblical evidence by Robert Gagnon in the cause of proving the traditionalist case, it must be admitted that the traditionalist apologetic, with certain pastoral issues as yet unresolved, must be considered a work in progress.

---

6   In more recent writing, published in the next chapter, Gagnon does look a little further at these issues [Ed.]

Chapter 10

Accommodation and pastoral concern: what does the biblical text say?

Robert A. J. Gagnon

Robert Gagnon is associate professor at Pittsburgh Theological Seminary, Pittsburgh, PA 15206-2596. This material was produced initially for D. Min. students at the seminary, and like all the material in this book, is copyright.

Ever since my book *The Bible and Homosexual Practice* was published in Autumn 2001, many mainline churches, regional denominational bodies, and Christian-affiliated colleges and seminaries have invited me to speak to this issue, sometimes as a single presenter, sometimes in dialogue or debate with other scholars. My experience in these discussions is that two questions generally come to the fore in people's minds. They are:

1   How seriously does Scripture treat the issue of homosexual practice?

2   Does Scripture indict committed homosexual unions?

Behind each of these questions lie several related concerns:

1 Doesn't the Bible treat all sins alike? Are we giving unfair attention to the issue of homosexual practice when we ordain people who commit other sins, such as people who are divorced and remarried? Aren't we all sinners anyway? Even if we think homosexual practice is a sin, is this really an issue worth dividing the church over? Doesn't the church have more important things about which to be concerned? After all, doesn't Scripture itself give relatively little attention to the matter in relation to other issues like helping the poor?

2 Although Scripture may have some hard things to say about homosexual practice, did Paul and other writers of Scripture really have in mind the kind of committed and loving homosexual relationships that we witness

today? Weren't the biblical injunctions aimed exclusively at exploitative practices – sexual relationships between a man and an adolescent boy (pederasty), man-male prostitution, and coercive sex between a man and his male slave? Moreover, isn't it true that the ancient world had no concept of homosexual orientation but rather presumed that those participating in homosexual practice were oversexed heterosexuals? Doesn't love and commitment at least moderate the severity of homosexual practice to a point where the church can tolerate committed homosexual unions among the laity and even ordained officers of the church?

The first concern is answered in this and the following chapter. The second is dealt with in related material which will be published later in 2012,[1] and is summarised before the references at the end of this chapter.

Here we look at the reason why the church is at a juncture that requires a detailed response to these questions.

The new 'Third' or 'Middle' Way that seeks to accommodate homosexual practice in the church

There are many in the church today who, though caring about Scripture and generally unenthusiastic about homosexual unions, are sliding down a slope of accommodation to homosexual practice in the life of the church. Undoubtedly this slide is partly motivated by a genuine desire to be 'pastoral' to persons in committed homosexual relationships. Equally clear, though, is that many also feel a need to find some compromise in order to shield themselves from the verbal abuse and loss of status that comes with adopting the historic (and, I dare say, scriptural) position. The culture at large in the Western world has been moving steadily toward codifying opposition to homosexual practice as the equivalent of virulent racism and sexism. The church feels the pressure of these developments, especially the elite of the church who crave respectability. No one wants to be labeled a bigot, much less have one's career jeopardized or be hauled into court on a charge of hate speech or discrimination.

1 Problems with the so-called 'Third' or 'Middle' Way

One way of trying to 'have one's cake and eat it', that is, to look faithful and yet remain a player in the church's hierarchy, is to latch onto a so-called 'third' or 'middle' way. This views homosexual practice as something less

---

1 Goddard, A. (ed.) 2012, forthcoming, *Living Truth: Christian Faith and Homosexuality*, Gilead Books.

than the perfect will of God but, at any rate, no worse than any other sin and thus within the realm of compromise. Vigorous supporters of homosexual unions sometimes encourage this kind of response from the church's centre. They do so as part of a strategy to split the forces opposed to homosexual unions and move an otherwise resistant church to incremental and transitional steps in normalizing homosexual practice. Here left-of-centre supporters of homosexual unions have proven to be "as wise as serpents" in relation to those who are "as innocent as doves." Yet Jesus wanted his followers to be both: wise about how the people of the world operate without being tainted by the world's evil (Matt 10:16).

We will see in a moment that the assumption of homosexual practice being no worse than any other sin is problematic. Even apart from this problematic assumption, however, there are two key problems with the obsessive compulsion to be perceived, virtually at all costs, as 'in the middle' on the issue of homosexual practice.

First, one may rightly raise the question: What does one mean by the 'middle'? Usually, those seeking shelter from a storm of public criticism have in view a sociological middle. And not just a sociological middle but a sociological middle truncated to a tiny spectrum of Western 'elite' within a particular denomination and/or a left-leaning, largely non-Christian wing of scholarship. Yet even from a sociological standpoint the advocacy of some limited acceptance or toleration of homosexual practice does not constitute a 'middle' position. When one factors in any or all of the following – the laity within one's own denomination, the broader church across denominational lines, and the church inclusive of the Third World –a position that tolerates or endorses unrepentant homosexual practice is distinctly left of centre.

Secondly, given Scripture's view of a remnant and its repeated call to leave behind sexual practices of the unbelieving world (e.g., Lev 20:26; 1 Thess 4:3-5; Rom 1:24-27 with 6:19-21 and 13:13; 1 Cor 6:11; cf. Eph 4:17-19; 5:3-8), the appropriate middle must always be a stance faithful to Jesus Christ and his apostolic witness, irrespective of how many people adopt a stance in opposition to it. Determining morality is not a popularity contest. Nor should moral standards shift because of the pressures of ridicule and even more severe forms of persecution.

Consequently, there seems little justification for referring to a stance that accommodates homosexual practice among ordained officers of the church as a 'middle' way. It is not the middle position but rather a position left of centre. Nor does the nomenclature 'third way' seem to fit since the practical result of the position is to support the ideological objectives of those who seek to normalize homosexual practice in the church. A so-called 'third way' simply provides the transitional bridge to the full acceptance of homosexual practice in the church.

2 What did 'being pastoral' mean to Jesus and the apostle Paul?

Because supporters of a 'third' or 'middle' way often justify accommodation to homosexual practice through an appeal to 'being pastoral', it is important to examine briefly what that expression would have meant, or not meant, to Jesus and the chief apostle to the Gentiles, Paul. We will start with Paul, not because he is more important than Jesus but because we have more and clearer evidence from Paul of what 'pastoral' meant in the context of an organized church setting. We will then assess whether Paul's approach differed markedly from the approach of Jesus, at least as presented in the Gospels. Here we will see that for neither Jesus nor Paul did 'being pastoral' mean toleration of unrepentant behaviors that Scripture abhors.

Paul

We see this clearly in the case of the incestuous man dealt with by the apostle Paul in 1 Corinthians 5. There 'pastoral' for Paul meant rendering a verdict that the offender not merely be kept from leadership roles in the church until he repented but, more, be temporarily suspended from participation in the life of the community (vv. 3-5). The example is *a propos* to the issue of homosexual practice inasmuch as Paul, in context, compared a case of adult-consensual incest to sex between males, adultery, and sex with prostitutes (1 Cor 6:9, 15-17). All for Paul were instances of severe "sexual immorality" (*porneia*) that put the offenders at risk of not inheriting God's kingdom. Consequently, they necessitated similar ecclesiastical discipline to prevent the loss of eternal life from being actualized. The link between a heightened risk of exclusion from God's kingdom and temporary disassociation from the believing community is evident from a comparison of the vice lists in 5:10-11, which advocate temporary disassociation, with the similar vice list in 6:9-10, which refers to the risk of not inheriting God's kingdom. Paul's discussion in 6:12-20, where he insists that adult-consensual incest in particular and sexual immorality in general cannot be compared to dietary regulations, clarifies why such a risk exists:

1 Sexual intercourse is unique in the degree to which it engages embodied existence, even when it involves the most commercial and least self-

invested sexual relationship, namely, sex with a prostitute; thus, "every [other] sin – whatever a person does – is outside the body."

2 Therefore sexually immoral acts affect holistically (not superficially) the persons involved, who become "one flesh" with each other.

3 God owns the body because he "bought us with a price" (i.e. Christ's death), made it to be a "temple" for the Holy Spirit, and through that Spirit joined us in "one spirit" with Jesus.

4 Accordingly, immoral sexual intercourse is particularly pernicious in the way it takes ownership of the whole person back from God, defiles the place where the Spirit dwells, and brings Jesus into a bizarre association with the immoral act.

Now I suppose one could argue that Paul was overly harsh and not at all 'pastoral' in his verdict, even though Paul clearly believed that it could be implemented "in the name [and power] of our Lord Jesus" (5:4). However, the contention that Paul was not 'pastorally sensitive', that is, that he did not model well the care for one's flock, appears hard to sustain in view of what we know about Paul from his own letters. Consider the following:

• Paul's supreme devotion to his converts, to a point of great personal hardship. Paul suffered extraordinarily for his converts (see the catalogue of hardships in 11:23-33; also 1 Cor 4:9-13; 2 Cor 6:4-10), as he and his co-workers shared with them "not only the gospel of God but also our own souls" (1 Thess 2:8). "I will very gladly spend and be utterly spent on behalf of your souls," he told the Corinthians (2 Cor 12:15). "If we are afflicted, it is on behalf of your encouragement and salvation" (2 Cor 1:6). "If I cause you pain, who is there to make me glad . . . ?" (2 Cor 2:2). To the Philippians he stated: "But even if I am being offered up as a drink offering to complement the sacrifice and temple-service of your faith, I rejoice and do so with you all" (2:17). To the Thessalonians, in a letter where he compared his relationship to them as that of a father, nursing mother, a brother, and an orphan, he declared his intense longing for them: "For what is our hope or joy or crown of boasting – isn't it indeed you – before our Lord Jesus at his coming? For you are our glory and joy. . . . For now we live if you stand firm in the Lord" (1 Thess 2:7, 11, 17, 19-20; 3:1, 5-10). There is no question that Paul devoted himself to those under his care in a way and to a degree that has scarcely been equalled in the history of the church.

- Paul's policy of accommodation to save the maximum number possible. In addition, Paul determined to "give no obstacle [i.e., nothing to trip or stumble over] in anything" that might hinder the path leading to salvation for the maximum number of people (2 Cor 6:2-3). Accordingly, he adopted a principle of adaptability, having "enslaved myself to all in order that I may gain more people," having become "all things to all people in order that I might save some" and, more, "that I might become a participant with them in the gospel" in receiving the prize of eternal life (1 Cor 9:19-27). Among other things, Paul applied this principle to matters of dietary observances and calendar regulations and to laboring day and night so as not to be a burden to his converts (1 Cor 8–10; Rom 14; 1 Thess 2; 2 Cor 11:7-11). He did not regard sexual offences, however, as matters of indifference to which the church might accommodate but rather viewed such offences as endangering the salvation of the perpetrators (cf. 1 Cor 6:12-20 within chs. 5-7; also 2 Cor 12:21; 1 Thess 4:3-8; Gal 5:19-21; Rom 1:24-27; 6:17; 13:13; cf. Eph 4:19; 5:3-5).

- Paul's emphasis on love and unity in the proper implementation of correction. Paul insisted on the importance of love and unity within the church (e.g., 1 Cor 1–4, 12–14), even exhorting that correction be done with gentleness, humility, self-introspection, and a desire to bear each other's burdens (Gal 6:1-5). He instructed his churches to tailor the intensity of the correction to the offender's degree of recalcitrance (1 Thess 5:14). Moreover, he cautioned his churches to have in view not only the purity of the community but also the speedy reintegration of those who are disciplined (compare 1 Cor 5:5; 2 Cor 2:5-11; 7:8-12; 2 Thess 3:14).

- Paul's strong preference for building up through encouragement over tearing down through discipline. As he viewed his own apostolic call in the light of Jeremiah's prophetic call, Paul strongly preferred to exercise his authority to "build up" his converts rather than "tear down" (2 Cor 10:8; 12:19; 13:10, alluding to Jer 24:6 and 1:10). Coming to them with a proverbial rod was always and only a last resort (1 Cor 4:18-21; 2 Cor 10:1-6; 13:1-4, 9-10). Nevertheless, for their sakes, he was willing to resort to it. For as a slave and soldier of Jesus Christ he was under orders to "tear down fortresses" of pride that people erect "against the knowledge of God," in order to "capture every thought for obedience to Christ and be ready to punish every disobedience, until such time as your obedience is brought to completion" (2 Cor 10:4-6; cf. 12:19-21).

So was Paul contradicting his own best principles when he advocated temporary disassociation from professed believers involved in serial unrepentant sin of an egregious sort – especially sexual sin? So far as I can discern, the differences between Paul and many 'mainline' pastors today who misinterpret 'being pastoral' as accommodation to sexual immorality are fourfold:

1 Paul loved those entrusted to his care more and gave himself to them more sacrificially.

2 Paul really believed that the eternal destiny of offenders was at stake.

3 Paul recognized that catering to extreme acts of sexual immorality would, over time, seriously erode the entire community's posture toward sexual purity (1 Cor 5.6-8).

4 Paul really believed that it was dangerous to provoke God to wrath, consistent with God's actions toward the rebellious wilderness generation of the Israelites (1 Cor 10).

On the last point, Paul believed that toleration of serious sexual sin and of idolatry could provoke God to take strong physical action against a community of believers (1 Cor 10:1-13, 21-22; 11:30-31). That is why we find the parallel exhortations in 1 Corinthians: "Flee sexual immorality (*porneia*)" (6:18) and "flee from idolatry" (10:14). Even in the shadow of the cross, the God of Jesus Christ was a God to be reckoned with. As Paul succinctly puts it, "we are not stronger than him (God), are we?" (11:22).

In short, being 'pastoral' for Paul had nothing to do with tolerating sinful conduct among the laity, much less the leaders, of the church. An analogue would be the remarks of the exalted Christ to some of the seven churches of Asia Minor, castigating them for "tolerating" sexual immorality and idolatry in their midst (Rev 2:14, 20). To be sure, as noted above, Paul believed that 'being pastoral' included tailoring the mode of correction to the degree of the offender's recalcitrance. He also believed that unbelievers had to have access to the community's worship services as one important venue for hearing the gospel and having the opportunity to be transformed (1 Cor 14:23). These approaches, however, are a far cry from today's situation of accommodating to serious sinful behavior and impenitence, even to the point of ordaining as leaders of the church persons who engage affirmingly in such behavior. For this reason the so-called 'third' or 'middle' way that claims to be 'pastoral' is unfaithful to the gospel of Jesus Christ. Lives are at stake. With an exasperated Paul we say: "Isn't it the case that you are to judge those inside (the church)?" (1 Cor 5:12).

Jesus

There is no strong evidence that Paul was significantly out of step with Jesus on the meaning of being 'pastoral'. For, while Jesus actively reached out in love to fraternize with sinners and tax collectors, he coupled this outreach with a call for repentance as an essential precondition for inheriting the kingdom of God (Mark 1:15 par.; 6:12 par.; Matt 11:20-21 par.; 12:41 par.; Luke 13:3-5). In the paradigmatic story of the woman caught in adultery Jesus prevented the crowd from stoning the woman – dead people don't repent – but clearly commanded the woman to "no longer be sinning" (John 8.11). This command is combined elsewhere in John with the warning "lest something worse happen to you" (i.e., loss of eternal life; John 5:14). In Matthew's Sermon on the Mount the saying about cutting off offending body parts in order to avoid being sent to hell full-bodied is sandwiched in between two sets of teaching on the importance of sexual purity (Matt 5:27-32).

Jesus viewed rebuke of the recalcitrant as an integral part of what it meant to love one's neighbour (compare Luke 17:3-4 // Matt 18:15, 21-22 with Lev 19:17-18). Indeed, he himself often rebuked others sternly (e.g., Mark 8:33 par.; Mark 11:15-19 par.; Matt 23:13-36). He repeatedly warned about the perils of the coming judgment for those who only hear his words but do not do them (e.g., Matt 7:13-27; for a long list of Jesus' judgment sayings in the Synoptic Gospels, minus material unique to Matthew, see pp. 6-14 in Gagnon, 2002b). Jesus combined such warnings with an intensification of God's ethical demands and a closing of loopholes in the Law of Moses (Matt 5:17-48). Finally, at least Matthew understood Jesus' teaching as necessitating standards for community discipline (18:15-20).

It is one thing to assert (rightly) that Jesus reached out to sinners but quite another to claim (wrongly) that Jesus would have accommodated to ongoing, self-affirming sinful practices of a severe sort among his company of followers. As with the woman caught in adultery, the "sinful woman" who washed Jesus' feet with her tears and who loved much because she was forgiven much obviously did not intend to continue her life of sin (Luke 7:36-50). Likewise, the parables of the lost son and of the penitent tax collector are stories about people who leave behind sinful lives, and do not continue in them (Luke 15:11-32; 18:9-14).

Conclusion

My point is simply this: the attempt to justify accommodation to homosexual practice (and thus to circumvent the witness of Scripture) by
appealing to a 'pastoral concern' is just an excuse to avoid, first, the hard
work of reclaiming believers for the kingdom of God and, second, the
attendant abuse from the world.

What it means to be 'pastoral' in any given situation is determined
by the severity of the offence and the willingness (or lack thereof) of the
offender to repent. If the offence is severe and the individual is determined
to substitute his or her will for the will of God expressed in the teachings
of Jesus and the united apostolic witness, then the church's discipline ought
to be invoked in a spirit of gentleness, humility, sadness, and concern for
the offender. Certainly it ought to go without saying that the church should
not be installing such offenders in a position of leadership or in any other
way sanctioning the sinful behavior (e.g., by offering blessing ceremonies
for unions that are constituted through such behavior).

So the question boils down to this: how serious is the Bible's stance
against homosexual practice? No one can claim to know what it means to
be pastoral to persons engaged self-affirmingly in a homosexual bond until
and unless one can answer this question.

Appendix: Does Scripture indict committed homosexual unions?

(a summary by the editors of the section of Gagnon's material which is published elsewhere)[2]

While the OT and later Judaic prohibitions on homosexual conduct are absolute, Gagnon focuses on Paul, who says most about the issue. Gagnon gives six arguments (in detail) for concluding that Paul's opposition was absolute and not limited to exploitative forms of practice:

1   Behind the two main passages of Romans 1:24-27 and 1 Corinthians 6:9 lie the creation texts of Genesis 1:27 and 2:24, with eight points of correspondence: human, image, likeness; birds, cattle, reptiles; male, female.

2   Paul's 'nature' argument in Romans 1:24-27 does not lend itself to any distinction between exploitative and non-exploitative homosexual behaviour.

3   In Romans 1:24-27, Paul emphasises mutuality, which indicates that he is not restricting his remarks to exploitative relationships.

4   He includes lesbianism, and lesbianism in antiquity was not about pederasty, prostitution or abuse of slaves.

5   The Greek words *malakoi* and *arsenokoitai* in 1 Corinthians 6:9 include all homosexual bonds, understood in their historic context.

6   The idea of caring homoerotic unions already existed in Paul's cultural environment (though even these were rejected by some Greco-Roman moralists).

Would knowledge of the modern concept of homosexual orientation have changed Paul's verdict?

No, for several reasons, including:

1   the fact that for Paul 'nature' was not about impulses but what was embodied.

2   the prevalence of ancient versions of the modern view that homosexual attraction is congenital, especially the desire of some males to be penetrated. The idea of an interplay of nature and nurture was common in the ancient world.

Gagnon also points out how strictly both Jesus and Paul took sexual purity. And he mentions a number of revisionist scholars who frankly admit that Paul would not have changed his views in the light of modern knowledge.

---

2   See footnote 1.

References and Bibliography

Bailey, J. Michael and Mustanski, Brian S.
2003   "A therapist's guide to the genetics of human sexual orientation." Sexual and Relationship Therapy 18.4: 429-36.

Bird, Phyllis A.
"The Bible in Christian Ethical Deliberation concerning Homosexuality: Old Testament Contributions." 142-76 in Homosexuality, Science, and the 'Plain Sense' of Scripture. Ed. D. L. Balch. Grand Rapids: Eerdmans.

Brooten, Bernadette J.
1996   *Love Between Women: Early Christian Responses to Female Homo-eroticism.* Chicago: University of Chicago Press.

Compton, Louis
2003   Homosexuality and Civilization. Cambridge: Harvard University Press.

Esler, Philip F.
"The Sodom Tradition in Romans 1:18-32." BTB 34:4-16.

Gagnon, Robert A. J.
Bible and Homosexual Practice: Texts and Hermeneutics. Nashville: Abingdon, 2002.

2002a   "Gays and the Bible: A Response to Walter Wink." Christian Century 119.17: 40-43.

2002b   "No Universally Valid Sex Standards? A Rejoinder to Walter Wink's Views." 16 pgs. Online: http://www.robgagnon.net/Reviews/homoWinkRejoinder.pdf.

2002c   "Are There Universally Valid Sex Precepts? A Critique of Walter Wink's Views on the Bible and Homosexuality," HBT 24:72-125. Online: http://www.robgagnon.net/articles/homoWinkHBTResp.pdf.

2003a   *Homosexuality and the Bible: Two Views*, with Dan O. Via. Minneapolis: Fortress.

2003b   "Notes to Gagnon's Essay in the Gagnon-Via Two Views Book." 50 pgs. Online: http://www.robgagnon.net/2Views/HomoViaRespNotesRev.pdf.

2003c   "Does the Bible Regard Same-Sex Intercourse as Intrinsically Sinful?" Pages 106-55 in *Christian Sexuality: Normative and Pastoral Principles.* Ed. R. E. Saltzman. Minneapolis: Kirk House.

2003d   "A Comprehensive and Critical Review Essay of Homosexuality, Science, and the 'Plain Sense' of Scripture, Part 2." HBT 25: 179-275. Online: http://www.robgagnon.net/articles/homoBalchHBTReview2.pdf.

2003e   "Response to Countryman's Review in Anglican Theological Review: On Careful Scholarship." 18 pages. Online: http://www.robgagnon.net/Reviews/homoCountrymanResp.pdf.

2005a   "A Faithful Journey through the Bible and Homosexuality? The Use of Scripture in Two 2003 ELCA Documents." 54 pgs. Online: http://www.robgagnon.net/articles/homoJourneyTogetherCritique.pdf.

2005b   "Old Testament and Homosexuality: A Critical Review of the Case Made by Phyllis Bird." ZAW 117: 367-94.

2005c   "Scriptural Perspectives on Homosexuality and Sexual Identity." Journal of Psychology and Christianity 24: 293-303.

2005d   "Sexuality." Pp. 739-48 in *Dictionary for Theological Interpretation of the Bible*. Eds. K. J. Vanhoozer, *et al*. London: SPCK; Grand Rapids: Baker Academic.

2005e   "Why the Disagreement over the Biblical Witness on Homosexual Practice? A Response to Myers and Scanzoni, What God Has Joined Together?" Reformed Review 59: 19-130. Online: http://www.westernsem.edu/wtseminary/assets/Gagnon2%20Aut05.pdf.

2006a   "Homosexuality." Pp. 327-32 in *New Dictionary of Christian Apologetics*. Eds. C. Campbell-Jack, G. J. McGrath, and C. S. Evans. Leicester, U.K.: Inter-Varsity Press.

2006b   "Does Jack Rogers's New Book 'Explode the Myths' about the Bible and Homosexuality and 'Heal the Church?' Part 3." 15 pgs. Online: http://www.robgagnon.net/articles/RogersBookReviewed3.pdf.

2006c   "Does Jack Rogers's New Book 'Explode the Myths' about the Bible and Homosexuality and 'Heal the Church?' Part 4." 16 pgs. Online: http://www.robgagnon.net/articles/RogersBookReviewed4.pdf.

2007a   "Is Rowan Williams wrong on the meaning of Romans?" Church of England Newspaper (The Record), 4 May 2007, pp. 22-23, online: http://www.churchnewspaper.com/Get-CEN-Online.aspx. Fuller version: "Rowan Williams' Wrong Reading of Romans (. . . and John 14.6)," 11 pgs. Online: http://www.robgagnon.net/articles/homosexRowanWilliamsResp.pdf.

2007b   "Did Jesus Approve of a Homosexual Couple in the Story of the Centurion at Capernaum?" 8 pages. Online: http://www.robgagnon.net/articles/homosexCenturionStory.pdf.

Greenberg, Moshe
Ezekiel 1-20. Anchor Bible. Garden City: Doubleday.
Ezekiel 21-37. Anchor Bible. Garden City: Doubleday.

Hubbard, Thomas K.
2003   *Homosexuality in Greece and Rome: A Sourcebook of Basic Documents.* Berkeley: University of California Press.

Loader, J. A.
"A Tale of Two Cities: Sodom and Gomorrah in the Old Testament, Early Jewish and Early Christian Traditions." CBET 1. Kampen: Kok.

Miller, James E.
1995   "The Practices of Romans 1:26: Homosexual or Heterosexual?" NovT 37:1-11.

Nissinen, Martti
Homoeroticism in the Biblical World: A Historical Perspective. Minneapolis: Fortress.

Schoedel, William R.
2000   "Same-Sex Eros: Paul and the Greco-Roman Tradition," 43-72 in Homosexuality, Science, and the "Plain Sense" of Scripture. Ed. D. Balch. Grand Rapids: Eerdmans.

Scroggs, Robin
1983   *The New Testament and Homosexuality: Contextual Background for Contemporary Debate.* Philadelphia: Fortress.

Williams, Craig A.
1999   *Roman Homosexuality: Ideologies of Masculinity in Classical Antiquity.* New York: Oxford University Press.

Wink, Walter
2002   "To Hell with Gays?" Christian Century 119.13: 32-34.

Chapter 11

How seriously does Scripture treat the issue of homosexual practice?

Robert Gagnon

It is my contention that homosexual practice is a more serious violation of Scripture's sexual norms than even adult-consensual incest, adultery, plural marriage, fornication, and divorce.

A Are all sins equally offensive to God in all respects?

At the outset there will be some readers who contend that it is unscriptural and un-Christian to argue that any sins are more severe than any other sins. The main problem with such a contention is that no one really believes it. In fact, most people in the mainline churches today who want to see some sort of accommodation made to committed homosexual unions do so by rationalizing that homosexual practice in a committed same sex relationship is 'not as bad' as promiscuous homosexual behaviour. Proponents of homosexual unions often recoil in horror at the thought of any comparison with adult-consensual incest or with adultery (to say nothing of bestiality or pedophilia) precisely because they operate with a notion that some sexual sins are truly more severe than others.

Thus when I hear people both (1) insisting that all sins are equal and (2) getting irate over any comparison of homosexual practice with loving adult-consensual incest or polyamory (or worse acts), I immediately know that such persons have not thought through the deep structure of their logic. For the two stances are mutually exclusive. If all sins are equal in all respects, then it makes no difference whether one compares homosexual practice to divorce or to adult-consensual incest or polyamory or even bestiality or pedophilia.

Whatever concessions have been made to fornication and divorce in the church, I still see the mainline churches in the West holding reasonably consistent positions against sexual unions involving more than two partners and certainly incestuous unions of a first-order severity (e.g., incest with one's parent, full sibling, or child), to say nothing of bestiality, sex with prostitutes, and sex with prepubescent children. Are we being unreasonable in giving precedence to some sins over others? Should we concede these other matters as well and be more consistently disobedient to the will of Christ? I personally don't know anyone who would argue such positions. The reason why is obvious: nearly everyone recognizes that making accommodations in some areas does not justify making accommodations for violations in more foundational matters. The church's current practices tacitly acknowledge a different weight given to different sins.

Now it is true that any sin, including sexual sin, can get one excluded from the kingdom of heaven if merit is the means of entrance. In that specific sense, all sins are equal. In addition, there are certainly other sins besides homosexual practice, including other sexual sins, that can get offenders excluded from the kingdom of God if practised in a serial, unrepentant manner (1 Cor 6:9-10; Gal 5:19-21). Yet none of these concessions means that the church should (or does) regard all sexual sins, let alone all sins of any type, as basically of equal import. Much less do they mean that God views all sins as equally abhorrent. I am confident that few Christians, at least when hooked up to a lie detector or given truth serum, would assert that God views the taking home of a company pen as endangering the eternal destiny of the Christian perpetrator in the same way that, say, raping and eating children would (I am thinking here of the serial killer, Jeffrey Dahmer, as an extreme example). The image is offensive, I grant. In fact, if you, the reader, feel any offence, this merely confirms my point: you don't really believe that all sins are equally heinous, either to God or to us.

In short, it is not true that all sins are in all respects equally offensive to God.

The point can be made easily from Scripture. To take a few examples:

1 In the Old Testament there is a clear ranking of sins. For instance, in Leviticus 20, which reorders the offences in ch. 18 according to penalty, the most severe sexual offences are grouped first (20:10-16). Among the first-tier sexual offences (along with adultery, the worst forms of incest, and bestiality) is same sex intercourse. Of course, variegated penalties for different sins can be found throughout the legal material in the Old Testament.

2 Jesus also prioritized offences, referring to "the weightier matters of the law" (Matt 23:23) and, of course, to the two greatest commandments

(Mark 12:28-31 par.). For instance, he viewed healing a sick person on the Sabbath as taking precedence over the Decalogue command to rest on the Sabbath when the two principles came into tension or outright conflict. His special outreach to economic exploiters (tax-collectors) and sexual sinners, all in an effort to recover them for the very kingdom of God that he proclaimed, was not so much a reaction to their abandonment by society as an indication of the special severity of these repetitive sins and the extreme spiritual danger that they placed perpetrators in (Gagnon 2001, 210-28). Another obvious instance of prioritizing some offences as worse than others is Jesus' characterization of "blasphemy against the Holy Spirit" as an "eternal sin" from which one "never has forgiveness" – in context referring to the Pharisees' attribution of Jesus' exorcisms to demonic power (Mark 3:28-30 par.).

3 Paul's attitude toward the case of incest in 1 Corinthians 5 also makes clear that he differentiated between various sexual offences, with some being more extreme than others. This is clear both from the horror in his tone at the case of incest (vv. 1-2) but, even more, from the fact that he had to arbitrate between competing values when he condemned the incest. If there were no ranking of priorities, then how could Paul have rejected out of hand a case of incest that was monogamous and committed? If the values of monogamy and commitment to longevity were of equal weight with a requirement of a certain degree of familial otherness, Paul could not have decided what to do. Would commitment to a monogamous, lifelong union cancel out the prohibition of incest? Obviously, this was not a difficult matter for Paul to decide. He knew that the incest prohibition was more foundational.

For those from the Reformed tradition it should be noted that such a view is 'reformed'. For example, the Larger Catechism of the Westminster Confession of Faith (1647) states the obvious: "All transgressions of the law of God are not equally heinous; but some sins in themselves, and by reason of several aggravations, are more heinous in the sight of God than others" (7.260; elaboration in 7.261; cf. the Shorter Catechism 7.083).

B Why homosexual practice is one of the most severe sexual sins

Having established the principle that some offences are more heavily weighted than others, the question arises: how big a violation does Scripture view same sex intercourse, particularly among sexual offences? I will argue that Scripture itself, understood in its historical context, indicates that homosexual practice is a more severe violation of God's will for sexual behaviour than polyamory (multiple-partner sexual bonds), incest, and adultery. Here are three main reasons why, in no particular order of significance.

B.1 The male-female prerequisite is the foundation or prior analogue for defining other critical sexual norms

Homosexual practice is a more severe violation of God's will for human sexual behaviour than (a) divorce/remarriage and (b) polygamy. Jesus himself clearly predicated his view of marital monogamy and indissolubility on the foundation of Gen 1:27 and 2:24 (Mark 10:6-9; Matt 19:4-6), texts that have only one thing in common: the fact that an acceptable sexual bond before God entails as its most foundational prerequisite – after, of course, the assumption of an intra-human bond – "male and female" (Gen 1:27) or, defined for age, "a man" and "his woman" (Gen 2:24). Jesus argued that the 'twoness' of the sexes ordained by God at creation was the foundation for limiting the number of persons in a sexual bond to two, whether concurrently (as against polygamy) or serially (as against repetitive divorce and remarriage). This is at one and the same time an argument from Scripture (an appeal to God's intention at creation) and an argument from nature (inferences from the existence of two primary sexes).

B.1.1 Polyamory

It is axiomatic that the foundation (a two-sexes prerequisite) must be more important than the regulation predicated on it (a monogamy principle). If the Western church is not inclined to tolerate faithful 'plural' unions among the laity (whether the traditional polygynous variety or non-traditional models such as 'threesomes'), much less tolerate such among its ordained leaders, it should be even less inclined to tolerate violations of the foundation upon which monogamy is based. In recognition of the illogic of holding the line on a two-partner limitation after eliminating its two-sexes foundation, some homosex-affirming quarters of the church have already begun advocating for 'polyamory awareness' and 'polyfidelity' (see Gagnon 2005e, 35-40).

B.1.2 Divorce/remarriage

By the same token, yielding at some points on the matter of divorce and remarriage (while still rejecting ordination for those involved in 'serial divorce and remarriage') is no justification for yielding ground on a two-sexes prerequisite that is prior and more significant. Clearly, too, the dissolution of an otherwise natural marital bond (i.e. divorce) is not more severe than the active entrance into an inherently unnatural union (e.g. homosexual practice). Active entrance into an incestuous bond would be a parallel case in point: I don't know anyone who views active entrance into an incestuous union between a man and his mother (or a woman and her brother, or a parent and child) as a lesser offence, or even equivalent offence, to the dissolution of a marital bond between persons unrelated by blood. And so it should be.

B.1.3 Incest

The principle by which same sex intercourse is rejected is also the principle by which incest, even of an adult and consensual sort, is rejected. Incest is wrong because, as Leviticus 18.6 states, it involves sexual intercourse with "the flesh of one's own flesh". In other words, it involves an attempted sexual merger with someone who is already too much of a formal or structural same on a familial level. The degree of formal or structural sameness is felt even more keenly in the case of homosexual practice, only now on the level of sex or gender, because sex or gender is a more integral component of sexual relations, and more foundationally defines it, than is and does the degree of blood relatedness. So the prohibition of incest can be, and probably was, analogically derived from the more foundational prohibition of same sex intercourse.

Certainly there was more accommodation to some forms of incest in the Old Testament than ever there was to homosexual practice. An implicit proscription of homosexual behaviour can be grounded in the creation narratives in Genesis 1–2 (as Paul certainly did, see below) but as regards incest at most only an implicit prohibition of intergenerational incest might be found. So adult, consensual homosexual practice is more severe than adult, consensual incest. Again, the point here is not in the first instance to establish a moral 'slippery slope', though acceptance of homosexual relations will grease the slope considerably and likely lead in the long run to a near-complete breakdown of formal or structural prerequisites for sexual bonds. Rather, the point is that if the church finds problematic the acceptance of incestuous unions of an adult, consensual, and committed sort, it should find homosexual unions even more problematic; the latter violate more deeply the principle upon which an incest prohibition is based – namely, the necessity of a certain amount of complementary otherness on the level of bodily structures.

B.1.4 Adultery

We have argued above that homosexual practice is a worse offence than committed, adult polysexual unions and, of course, divorce and remarriage, since the violation of foundational matters is worse than the violation of structures built on the foundation. We have also argued that homosexual practice is a worse violation of God's will than committed, adult incestuous unions, on the following principle: among two things related by analogy the violation of the one that more deeply embeds the principle upon which the analogy is based is more serious than the violation of the other. A similar argument can be made that homosexual practice is a worse offence than even adultery.

Adultery at least cannot be a worse offence than incest and thus homosexual practice since adultery becomes an applicable offence only when the sexual bond that the offender is cheating on is a valid sexual bond. Needless to say, it would be absurd to charge a man in an incestuous union with adultery for having sexual relations with a person unrelated by blood outside the committed incestuous bond. To do so would wrongly presume the validity of the incestuous bond. The same point applies to cheating on a homosexual bond; especially, for example, as regards a man in a homosexual relationship 'cheating' by having sex with a woman. One can't cheat against a union that is structurally invalid, and thus immoral, from the beginning – or at least the notion of cheating must be considerably diluted (much as the idea of 'cheating' on a mistress must, by definition, be diminished in significance).

So, in summary, it is evident that the male-female prerequisite is the foundational prerequisite for defining most other sexual norms.

B.2 Same sex intercourse radically offends against God's intentional creation of humans as "male and female" (Gen 1:27) and the definition of marriage as a union between a man and a woman (Gen 2:24)

Since Jesus himself defined these texts as foundational for matters of human sexual ethics (Mark 10:6-8 par. Matt 19:4-6), Jesus' church must treat an offence against them as a major violation of Christian sexual ethics.

Genesis 1:27 brings into close connection "the image of God" and creation of humans as "male and female": "in the image of God he (God) created [the human]; male and female he created them." The language of

Genesis 1:27 suggests two points of importance. First, though animals too participate in sexual differentiation and pairing, human sexual differentiation and pairing is uniquely integrated into God's image. This makes it possible for humans to enhance or to efface that image through their sexual behaviour. The alternative is to argue, falsely, that one's sexuality is wholly disconnected from God's image, thereby making it possible for one to engage in every kind of sexual misbehaviour, including adultery, bestiality, and paedophilia, without doing any harm to the imprint of God's image. Secondly, a male-female sexual pairing manifests the fullness of the imprint of God's image on the sexual dimension of human life. While male and female each bear the stamp of God's image on their sexuality and have independent integrity as such, they do so as 'angular' and complementary expressions of that image.

Genesis 2:21-24 adds to this point with a beautiful picture of the reality that man and woman are complementary sexual 'other halves'. The sole differentiation produced by the removal of a "side" from the original human is the differentiation of the sexes ("side" is a better translation than "rib" of Hebrew tsela'; see Gagnon 2005b, 386-89). The principle of two sexes becoming one flesh is thus grounded in the picture of two sexes emerging from one flesh (2:24). What is required in the story line of Genesis 2:21-24 is not merely a joining or merger of two persons but a rejoining or remerging of the two sexes into one. It matters little how literally or metaphorically one takes the image. We are, after all, dealing with transcendent realities that, by necessity, require a certain amount of metaphor. The image conveys the essential point that man and woman are the two essential and complementary parts in a holistic picture of human sexuality. As an aside, it is a misnomer to refer to the phenomenon of the 'intersexed' as a 'third sex' since persons who exhibit extreme androgyny merely possess an amalgam of the two sexes. In addition, this very rare phenomenon no more justifies the elimination of a two-sexes prerequisite than does the equally rare phenomenon of conjoined ('Siamese') twins justify the elimination of a monogamy principle.

Those who contend that Genesis 1:27 and 2:24 are merely descriptive texts and carry no prescriptive implications for a male-female prerequisite or no proscriptive implications for rejecting homosexual bonds have to contend with Jesus and Paul. Jesus gave priority to Genesis 1:27 and 2:24 when he defined normative and prescriptive sexual ethics and indeed predicated his 'two and only two' rule for the number of persons in a sexual bond on the twoness of the sexes ordained at creation. Paul clearly had the creation texts in the background of his indictment of homosexual practice in Romans 1:24-27 and 1 Corinthians 6:9 (see below).

The main counterargument against the position outlined above is that viewing male and female as two incomplete parts of a sexual whole made in God's image leads to a denigration of singleness, including Jesus' and Paul's single state, and so a denigration of Jesus as the image of God. However, this argument is misplaced, for at least six reasons.

(1) The truth of two primary sexes. It is axiomatic and undeniable that a male or a female is only one half of a complete sexual whole since, obviously, there are two primary sexes. This is just another way of stating the elementary point that women bring out dimensions of God's image lacking in men and vice versa.

(2) The impact of sexual behaviour on God's image in humans. It is equally axiomatic and undeniable that one's sexual expression has powerful potential to honour or to dishonour, to enhance or efface, one's own creation in God's image. Sexuality and divine image are interconnected in humans. Unlike some pagan conceptions of sexuality that largely disconnect sexual behaviour from religious devotion, the Judeo-Christian conception of sexuality thoroughly integrates the two dimensions so that sexual purity becomes a vital component of one's spirituality.

(3) "Made in God's image" as a relative quality. It is legitimate to speak of the two sexes as complementary, and so incomplete, representations of God's image in the restricted sphere of sexuality without denying the broader integrity of an individual's creation in God's image. In a similar way one can speak of God's image as more fully represented in a community of believers than in any single individual in isolation without denying that the individual too is made in God's image.

(4) The single state as a non-moral deficit. Both Jesus and Paul viewed the single state as a form of deprivation or deficit, though recognizing the value of a sexually unattached life for the advancement of God's kingdom (Matt 19:10-12; 1 Cor 7:7-8, 25-40). They also recognized a distinction, as persons do today, between foregoing a valid sexual union, which is an experience of deprivation but no sin, and willfully entering into a structurally incompatible union, which is sin. One's status as a single sex is not a moral deficit in God's image but a non-moral deficit, since God himself ordained distinct sexes.

(5) Active entrance into a structurally incongruous union as a moral violation that assaults the image of God stamped on humans. While a state of singleness violates no boundaries, a discordant sexual merger does disrupt formal or structural congruities and thus dishonor the human that God created one to be. Obvious instances of the latter that presumably even advocates for homosexual unions would have to acknowledge include attempted sexual unions involving close blood relations, three or more persons concurrently, an adult and a child, or a human and an animal.

(6) Homosexual practice as a denial of the integrity of one's maleness or femaleness made in God's image. It is same sex sexual activity, not singleness, that compromises one's integrity as a sexual being made in God's image. For the logic of a same sex sexual bond is that each partner is only half his or her own sex since a sexual bond by its very nature involves bodily integration of two discrete halves. This dishonors the integrity of God's image imprinted on maleness, if one is male, and on femaleness, if one is female. The picture in Genesis 2:21-24 of a woman being formed from what is pulled from the man/human illustrates the point that the missing element from one sex is not another of the same sex but rather one from the only other sex. The story conveys the self-evident point that on a sexual level men and women are configured bodily – and here I mean 'bodily' in a holistic sense – as open-ended to a person of the only other sex, not a person of the same sex.

We find this perspective in a number of early Jewish texts that allude to woman's creation from the "side" or "rib" (Gk. *pleura*) of the first human and thus to woman as the only suitable being with whom a man may be rejoined. For example, Philo of Alexandria (a first-century Jewish philosopher) writes about the creation of woman in Genesis 2:21-24 (albeit allegorically): "And which side did he take? For we may assume that only two are indicated" (Philo, Allegorical Interpretation 2:19-21); "Love . . . brings together and fits into one the divided halves, as it were, of a single living creature" (*Creation* 152). In 4 Maccabees 18:7 the mother of seven sons about to be slaughtered by Antiochus IV for her faith declared: "I was a pure virgin and . . . guarded the side (or: rib) that had been built up (i.e. from the man)." Similarly in the Apocalypse of Moses 29:9-10, Eve asks Adam to kill her so that God and his angels will no longer be angry at him, with Adam responding: "Why . . . should I commit murder and bring death to my side (or: rib) . . . against the image which God made?" (cf. 42:2-3 which refers to Eve's death as the time when Adam's "side/rib would return to him"). In each of these texts woman is represented as an integral part of a "single living creature," the missing element to man so far as sexuality is concerned.

For further discussion of the significance of the creation texts in the 'homosex' debate, see Gagnon: 2005b, 386-89; 2005a, 25-29; 2005e, 40-41, 56-57, 65-67; 2003c, 111-27; 2003d, 206-13, 242-46; 2001, 56-62, 193-96, 289-93.

B.3 Every text that treats the issue of homosexual practice in Scripture treats it as a high offence abhorrent to God.

This is evident from an examination of a number of texts.

B.3.1 A triad of stories about extreme depravity

Ham's offence against his father Noah (Gen 9:20-27), attempted sexual assault of male visitors by the men of Sodom (Gen 19:4-11), and the attempted sexual assault of the Levite passing through Gibeah (Jdg 19:22-25), feature a real or attempted act of man-male intercourse as an integral element of the depravity. Initially I will treat the first two stories.

B.3.1.1 Ham's act against Noah

The arguments for reading the Ham episode as a sexual act rather than as merely voyeurism include the following (for further documentation see Gagnon 2001, 63-71): (a) the expression "see the nakedness of" (Gen 9:22) appears elsewhere as a metaphor for sexual intercourse (Lev 20:17); (b) Noah "came to know what his youngest son had done to him" (Gen 9:24; the Babylonian Talmud records a debate about the meaning of this phrase in which one rabbi suggests homosexual relations, the other castration; Sanhedrin 70a); (c) the severity of the curse and its placement on Ham's son rather than Ham himself better suits an act of sexual assault on Ham's part (note the subtext: the curse falls on Ham's 'seed'/son because Ham offends with his 'seed'/sperm); (d) the same narrator subsequently tells a similar story of Lot's daughters having sex with their drunken father (Gen 19:30-38); (e) a similar story of incestuous Same sex rape as a means to establishing familial dominance exists in the Egyptian tale of Horus and Seth; and (f) the narrator shortly after links the Canaanites, i.e. Ham's descendants, to the Sodom story (Gen 10:19), suggesting that the narrator understands both stories in a similar light. Both Hermann Gunkel and Gerhard von Rad, the greatest OT scholars of the 19th and 20th centuries respectively, understood

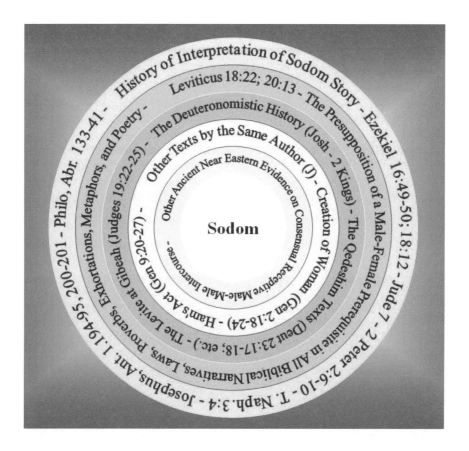

Ham's offence as sexual assault of his father, as has recently Martti Nissinen, a Finnish OT scholar who has written the most significant book by a biblical scholar defending homosexual relations (1998).

B.3.1.2 Sodom

The usual counterargument to the use of these stories, particularly the Sodom narrative, as witnesses against homosexual practice is to claim that these stories indict only coercive acts of male-male intercourse. These stories allegedly have no negative implications for loving homosexual bonds entered into by those who are homosexually oriented. The problem with this argument is that it is tantamount to alleging that a story about a man having coercive intercourse with his mother or father, such as the Ham story, has no negative implications for a mutually loving sexual relationship between an adult and parent.

Whether the male-on-male act of intercourse constitutes a compounding offence or a coincidental act that is merely incidental to the evil of rape can only be settled by an examination of the historical and literary context. Here context is decisive that the narrators (the Yahwist and the Deuteronomistic Historian) regarded the attempt at treating a man sexually as though he were the sexual counterpart to men, i.e. a woman, as inherently dishonouring (on Sodom and the Levite at Gibeah see Gagnon 2001, 71-100; 2005b, 374-78; 2005e, 46-49).

(1) The ancient Near East generally regarded with great scorn a man who willingly offered himself as the passive receptive partner in male-male intercourse (Gagnon 2001, 44-56).

(2) Most scholars agree that the narrator of the Sodom story also narrated the description of the creation of man and woman in Genesis 2 (i.e. the Yahwist), a text that has proscriptive implications for same sex intercourse.

(3) The story of Ham has close ideological links with Leviticus 18 since both texts explain that the Canaanites were expelled from the land or subjugated for heinous sexual offences. Clearly the editors of Leviticus 18 have not limited their critique of incest or of man-male intercourse to coercive forms (18:6-18, 22).

The discussion below will introduce additional layers of context, including:

(4) The history of the interpretation of the Sodom story;

(5) The Deuteronomistic parallel of the Levite at Gibeah and the relevance of the *qedeshim* texts;

(6) The Levitical prohibitions in their historical context alongside the universal presumption in ancient Israel of a male-female prerequisite.

B.3.2 History of the interpretation of Sodom

Subsequent history of interpretation of the Sodom episode also indicts man-male intercourse *per se*, not just man-male intercourse conducted as rape, as a major factor in God's judgment. This is clear enough in two first-century Jewish authors: Philo of Alexandria (Abraham 135-37 and Questions on Genesis 4:37; Gagnon 2001, 172, 177) and Josephus (Antiquities 1.200-201; Gagnon 2001, 177), among other early Jewish texts (e.g., the Testament of Naphtali 3:4, for which see Gagnon 2003e, 12-13; Jubilee 16:5-6; 20.5-6; 2 Enoch 10:4; 34:1-2, for which see Gagnon 2001, 88-89 n. 121). It is sometimes argued by supporters of homosexual unions that most, if not all, biblical texts that refer directly to Sodom say nothing about homosexual practice but rather comment on inhospitable treatment of the vulnerable in their midst: the poor, resident aliens, and visitors. The truth is that most texts in the canon of Scripture that refer to Sodom simply mention it and Gomorrah as places of great evil that God utterly destroyed (Gagnon 2001, 79 n. 103). Isaiah 1:7-17 alludes to Sodom and Gomorrah in the context of discussing social injustice but this merely picks up one theme of the Sodom cycle without excluding other themes. There are a number of biblical texts that allude to the immorality of homosexual practice at Sodom.

B.3.2.1 Ezekiel 16:49-50

According to Ezekiel 16:49-50, Sodom "did not take hold of the hand of the poor and needy. And they grew haughty and committed an abomination (to'evah) before me and I removed them when I saw it." Is the reference to "committing an abomination" to be identified with "not taking the hand of the poor and needy"? The evidence indicates that it is to be identified rather with man-male intercourse.

(1) The vice list in Ezekiel 18:10-13, consisting of ten vices, indicates otherwise since it clearly distinguishes between the offence "oppresses the poor and needy" (fifth vice) from the offence "commits an abomination" (ninth vice).

(2) The two other singular uses of to'evah in Ezekiel refer to sexual sin (22:11; 33:26).

(3) All scholars of Ezekiel agree that Ezekiel knew, and shared extraordinary affinity with, either the Holiness Code (Lev 17–24) or a precursor document. Certainly the Levitical prohibitions of man-male intercourse are absolute (see below).

(4) The phrase "committed an abomination" in Ezekiel 16:50 is identical to the phrase in Leviticus 20:13 that refers to man-male intercourse.

(5) The conjunction in Ezekiel 18:12-13 of a singular use of *to'evah*, as a reference to a single specific offence, with a plural use of *to'evoth*, as a summary description of all preceding offences, is exactly what we find in Leviticus 18:22 (man-male intercourse) and 18:26-30.

The medieval Jewish commentator Rashi also understood the text as a reference to homosexual practice, as have some modern commentators (e.g., Greenberg 1983, 289 and 1997, 685; Loader 1990, 37, 72-74). It is apparent, then, that Ezekiel in 16.50 was interpreting the Sodom episode partly through the lens of the absolute prohibition of man-male intercourse in Leviticus 18:22 and 20:13, indicating that he understood the same sex dimension of the rape to be a compounding offence. This strengthens the ideological nexus between the Yahwist's interpretation of the Sodom episode and the absolute sex prohibitions in Lev 18 and 20 (Gagnon 2001, 79-85).

B.3.2.2 Jude 7 and 2 Peter 2:6-7, 10

According to Jude 7 the men of Sodom "committed sexual immorality (ekporneusasai) and went after other flesh." Some have argued that "committed sexual immorality" in Jude 7 refers to sex with angels, not sex between men, because that is what the next phrase, "went after other flesh," clearly refers to. In effect, such an interpretation understands the two verbs here (Greek participles, to be precise) as an instance of 'parataxis'. In parataxis one of two clauses conjoined by 'and' is conceptually subordinated to the other; thus, "they committed sexual immorality by going after other flesh." But a paratactic construction in Greek can just as easily make the first clause subordinate; in this case, "by [or: in the course of] committing sexual immorality they went after other flesh." In other words, in the process of attempting the sexually immoral act of having intercourse with other men, the men of Sodom got more than they bargained for: committing an offence unknowingly against angels (note the echo in Hebrews 13.2: "Do not neglect hospitality to strangers for, because of this, some have entertained angels without knowing it"). This is apparently how the earliest 'commentator' of Jude 7 read it. For 2 Peter 2:6-7, 10 refers to the "defiling desire/lust" of the men of Sodom. Since the men of Sodom did not know that the male visitors were angels – so not only Genesis 19:4-11 but also all subsequent ancient interpreters – the reference cannot be to a lust for angels but rather must be to a lust for men. So both Jude 7 and 2 Peter 2:6-7 provide further confirmation in the history of interpretation that the Sodom narrative is correctly interpreted when one does not limit the indictment of male homosexual relations to coercive forms (see further Gagnon 2003e, 10-13; 2001, 87-89).

B.3.2.3 Romans 1:24-27

We will show below that in Romans 1:24-27 Paul had in view Genesis 1:27 and the Levitical prohibitions of homosexual practice. Here we make the case for echoes to the cycle of traditions about Sodom. Like many significant NT texts (e.g., Jesus' words at the Last Supper), there are here echoes to multiple OT texts. (Scholars refer to such echoes, whether multiple or not, as instances of intertextuality.) Romans 1:24-27 is a veritable echo chamber of the most important OT texts impinging on homosexual practice: creation, Sodom, and the Levitical prohibitions. Philip Esler (2004) has made a convincing case for echoes to the Sodom cycle (see already Gagnon 2003e, 12-13), though at times he overreaches in some alleged allusions and errs both in excluding additional echoes to the creation story (Esler shows no awareness of my work on this) and in asserting that Paul's reference to lesbian intercourse in Romans 1:26 derived from the "daughters of Sodom" in Ezekiel 16:46-55 (the phrase has nothing to do with homosexual practice). Note the following echoes to the Sodom cycle in Romans 1:18-32, a few of which I have added to those supplied by Esler:

(1)   Romans 1:18 refers to God's "wrath" being revealed "from heaven" against all "irreverence" (or: godlessness, impiety, *asebeia*) and "unrighteousness" (or: injustice, *adikia*). Similarly, Deuteronomy 29:23 states that God overthrew Sodom "in his wrath and anger." According to Genesis 19:24, God rained on Sodom sulfur and fire "from heaven." In Genesis 18:23, 25, Abraham pleads with God not to lump the righteous with "the irreverent" or "godless" at Sodom (cf. Josephus, Jewish War 4.484). Lot implores the men of Sodom: "don't do this unrighteous (or: unjust) thing to these men" (Gen 19:8; cf. Philo, Abr. 133; 3 Macc 2:4-5).

(2)   Romans 1:19-23 focuses on the Gentile sin of idolatry, a sin loosely associated elsewhere with Sodom (perhaps implicit in Deut 29:23-28; 32:32; Isa 1:2-3; Jer 27:33-40; Jub. 20:5-8; T. Naph. 3:3-4).

Romans 1:24-27 refers to same sex intercourse as a dishonoring of their bodies, an indecent act, and a product of unclean desires (*epithumiai*; cf. the descriptions of Sodom in Josephus, Ant. 1:201; Philo, Abr. 135). It also refers to same sex intercourse as an act "contrary to nature." Philo employs the against-nature theme in his interpretation of the Sodom story (Abr.

135, 137). Similar to Romans 1:19-27, the Testament of Naphtali 3:4, like Romans 1:19-27, immediately follows an indictment of idolatry with an indictment of Sodom for its unnatural intercourse.

(3) Romans 1:29-31 lists a series of vices characteristic of the Gentile world, some of which factor prominently in the traditions about Sodom: "arrogant" (or: haughty, *huperephanoi*; Ezek 16:49; Sir 16:8; 3 Macc 2:5; Josephus, Ant. 1:194-95) and "insolent" (*hubristai*; Josephus, Ant. 1:194); "wickedness" (*poneria*; cf. Gen 13:13; 19:7; Josephus, Ant. 1:199) and "badness" (*kakia*; 3 Macc 2:5).

Given the fact that Sodom was widely regarded in ancient Israel and early Judaism as a byword for God's terrifying wrath against human iniquity, it is not at all surprising that Paul alludes to it in his description of divine wrath against human unrighteousness in Romans 1:18-32. Indeed, Paul refers to Sodom as just such a byword in his citation of Isaiah 1:9 in Romans 9:29. The big difference, of course, is that Paul in Romans 1:18-32 is describing a preliminary stage of that wrath: the "handing over" of human beings to their controlling, self-dishonoring desires (1:24, 26, 28) – a handing over that heaps up sins and leads to a Sodom-like, cataclysmic judgment on the Day of (ultimate) Judgment (2:6).

Paul in Romans 1:24-27 does not limit his indictment of same sex intercourse to rape, as shown by his references to lesbianism in 1:26 and men being "inflamed with their yearning for one another" in 1:27. Consequently, his series of intertextual echoes to the Sodom tradition in 1:18-32 indicate that he understood the Sodom story as an indictment of homosexual practice *per se*.

B.3.2.4 Jesus on Sodom

If historical context means anything, Jesus' remarks about Sodom must be read in light of the texts cited above. When he declared that it would be "more tolerable on the Day (of Judgment) for Sodom" than for the towns that did not welcome his messengers (Luke 10:10-12 par. Matt 10:14-15), he was acknowledging Sodom's role in Scripture and tradition as the prime example of abuse of visitors. This abuse included the ghastly attempt at treating males as though they were not males but sexual counterparts to males (i.e. females). Jesus merely added a novel twist: As bad as the actions of the men of Sodom were, failure to welcome him and his emissaries was worse still because "something more than" angelic visitation was here (Luke 11:29-32 par. Matt 12:39-41).

B.3.3 The Deuteronomistic references to the qedeshim and the Levite at Gibeah

Legal material from Deuteronomy and narrative material from Deuter-onomistic History (Joshua through 2 Kings) disparage the homoerotic associations of the *qedeshim* (pronounced k-day-'sheem). The word literally means "consecrated men" but refers in context to male cultic figures who sometimes served as the passive receptive sexual partners for other men (i.e. homosexual cult prostitutes: Deut 23:17-18; 1 Kgs 14:21-24; 15:12-14; 22:46; 2 Kgs 23:7; cf. Job 36:14). Even Phyllis Bird (2000, 170-76), an OT scholar who writes on behalf of homosexual unions and has done extensive work on the *qedeshim*, concedes that the Deuteronomistic Historian was especially repulsed by the consensual, receptive intercourse that these figures had with other men. The reference to such figures as "dogs" (Deut 23:18) matches the slur made against parallel figures in Mesopotamia (the *assinnu, kurgarrû,* and *kulu'u*), called both "dog-woman" and "man-woman" because of their consensual attempts at erasing masculinity and being penetrated by other men (compare Rev 22:15, "dogs," to Rev 21:8, "the abominable").

It will not do to dismiss the references to the *qedeshim* as irrelevant because of the cultic associations, the exchange of money, or the absence of orientation, for several reasons.

(1) The Deuteronomic and Deuteronomistic description of their behaviour as an "abomination" (*to'evah*, an abhorrent or detestable act) links these texts ideologically to Leviticus 18:22, where the same tag is applied absolutely to all man-male intercourse and not limited to intercourse in a cultic context for pay.

(2) The disgust registered by these narrators for the qedeshim parallels the disgust registered in Mesopotamia for similar figures precisely on the grounds of their attempt to define themselves sexually as women in relation to men rather than as the men that they are.

(3) Despite the revulsion with which such figures were held in the ancient Near East, this was still one of the most accepted forms of homosexual practice (not the least), because it was believed that their androgynous demeanor was beyond their control (i.e. due to a goddess figure with androgynous traits). This has links to today's claim that homosexual attraction is beyond a person's control.

So although there is no exact one-to-one correspondence between the qedeshim and homosexual persons today, Deuteronomistic abhorrence of the qedeshim was not confined to men who experienced no same sex attraction or who were affiliated with a foreign cult and received compensation. It was primarily focused on men who feminized themselves to attract male sex partners – which, incidentally, is also the focus of Paul's term malakoi ("soft men") in 1 Corinthians 6:9. All of this is relevant to a proper interpretation of the Sodom narrative.

Since the Deuteronomistic Historian's attitude toward the qedeshim makes it clear that he would have been repulsed by a consensual act of man-male intercourse, it is evident that in telling the story of the Levite at Gibeah the Deuteronomistic Historian was indicting man-male intercourse *per se* and not only coercive forms of man-male intercourse. Since too the story of a Levite at Gibeah in Judges 19:22-25 is in many respects a carbon copy of the Sodom narrative in Genesis 19:4-11 (there are even some verbatim agreements in the Hebrew), how the narrator of Judges 19:22-25 interpreted the attempt of the men of the city to have intercourse with a male visitor provides our earliest commentary of how the Yahwist would have interpreted the similar event at Sodom. In other words, the Yahwist is likely to have viewed the man-male dimension of the attempted act as a compounding factor in underscoring the depravity of the inhabitants. (On the *qedeshim*, along with critiques of Nissinen and Bird, see Gagnon 2005b, 373-75; 2001, 48-49, 100-10; 2005e, 48-49.)

We now see an interconnected ideological nexus in the OT as regards the issue of man-male intercourse, linking Deuteronomy and the Deuteronomistic History, the Yahwistic material in the Pentateuch, the Levitical sex laws, and Ezekiel. These links are picked up also by Jesus, Paul, and the authors of Jude and 2 Peter.

B.3.4 The Levitical prohibitions in their ancient context

The Levitical prohibitions of man-male intercourse (18:22; 20:13) are often cavalierly dismissed as the antiquated remains of ceremonial law. As it happens, there are a number of strong arguments against such a presumption.

(1) Part of a broader OT witness. As is evident from the material cited above, the restriction of sexual activity to male-female bonds in Leviticus 18:22 and 20:13 was not an isolated view within ancient Israel. Indeed, every text in Scripture treating sexual matters, whether narrative, law,

proverb, poetry, moral exhortation, or metaphor, presupposes a male-female prerequisite for all sexual activity. For example, in OT legal material there are constant efforts at distinguishing appropriate forms of other-sex intercourse from inappropriate forms but nothing of the sort for same sex intercourse. The reason for this is apparent: Since same sex intercourse was always unacceptable, there was no need to make such distinctions. Another example involves metaphor: Even though ancient Israel was a male-dominated society, it imaged itself in relation to Yahweh as a female to a husband, so as to avoid the imagery of a man-male sexual bond.

(2) A first-tier offence and 'detestable act.' In Leviticus 20, where the sex laws in Leviticus 18 are rearranged according to severity of offence, the prohibition of man-male intercourse is listed among first-tier, capital offences, alongside other sexual offences that we continue to reject today: adultery, the worst forms of incest, and bestiality (20:10-16). Although in the concluding summary (Lev 18:26-27, 29-30) the sexual offences in Leviticus 18 are collectively labeled "abominations," "abhorrent "or "detestable acts" (to'evoth), only man-male intercourse is specifically tagged with the singular to'evah. Outside the Holiness Code in Leviticus 17–24 the term is normally used for various severe moral offences (not merely acts of ritual uncleanness; cf. Gagnon 2001, 113, 117-20), including occasionally homosexual practice (Deut 23:18; 1 Kgs 14:24; Ezek 16:50; 18:12; probably also Ezek 33:26).

The severe character of this offence is amply confirmed in early Jewish texts of the Second Temple period and beyond (Gagnon 2001, 159-83) and in early Christian texts after the New Testament period, where only bestiality appears to rank as a greater sexual offence, at least among 'consensual' acts. There is, to be sure, some disagreement in early Judaism over whether sex with one's parent is worse, comparable, or less severe, though most texts suggest a slightly lesser degree of severity (Gagnon 2003b, 3-4 n. 17). While Scripture makes some exceptions, particularly in ancient Israel, for some forms of incest (though never for man-mother, man-child, man-sibling) and for sexual unions involving more than two partners (though a monogamy standard was always imposed on women), it makes absolutely no exceptions for same sex intercourse.

(3) The marks of moral, not ritual, impurity. The Levitical prohibitions of man-male intercourse bear the marks of treating moral, not merely ritual, impurity. Unlike purely ritual impurity concerns (e.g. genital discharges, corpse impurity) and like moral impurity concerns (e.g., incest, adultery,

bestiality), the prohibition of male homosexual practice (i) is not contagious through physical contact, (ii) is not rectified merely by ritual bathing, and (iii) treats only intentional acts (Klawans 2000, 22-34, 41-42). Moreover, (iv) purity language appears often in Jewish and Christian tradition in connection with sexual offences because additional psychological supports to civil penalties are needed to combat offences in society that are intensely pleasurable, private, and self-justifying.

(4) Implicit motive for proscription: sexual discomplementarity. The reason for the proscription is implied in the proscription itself and underscores the absolute character of the prohibition: another male shall not be made into a man's sexual counterpart, a woman ("you shall not lie with a male as though lying with a woman").

(5) Appropriation in the NT. These prohibitions are clearly appropriated in the New Testament. The term *arsenokoitai* ("men lying with a male") in 1 Corinthians 6:9 was formulated from the Greek version of Leviticus 18:22 and 20:13 (see below). In Romans 1:24-27 Paul uses two terms, "uncleanness" and "indecency," that appear frequently in the discussion of sex laws in Leviticus 18 and 20.

(6) Why cloth mixtures and menstrual law are second-rate analogies. The attempt to compare the prohibition of homosexual practice with the prohibition of wearing a garment made of two different materials and the like (Lev 19:19) or with the prohibition of sex with a menstruant (Lev 18:19; 20:18) shows a preference for more remote analogues over closer analogues (on problems with the sex-with-a-menstruant parallel, see Gagnon 2002c, 100-103). For the prohibitions of adultery (Lev 18:20; 20:10), bestiality (Lev 18:23; 20:15-16), and especially adult incest (18:6-18; 20:11-12, 14, 17, 19-21) have far more points of close correspondence with the prohibition of homosexual practice. The choice of distant analogies over close analogies suggests a manipulation of analogical reasoning in order to achieve a desired ideological outcome. For example:

(a) There is no comparison as regards the severity of the offence. The penalty for wearing a garment made of two different kinds of cloth was probably only the destruction of the garment (cf. Deut 22:9-11 where the penalty for sowing one's vineyard with two different kinds of seed is merely the forfeiting of the yield). Although the Levitical Holiness Code treats sex with a menstruant as a serious offence, even it categorizes it as a second-tier offence (20:18).

(b)   There is no comparison as regards the absoluteness of the prohibition and the degree to which the prohibition was more than merely
symbolic. The prohibition of cloth mixtures was not absolute since
mixtures of linen and wool were enjoined for some Tabernacle cloths,
parts of the priestly wardrobe, and the tassel worn by laity, apparently
on the assumption that cloth mixtures symbolized 'penetration' into
the divine realm, which were inappropriate in non-sacral contexts
(Gagnon 2003b, 12 n. 42, citing Jacob Milgrom). One may contrast the
prohibitions of incest, adultery, male-male intercourse, and bestiality,
which were absolutely maintained and hence much more than merely
symbolic in character. As regards intercourse with a menstruant, it
is important to note that this is the only sexual offence in Lev 18 and
20 that elsewhere in Leviticus, outside the Holiness Code, overlaps
with permitted ritual impurities in the Priestly Source (P; Lev 15:24).
In addition, the main issue as regards sex with a menstruant is the
interaction of fluids, not the legitimacy of the sexual union per se
(as with adultery, man-male intercourse, incest, and bestiality). It
does not approach the degree of unnaturalness associated with incest,
man-male intercourse, and bestiality, since it happens inadvertently
in the course of normal sexual activity.

(c)   There is no comparison as regards pervasive canonical witness.
Neither the prohibition of cloth (or seed, or animal) mixtures nor the
prohibition of intercourse with a menstruant is clearly carried over into
the NT. Both also have significantly more constricted OT support than
the prohibitions of incest, adultery, and man-male intercourse.

(d)   There is no comparison as regards the socio-scientific case today
for circumventing the biblical prohibitions. Even proponents of
homosexual practice would have to admit that the case against maintaining the prohibitions of cloth mixtures and sex with a menstruant
are on a wholly different level than the case against maintaining the
prohibition of homosexual practice. Indeed, as we have seen, the
philosophic and scientific case for maintaining the prohibition of
homosexual practice resembles at key points the case for maintaining
prohibitions against adult consensual incest and polyamory.

For further discussion of Leviticus 18:22 and 20:13 and their hermeneutical
relevance, see Gagnon 2005e, 51-54; 2005a, 44-49; 2005b, 378-85; 2003a,
62-68; 2003b, 10-14; 2001, 111-46.

B.3.5 Silence of the Lamb? The witness of Jesus

Just as we have no sayings of Jesus on incest and bestiality, so too we have no explicit sayings of Jesus on homosexual practice. The reason for this is historically self-evident: His ministry was to fellow Palestinian Jews, not to Gentiles in the Greco-Roman Mediterranean basin. Simply put, no Jew in first-century Palestine was advocating for homosexual practice, incest, and bestiality, much less engaging in them. Running around first-century Palestine saying, "Stop lying with a male, or with your mother, or with an animal" would not have been the best use of Jesus' time since he would only have been 'preaching to the choir'. The expansion of the discussion of sexual issues in Paul is a natural byproduct of Jewish ministry primarily to a Gentile world. Even so, there are at least a dozen reasons why we can confidently conclude that Jesus was strongly opposed to homosexual practice of any sort (see further Gagnon 2001, 185-228; 2005e, 56-62; 2003a, 68-74). Numbers 2 through 6 and 12 below have to do with contextual factors, while nos. 1 and 7 through 11 treat specific sayings of Jesus.

(1) Jesus' adoption of a back-to-creation model for sex in which he predicated marital monogamy and indissolubility on the 'twoness' of the sexes brought together in a sexual union in Genesis 1–2 (Mark 10:2-12 par. Matt 19:3-9).

(2) Jesus' retention of the Law of Moses even on relatively minor matters such as tithing (cf. Matt 23:23 par. Luke 11:42), to say nothing of a foundational law in sexual ethics; and his view of the Old Testament as holy Scripture – Scripture that, as we have seen above, was strongly and absolutely opposed to man-male intercourse.

(3) Jesus' further intensification of the Law's sex-ethic in matters involving adultery of the heart and divorce (Matt 5:27-32), suggesting a closing of remaining loopholes in the Law's sex-ethic rather than a loosening and, in his saying about cutting off body parts, warning that people could be thrown into hell precisely for not repenting of violations of God's sexual standards (5:29-30).

(4) The fact that the man who baptized Jesus, John the Baptist, was beheaded for defending Levitical sex laws in the case of the adult-incestuous union between Herod Antipas and the ex-wife of his half-brother Philip, a woman who was also the daughter of another half-brother (Mark 6:16-18).

(5) Early Judaism's univocal opposition to all homosexual practice (Gagnon 2001, 159-83).

(6) The early church's united opposition to all homosexual practice. This, combined with nos. 2 to 5 above, completes the historical circle, underscoring the absurdity of positing a pro-homosex Jesus without analogue in his historical context: cut off from his Scripture, cut off from the rest of early Judaism, cut off from the man who baptized him, and cut off from the church that emerged from his teachings.

(7) Jesus' saying about the defiling effect of desires for various forms of sexual immoralities (Mark 7:21-23), which distinguished matters of relative moral indifference such as food laws from matters of moral significance such as the sexual commands of his Bible and connected Jesus to the general view of what constitutes the worst forms of *porneia* in early Judaism (same sex intercourse, incest, bestiality, adultery).

(8) Jesus on the Decalogue prohibition of adultery (Mark 10:17-22), which presupposed a male-female prerequisite for valid sexual bonds both in its Decalogue context and in its subsequent interpretation in early Judaism as a rubric for the major sex laws of the Old Testament.

(9) Jesus' saying about Sodom which, understood in the light of Second Temple interpretations of Sodom (Matt 10:14-15 par. Luke 10:10-12), included an indictment of Sodom for attempting to dishonor the integrity of the visitors' masculinity by treating them as if they were the sexual counterparts to males.

(10) Jesus' saying about not giving what is "holy" to the "dogs" (Matt 7:6), an apparent allusion to both Deuteronomic law (Deut 23:17-18) and texts in 1–2 Kings that indict the *qedeshim*, self-designated "holy ones" identified as "dogs" for their attempt to erase their masculinity by serving as the passive-receptive partners in man-male intercourse.

(11) Jesus' comparison of "eunuchs for the kingdom of heaven" with "born eunuchs" (persons who are asexual and/or homosexual), a comparison that presumes that "born eunuchs" are not permitted sexual relationships outside a man-woman bond (Matt 19:10-12; cf. Gagnon 2006c, 5-6).

(12) The fact that Jesus developed a sex ethic that had distinctive features not shared by the love commandment (love for everyone does not translate into having sex with everyone), reached out to tax collectors and sexual

sinners while simultaneously intensifying God's ethical demand in these areas, insisted that the adulterous woman stop sinning lest something worse happen to her (i.e., loss of eternal life; cf. John 8:3-11; 5:14), appropriated the context of the "love your neighbour" command in Lev 19:17-18 by insisting on reproof as part of a full-orbed view of love (Luke 17:3-4), and defined discipleship to him as taking up one's cross, denying oneself, and losing one's life (Mark 8:34-37; Matt 10:38-39; Luke 14:27; 17:33; John 12:25).

Some have argued that the story of Jesus' distance-healing of a centurion's 'boy' communicates Jesus' acceptance of homosexual relations, assuming that the centurion must have been having sex with his 'boy' (i.e., slave) and that Jesus' silence on the matter suggests affirmation. Even on the (incorrect) assumption that the centurion was having sex with his slave, the additional assumption of Jesus' affirmation does not follow, since it would make Jesus a supporter of one of the most exploitative forms of homosexual practice in the ancient world: a coercive sexual relationship between a master and his young male slave. But as it is, not even an assumption of sex between the centurion and his slave can be sustained since none of the earliest extant interpreters of the text understood it in this manner (John, 'Q',[1] Matthew, and Luke) and the earliest recoverable version of the story that stands behind John 4:46-53 and Matthew 8:5-13 (par. Luke 7:1-10) suggests a story about a Jewish official requesting a healing for his son (Gagnon 2007b).

B.3.6 The witness of Paul

We discuss Paul's perspective in more detail elsewhere[2] in our treatment of whether Scripture indicts only exploitative forms of homosexual practice. Here it will suffice to make the point of how seriously Paul regarded homosexual practice.

B.3.6.1 Romans 1.24-27

Paul in Romans 1:24, 26-27 singles out homosexual practice as an especially reprehensible instance – along with idolatry (1:19-23, 25) – of humans suppressing the truth accessible in the material creation set in motion by the Creator. He refers to it as an act of sexual "uncleanness" or "impurity" (*akatharsia*), an "indecency" or "shameful act" (*aschēmosune*), a "dishonoring (*atimazesthai*) of their bodies among themselves," the

---

1   A textual source thought to lie behind parts of the synoptic gospels.

2   Goddard, A. (ed., 2012, forthcoming, *Living Truth: Christian Faith and Homosexuality*, Gilead Books.

product of "dishonorable passions" (*pathē atimias*), and an act "contrary to nature" (*hē para phusin*) that, in part, was its own "payback" (*antimisthia*).

Twice later in the letter, in 'intratextual' echoes, he alludes back to 1:24-27. In 6:19 he tells his audience to put themselves no longer at the disposal of the "sexual impurity" (*akatharsia*) that had characterized their pre-Christian life, for to continue in such behaviour was to engage in acts of which they should now be "ashamed" (echoing the shame language of 1:24-27) and which lead to the loss of eternal life (6:19-23; cf. 1:32). In 13:13-14 he insists that believers "lay aside works of darkness" such as "immoral sexual activities (*koitai*) and licentious acts (*aselgeiai*)" and thereby to "make no provision to gratify the sinful desires of the flesh." This, in turn, connects up with the concluding answer to Paul's question, "Should we sin because we are not under the law but under grace?" asked in 6:15: "If you live in conformity to (the sinful impulse operating in) the flesh, you are going to die. But if by the Spirit you put to death the deeds of the body, you will live" (8:13). "*Koitai* literally means, "lyings" or "beds," a term that obviously links up with *arsenokoitai*, "men lying with a male," in 1 Corinthians 6:9 as a particular instance of an immoral "lying." Aselgeiai refers to a lack of self-restraint with respect to refraining from prohibited sexual behaviours – obviously including those mentioned in 1:24-27 and 6:19-22, to which they were once enslaved and "given over" by God.

Some (post-)modern interpreters have attempted to dismiss Paul's words in Romans 1:24-27 on the grounds that he subsequently widens the net of culpable sin to include an array of more ordinary vices in 1:29-31 and then indicts the Jewish interlocutor in ch. 2 who judges the Gentiles in 1:18-32 while himself sinning against an even clearer knowledge of the truth. However, the subsequent allusions back to 1:24-27 in 6:19 and 13:13 show that Paul is not telling his audience to stop passing judgment on sexually immoral acts in the community of believers. Indeed, a message to "stop judging" could hardly be applied to parallel case of idolatry in 1:19-23. Moreover, Paul positively insists in the case of the incestuous man in 1 Corinthians 5 that the community do its job precisely by passing Christ's judgment on the immoral person in their midst (5:12). For the issue of whether the context of Romans 1:24-27 speaks against judgment of sexual immorality, see, further, Gagnon 2001, 277-84; 2007a.

B.3.6.2   1 Corinthians 6.9

In 1 Corinthians 6:9 Paul lists "soft men" (*malakoi*) and "men who lie with a male" (*arsenokoitai*; cf. also 1 Tim 1:10) among a series of sexual offenders that include adulterers and the persons who engage in incest or who have sex with prostitutes (*pornoi*, cf. 5:9-11; 6:15-16). The non-sexual offenders on the list (thieves, the greedy, drunkards, slanderers) allude to those who engage in habitual, unrepentant, and particularly exaggerated forms of offences. For example, the "greedy" (*pleonektai*) refers not just to persons with a desire for a little more money but, more, to persons who exploit, defraud, cheat, extort, or generally take advantage of another for personal gain, including unjust seizure of the property of others. Such persons, Paul makes clear, whether they claim to be believers or not, "shall not inherit the kingdom of God" if they do not repent (6:9-10). He makes a similar point in 2 Corinthians 12:21 where he expresses concern that he "may have to mourn over many who have continued in their former sinning and did not repent of the sexual uncleanness (*akatharsia*), sexual immorality (*porneia*) and sexual licentiousness (*aselgeia*) that they practised." Mourning is a propos over loved ones who face the prospect of losing eternal life (cf. 13:5-6; 7:9-10).

C Why emphasize the severity of homosexual practice?

My purpose in evaluating, from Scripture's perspective, the severity of engaging in same sex intercourse is not to exhort believers to hate those who engage in homosexual behaviour. Rather, it is to make three points.

C.1 Love in truth

My first purpose is to ensure that the church inform its practice of love with knowledge of the truth so that we truly do the loving thing for those who participate in homosexual practice. In Paul's words, what matters is "faith working through love" and "obeying the truth" (Gal 5:6-7) and "keeping the commands of God" (1 Cor 7:19). "Love does not rejoice over wrongdoing (or: unrighteousness, *adikia*) but rejoices in conjunction with the truth" (1 Cor 13:6). Paul often prayed for his converts that their love "would abound still more and more in a deeper knowledge and in full insight" (Phil 1:9; cf. Phlm 6). Many Christians have attempted to respond in love towards persons who act on homosexual urges, including ordained officers, by either tolerating the behaviour or, worse, affirming it. If, however, same sex intercourse is a high offence in the sexual realm toward God, then there can be no question of viewing toleration or acceptance of homosexual bonds as an act of love. Augustine was right when he explained the meaning of his dictum "love and do what you want" by citing the example of a father who disciplines rigorously his child, while a "boy-stealer" caresses a boy. Which expresses love? The one who disciplines (*Ten Homilies on the First Epistle of John* 7:8). He later elaborates:

> If any of you perhaps wish to maintain love, brethren, above all things do not imagine it to be an abject and sluggish thing; nor that love is to be preserved by a sort of gentleness, nay not gentleness, but tameness and listlessness. Not so is it preserved. Do not imagine that . . . you then love your son when you do not give him discipline, or that you then love your neighbour when you do not rebuke him. This is not love, but mere feebleness. Let love be fervent to correct, to amend. . . . Love not in the person his error, but the person; for the person God made, the error the person himself made. (7.11; NPNF, slightly modified)

Tolerating or accepting the behaviour would only convey to the perpetrators that the sin is 'no big deal', leave the individual exposed to the wrath of God, and put such a one at risk of exclusion from an eternal relationship with God – not to mention the harmful effects of undermining the community's resolve to resist sexual impurity (1 Cor 5:6-7: a little leaven leavens the whole lump of dough) and provoking God's judgment on the community as a whole.

It would also short-circuit whatever work God was doing in the person's life through the experience of hardship or deprivation. Mainline denominations mostly appear to understand grace as a power that licenses believers to carry out their desires without the imposition of 'legalism'. But Paul viewed grace as a power that freed people from the gratification of sinful desires and enabled God to form Christ in them through difficult experiences. Thus, as Paul learned from God in the case of his "thorn in the flesh": "My grace is sufficient for you, for [my] power is being brought to completion in circumstances of weakness." Grace here meant not deliverance from deprivation and hardship but a fuller experience of Christ's power and blessed presence in and through difficult times. "So", Paul concluded, "I will all the more gladly brag in my weaknesses, in order that the power of Christ might dwell [or: set up its tent] on me" (2 Cor 12:9). In seeking to accommodate the gratification of homosexual desire among some the 'third' or 'middle' way is undoing the opportunity God is granting of a deeper experience of his presence.

C.2 Ordination issues

My second purpose is to remind policymakers in the church that the relative severity of an offence has implications for polity decisions. As noted above, churches do not treat all sexual offences as equal when it comes to decisions of ordination (and sometimes even membership) but rather make distinctions on the basis of the severity of the offence, its repetitive character, and whether the offender has expressed repentance. Churches will ordain persons who have, and occasionally entertain, lustful thoughts – though I'm not sure one will find many churches ordaining persons who affirm and promote such thoughts. They will ordain persons who have been divorced and remarried, though I know of none who will ordain persons who have had five or more divorces and remarriages and plan to continue the cycle with the fewest negative side effects. Some churches may even ordain heterosexual persons in a committed sexual bond outside of marriage. However, few if any churches will ordain – at least not as of today – persons who are in committed sexual bonds involving close blood relations, more than two persons concurrently, or an adult and an adolescent or child. Few if any will ordain persons who are actively engaged in adulterous behaviour. So knowing the severity of the sexual offence is an important factor in deciding what ordination decisions should be taken when violations are committed – and not only committed but committed repeatedly and, worst of all, unrepentantly.

C.3 Denominational unity

My third purpose is to inject in current ecclesiastical conflicts a sobering note about the impact on intra-denominational unity. The more severe the sexual offence, the more acute the question of whether churches and individuals should stay in a denomination that tolerates or perhaps even promotes such offences among its ordained officers. For I know of few reasonable persons who would stay indefinitely within a denomination that tolerated or promoted repetitive and unrepentant incest, adultery, or polyamory among its ordained officers. If same sex intercourse is treated by Scripture as worse than these sexual offences, then serious issues about denominational unity are posed by a denomination's toleration or affirmation of homosexual practice among its ordained officers.

For references and bibliography, see the end of the previous chapter

Wisdom and obedience

Chapter 12

The celibate path: a Christian's journey with homosexuality

Calum MacKellar

Dr MacKellar holds a doctorate in biochemistry from the University of Stuttgart in Germany and is both a visiting professor of bioethics at St Mary's University College in London and the director of research of a medical ethics charity in Edinburgh. He is also an elder in the Church of Scotland.

Early years as a homosexual

The first ever thoughts that I can recall were homosexual ones. At the age of three, I remember being completely overwhelmed by my feelings of attraction at the sight of some young men (and not other boys my own age). I still do not understand how these feelings came about.[1] All I know is that my homosexuality was then, and continues to be, the cause of an incredible amount of suffering and despair.

My teenage years in the 1970s were probably the worst, as I felt that if anyone, including my parents, learned about my orientation, I would be completely rejected since having a homosexual orientation was considered completely unacceptable in those days. Things were especially difficult when I was an older teenager and many of my high school friends seemed to be growing into male models. The torment of the attraction and the loneliness which resulted were very profound. And 'falling in love' with some of them just multiplied the problem!

But I also grew up in a Christian home and was fortunate to become a Christian when I was a child. Looking back, I do not know how I would have survived without God. In a way, he was always there and I was never too afraid to throw all my despair and suffering on to him. I was convinced

---

1   The incredibly overwhelming feelings of attraction to other adult young men have always been present since the age of three to the same extent including in kindergarten, primary school, high school, university and beyond.

that God loved me and wanted to be my friend no matter what went on in my head. And though I could not speak to my Christian parents (or my robustly heterosexual brothers) about what was going on inside, I knew that I could always cry out to God.

Slowly, through learning to read the Bible, I realised that God was also averse to homosexual relationships. At the time, this did not surprise me, and it still doesn't. How could a God of love and goodness be in favour of the deeply painful feelings I experienced of being overpowered by another person? Is this what the world calls love? But why was there so much suffering? This was a question that never went away. What was the cause of this deep suffering and despair?

I was 24 years old when I first felt safe enough to speak of my homosexual struggles to a Christian counsellor. And this was only because I knew he had also experienced difficulties in this area. I now know that waiting to speak about my struggles until this age was far too old to 'come out' but in those days, neither society nor the church accepted any form of homosexual orientation.

At first, when I first started discussing this, I was encouraged to pray for my orientation to be changed, something which I very much wanted. But nothing happened – at least, not yet. As a result, I went into a deep depression which lasted for a number of years. I did not understand God or the lack of progress, and this compounded my deep suffering and resulted in despair. All this, moreover, was not helped by some Christian psychotherapists who, becoming frustrated by the lack of success in changing my orientation, eventually criticised my faith and my relationship with God.

Now, I remain convinced that God can change my orientation but have also learned, over the years, to accept God's will even though I often do not understand where he is taking me. Even when I cried out to God in despair, I never lost my love for him. I found it difficult to rebel against a God who had died such a horrific death on a cross, out of love for me – a God who also continues to love and suffer with me, and who helps me to love him.

But being a Christian while also being affected by homosexuality is not easy. My mind sometimes feels like a battlefield, with my loving relationship with God on one side, and sometimes overwhelming feelings of homosexuality on the other. And these battles are often very lonely experiences since being a homosexual person is still a very difficult 'state' to be in for many churches.

My own reflections on homosexuality

The following short sections reflect some of my own personal journeys over many years with respect to the manner in which I see the church, the origins of homosexuality and the theology relating to it. I would, however, like to emphasise that I come to these questions as a scientist and ethicist affected by homosexuality, and not as a person who has studied theology.

The church and the family of God

For many hundreds of years, most Christian churches have simply ignored the issue of homosexuality. This is probably because they considered the topic too uncomfortable or taboo and may not have had enough courage, understanding or love to seek to help the people affected. In other words, many Christians may have denied their responsibility to be a light of love and compassion to the world in this area of deep suffering and despair. It should therefore come as no surprise that many homosexual people still feel a great deal of anger towards the churches, and often view them as largely responsible for their condemnation and rejection by society.

In the past 15 to 25 years, however, the Christian churches have begun making a serious attempt to understand homosexual people better – both those in their congregations, and those outside the church. Unfortunately, this did not happen because they finally woke up to the deep suffering and pain in their midst, but because of growing pressure from the secular homosexual lobby at the end of the 20th century and beyond. Nevertheless, the situation is now a lot more positive and many Christians (but not all) have now learned to move towards homosexual people with love and compassion.

In some churches, this spirit of love and compassion towards homosexual persons has been expressed by simply accepting homosexual relationships. Other churches, however, have not gone down this road, but have stressed that it is also important to consider how God himself might be affected by such same sex relationships between two persons. And if one comes to a theological and biblical understanding that suggests that God may indeed be deeply opposed to homosexual relationships, the question then arises as to whether love between two homosexual people should have priority over love for God.

Some Christian churches, therefore, have continued to oppose homosexual relationships while also seeking to become more loving and supportive towards homosexual people in their community. Homosexual persons may also agree with their church that Same sex relationships are wrong and, as a consequence, are suffering very deeply because of their predicament. For example, some Christian homosexual men have indicated that they are in torment because of their strong attraction to other Christian men in the church and often do not know what to do with this painful attraction. Some may even be uncertain whether to talk about their situation to their pastor or other Christian friends. They may not tell anyone of this feeling of despair for many years.

In addition, some homosexual Christians may suffer from a deep sense of loneliness as they seek to battle against their own thoughts. They may feel that they do not really fit into a church that often emphasises the importance of the biological family model. A family model which provides love and belonging to family members in which they have no part. They then seek to survive in a church where they increasingly feel abandoned, lonely and unloved by anyone in any meaningful way.

Being a single homosexual in the church

Over the years, I have attended a number of Christian churches, and my experience of being a single person in church has varied quite considerably from one congregation to another.

Some were very welcoming and genuinely made me feel that I was part of a caring community. Others were more formal with a certain amount of 'safety distance' between members. And it was in the latter type of church that I experienced the most difficult sermons, which repeatedly claimed that the congregation was my 'real' family and that I had found my 'home'. I was always acutely aware, however, that in reality, most of the many people attending these churches would always put their children, wives, husbands, parents or even the dog first, and that I would always come a very long way down the list of people to help, value and love.

These 'pretend family' sermons, in my view, demonstrated a complete misunderstanding of the loneliness which sometimes exists in churches and what it actually means to be a genuine family of God.

Because of the contrast between the official message and the reality, going to church was sometimes the most difficult experience of the week. It just served to emphasise how alone I felt in a community or communion where people were supposed to belong to one another. I knew that I would go to church alone and come back alone while often wondering whether anybody in the congregation would actually miss me, in any way, if I happened to die during the night.

But I do know that God loves me as a child. He loves me so much that he was prepared to give everything he had – even his Son who died on a cross for me. And I have also learned, over the years, to accept my situation of being alone with God even though I do not always like or understand it. I often long for the physical and emotional closeness and affection that I see in couples and families, and to be part of something so positive and full of love. But perhaps, to an extent, the grass is always greener on the other side, as I know that deep loneliness can sometimes also exist within couples or families.

Going to church on a Sunday is still an extremely difficult time for me because a number of young men are always present. The despair arising from attending church is sometimes unbearable and I often become so tired of being what I am. I do not understand God! I sometimes still 'fall in love' with some of my male Christian friends, not only because of their good looks but because of 'who they are' including all their masculine character, sensitivity and compassion.

However, I have learned in time that God's church is far bigger than the places I go to on a Sunday. And even if most people in the congregation will never want to see me as part of their 'real' family, one amazing thing about God is that even though he never seems to want to take away the problem he always provides alternatives.

In this respect, I have been blessed by God with some incredible Christian brothers and sisters, even though many of them are hundred or even thousands of miles away, whom I can contact at any time when the storm in my mind becomes unbearable. Friends and members of my Christian family and church to whom I belong and who rejoice in my existence: who love and accept me unconditionally in their walk with me along the storms of the road of life and who remain with me when I fall and everything goes wrong. These friends have also now become a sort of family to me with brothers and sisters replacing the wife and children, which I will never have. In a way, God has not taken away my problem, but given me loving friends, instead, who can carry this burden with me during the years of my life. In a way, the gifts that God has given me in these persons are the greatest gifts of my life.

Twenty years ago, I never thought that I would have a family of any kind and that my life prospects were hopeless. But God, in his own way, can provide solutions where we only see despair. He also loves in a way that no one else can love.

I also know that I am myself part of the imperfectness of imperfect churches. I know that I, too, have a responsibility to seek to love others with the sacrificial love of God and be a brother to all around me, including those in my 'Sunday' church even if this is not always easy.

Many churches have a very long way to go before they can be a real family united by the communion of unconditional love. But nothing is impossible with God's help, and I believe he will help each congregation grow into a family which can then be a real witness to all those who seek to belong to God.

For about 20 years, I have also been a member of a Christian fellowship group organised by a charity called the True Freedom Trust, which seeks to meet the needs of homosexual people in ways which they do not find in their own church communities. And this group remains a lifeline to me.

Homosexuality: social and biological aspects

For a very long time, I have wondered what had caused my homosexuality. As already mentioned, I was already attracted, when I was three, to certain young men of 15-16 years and older.

There is still a lot of research taking place into the causes of homosexuality and heterosexuality, which has so far been inconclusive. It is also notable that, over the years, there have been far more studies into the causes of homosexuality than heterosexuality. I have often asked myself why the heterosexual majority did not try first to understand their own feelings towards the opposite sex before trying to understand homosexuality. Are the causes of heterosexuality biological? Did heterosexuals choose to be so oriented at one stage in their lives? One suggested cause of homosexuality is an imbalanced relationship between a child and one of his or her parents. Could this also be a cause of heterosexuality?

I do not know the answers, but I believe, as a scientist, that understanding heterosexuality may be the key to understanding homosexuality though it is largely accepted that there is unlikely to be a unique cause for either of these sexualities. Instead, the sexuality of a person is likely to be determined by several factors, including both biological and social-environmental aspects.[2]

---

2   Studies relating to the biological aspects of homosexuality have often been undermined by a questionable methodology which assumed that all homosexual people would have similar reasons for their sexuality. This would be on a par with putting all people with cancer (including lung, skin and breast cancer) into one group and then trying to determine similarities between the different affected people.

What appears certain, however, is that there must be a biological aspect to the homosexuality of at least some people, since every study so far has shown male homosexuality to be 2-3 times more prevalent than female homosexuality. In other words, there is something in the make-up of a biological man, as opposed to a biological woman, which makes him more prone to homosexuality. A kind of biological predisposition that may be triggered if certain factors come into play.

But accepting that homosexuality has a biological element should not affect how we view the morality of homosexual practice. In the same way, the fact that a tendency for aggressiveness in a person can sometimes be shown to have a biological root does not mean that it should be viewed as morally acceptable by society.

The possibility of a homosexual person being able to change his or her sexuality has also been the subject of a lot of debate and research over the years. It should be noted, in short, that although steady changes towards heterosexuality and more dramatic miracles do indeed take place, they clearly do not happen to all those affected by homosexuality for reasons only known to God .

Sexual identity

In considering relationships between men and women, it may be helpful to stress that biomedical science has not yet found an accepted definition of a 'man' and of a 'woman' as such. Indeed, science has often found it difficult to distinguish between:

(a) the manner in which a person considers his or her own sexual identity (i.e. male or female),[3]

(b) the manner in which other people consider the sexual identity of a person,

(c) the physiological aspects of a person such as his or her sexual organs,

(d) the genetic aspects of a person, such as his or her XY or XX chromosomes,

---

Therefore, it is important for any research into the subject to first separate the different kinds of homosexual people to be studied; for example, whether they were affected from earliest childhood or after the beginning of adulthood.

In addition, it should be noted that even if different biological reasons for homosexuality are considered, the results will still be difficult to interpret since social-environmental aspects such as the lack of adequate male role models in childhood may sometimes also be present.

3   The manner in which a person considers his or her own sexual identity may be determined by factors in his or her social environment and male or female neurology.

(e) the neuro-psychological make-up of a person controlling the attraction of a person towards another sexual identity.

For example, this make-up results in most heterosexual people being unconsciously attracted (amongst other traits) to:

(1) another human person (as opposed to an animal),

(2) a person of the opposite sex (as opposed to the same sex) or

(3) a young person (as opposed to a very old person).

In other words, most heterosexual people are 'wired' to (1) be attracted to another person (as opposed to not being attracted to anyone) and (2) only be attracted to specific kinds of people without being conscious of (or even understanding) the manner in which this 'falling in love' or attraction takes place.

The difficulty in determining the 'sex' of a person arises because, in some cases, a real mixture of the sexual aspects mentioned above may be found in a particular person. For example, until a few years ago, genetic tests were undertaken on women tennis players at Wimbledon to determine whether or not they really were 'women'. But these have now been stopped for ethical reasons because it is possible for someone to have male genes, but female sexual organs.

In addition, from a theological perspective, an adequate determination of a person's gender with respect to the aforementioned traits is also still ongoing. In this regard, it may be possible to ask, from a theological perspective, whether it may not be the manner in which a person considers his or her own gender (i.e. male or female) which may be determinative.

Theological basis of heterosexuality and homosexuality

Personally, I now believe that my homosexuality is most likely to be the result of how my biological brain was 'wired-up' and that I may now be constrained to a life of celibacy. But even if the whole world accepted homosexuality as morally acceptable, including the established church, I know that homosexual feelings of attraction would still be a cause of suffering to me although I do not know why. I also know that, whatever the consequences of the 'wiring-up' in my head, only the love of God is deep enough to fill whatever I am really seeking!

Since becoming a Christian I have often also tried to understand why God would be so opposed to homosexual relationships. Of course, I love God and am prepared to follow his precepts out of love even though I do not understand them. I trust that God is far more loving and greater than my understanding. But it is far easier to resist homosexual practices if there is clear evidence that it causes suffering to other people (including God) than if one is just following biblical precepts.

In the following paragraphs I have tried to present my own understanding of why God is so opposed to homosexuality. I have tried to understand why God is against something which, from the world's perspective, can only be seen as positive, pleasurable and good with no negative consequences. Something which, it is suggested, is actually considered as being edifying for both homosexual partners.

But would God suffer because two human beings are in a homosexual relationship?

Interpretation of the Bible

This article will not seek to re-examine the excellent biblical interpretation, already in existence, which clearly indicates that many passages in the Bible are opposed to homosexual practice but not to homosexual people.[4]

Why have two sexes?

Again, in many theological discussions about homosexuality, the topic has often been studied on its own without first seeking to understand the full theology behind heterosexuality. From a theological perspective, it is indeed important to first ask why heterosexuality should exist at all and how the 'falling in love' or attraction between heterosexuals should be understood and interpreted.

In this regard and in order to better understand some of the reasons behind the relevant issues of homosexuality, it may be useful, initially, to understand the background of the existence of sexual differences between men and women. God had a good reason to not just create human unisex hermaphrodites capable of procreating amongst themselves in a similar manner to snails.

But what was this reason? And again why were homosexual relationships perceived as being wrong?

I still did not understand why this would cause offence to God.

---

4   Mark Bonnington and Bob Fyall, *Homosexuality and the Bible*, Grove Books Ltd., 1998. David Wright, *The Christian Faith and Homosexuality*, Cutting Edge Series, Rutherford House, 1994. Robert A. J. Gagnon, *The Bible and Homosexual Practice: Texts and Hermeneutics*, Abingdon Press, 2002. See also other chapters in this book.

The meaning of an exclusive relationship

Many years ago, I was asked by a homosexual academic researcher whether I believed that a homosexual relationship would still be wrong if there was never any physical contact. This could happen, for example, if one or both the homosexual partners were disabled. I remember hesitating for a long time over this question, but as I discussed it with friends I slowly realised that it was not so much the sexual act which was so offensive to God but the relationship between the partners itself, of which the sexual act was an expression. In other words, it was the important exclusive relationship that existed that was significant. And of course these exclusive relationships could just as well exist between married heterosexual or between homosexual persons even though no sexual intercourse may take place in either case for a number of reasons.

The exclusivity and unity of a relationship

In characterising these exclusive relationships, it should be noted that every such relationship between a man and a woman involves an act of mutual self-giving which contains a spiritual as well as a physical aspect. As a result, the physical bodies and also the characters of the man and woman form a very deep complementary unity and completeness. However, it is not only the sexuality of the partners that forms and expresses this unity but also the manner in which both partners love each other. Indeed, the very manner in which the man loves the woman in marriage is quite different (but complementary) to the manner in which the woman loves the man though the intensity of these loves may be similar. There is thus both a very strong complementarity in communion of both the sexual characters in marriage but also of the manner in which their different relationships of love towards each other are expressed.

Even though the deeper meaning may be hidden if one or both of the participants only appreciates the pleasure of the sexual encounter, there is still a sense that he or she is giving in a manner that is unconditional, complete and total. In other words, during an exclusive relationship and sexual intercourse in particular, the body gives its whole self to the other unconditionally. This is the basis of the Biblical expression "to know" (to know the other unconditionally).

Another interesting aspect of a sexual relationship is that no person is able to 'fall in love' with more than one person at any time. It is an exclusive relationship between two people and so implies a real commitment by

THE CELIBATE PATH: A CHRISTIAN'S JOURNEY

the partners to remain faithful to each other with no other person being involved. No other type of relationship is characterised by such exclusivity. Parents can love many children at the same time, and brothers and sisters can love many people at the same time. But the fact that sexual relationships are physically and spiritually exclusive makes them completely different to all others.

But why are the relationships between two partners so exclusive? Is there a deeper Christian understanding of exclusive relationships of the kind that exist in marriage? Perhaps at this stage, it may be helpful to try to examine how these relationships relate to some aspects of the relationship between humanity and God.

In this respect, it may be useful to note that the apostle Paul experienced a glimpse of the mystery of the relationship of love which is made possible between two persons of different sex when he studied the relationship of love which is made possible between Christ and his 'bride' the church, as indicated in Ephesians 5:

> Submit to one another out of reverence for Christ. Wives, submit to your husbands as to the Lord. For the husband is the head of the wife as Christ is the head of the church, his body, of which he is the Saviour. Now as the church submits to Christ, so also wives should submit to their husbands in everything.
>
> Husbands, love your wives, just as Christ loved the church and gave himself up for her to make her holy, cleansing her by the washing with water through the word, and to present her to himself as a radiant church, without stain or wrinkle or any other blemish, but holy and blameless. (vv. 21-27)
>
> This is a profound mystery – but I am talking about Christ and the church. However, each one of you also must love his wife as he loves himself, and the wife must respect her husband. (vv. 32-33)

Clearly, this passage indicates that the bond between a man and a woman in marriage is like, or a model of, the bond which Christ has with his church. However, it can also be suggested that this bond between a man and woman is not only like that of Christ and the church but actually is the same bond, though expressed in a different way and between different actors. Accordingly, the relationships between (a) a woman and a man and (b) Christ and his church may somehow, and in a very mysterious way, be 'inter-linked' and 'interdependent' since they come from the same 'source' of love in God through creation (as both these relationships are the result of creation).

In a way, the relationship between a man and a woman is an eikon of the relationship between Jesus and the church and in ancient thought, the eikon was not considered only a copy of the reality being portrayed, but was thought somehow to participate in the very substance of the reality it symbolised. It is not just a reflection of reality, but is that same reality.[5]

This means that the heterosexual relationship between a man and a woman is the same reality in inherent correspondence with that of Jesus Christ and his church.

The one flesh aspects of a sexual relationship

The correspondence between the husband-wife relationship and the Jesus-church relationship is also expressed in the 'one flesh' terminology used in the Bible. The following passages characterise this meaning well, though it should be emphasised that it is the relationship that is central to the 'one flesh' experience, while the physical aspects are expressions of the relationship. For example:[6]

> But at the beginning of creation God "made them male and female". "For this reason a man will leave his father and mother and be united to his wife, and the two will become one flesh." So they are no longer two, but one. Therefore what God has joined together, let man not separate. (Mark 10:6-9)

> The body is not meant for sexual immorality, but for the Lord, and the Lord for the body. By his power God raised the Lord from the dead, and he will raise us also. Do you not know that your bodies are members of Christ himself? Shall I then take the members of Christ and unite them with a prostitute? Never! Do you not know that he who unites himself with a prostitute is one with her in body? For it is said, 'The two will become one flesh.' But he who unites himself with the Lord is one with him in spirit.

---

5   The Greek word *charakter* (representation) in Hebrews 1:3, "the exact representation of his being", is an even more categorical .word than *eikon*, in expressing the inherent correspondence and identity of the image to the nature of what is being represented. See F. F. Bruce, *The Epistle to the Hebrews* (New London Commentary on the New Testament 1964, 6).

6   See also Gen 2:2.

Flee from sexual immorality. All other sins a man commits are outside his body, but he who sins sexually sins against his own body. Do you not know that your body is a temple of the Holy Spirit, who is in you, whom you have received from God? You are not your own; you were bought at a price. Therefore honour God with your body. (1 Cor 6:12-20)

The expression 'one flesh' can be seen here as an image or metaphor for the closeness, unity and exclusivity of the marriage partnership. The gift in sexual intercourse which expresses the 'one flesh' relationship is not just a 'physical' gift; the physical and the 'soul' can never be separated in a whole person. It is a whole person that experiences the exclusive relationship expressed in sexual intercourse with another whole person. In addition, the couple's intercourse, expressing the 'one flesh' union, may also result in a 'one flesh' child, who is a personal expression (amongst many other realities) of the 'one flesh' aspect of such a relationship.

The 'one flesh' aspects of Christ and his body, the church

As already indicated, the relationship between the Church and Christ can be viewed as similar to a bride and groom. In addition, the church is also recognised in the Bible as the 'body of Christ', for example,[7] in the following passages:

Now you are the body of Christ, and each one of you is a part of it. (1 Cor 12:27)

Now I rejoice in what I am suffering for you, and I fill up in my flesh what is still lacking in regard to Christ's afflictions, for the sake of his body, which is the church. (Col 1:24)

This means that while Jesus can be seen, in one sense, as the husband of the church, which is his bride, the church also becomes a body joined with Jesus' body in 'one flesh', just as a husband and wife become one through the sexual act expressing their exclusive relationship. This is dramatically expressed and celebrated through the act of communion where Jesus indicates that his body does indeed become, in a very real way 'one flesh' with the communion of members of his church, through the physical bread and wine. These elements literally become part of the flesh and blood of church members and symbolically reflect Jesus' body which he offered to

---

7   See also Eph 4:11-13.

the church. In other words, by consuming this bread and wine the church expresses this 'one flesh' relationship with Jesus.[8]

In the same way, a husband and a wife become 'one flesh' in their relationship. This is also experienced in that the husband's body does indeed become, in a very really expressive sense 'one flesh' through the exclusive relationship expressed in sexual intercourse with his wife. His wife then also becoming 'one flesh' with her husband.

In this manner, communion between Jesus Christ and his church and between a husband and his wife are expressions of the same reality at the very deep and wonderful 'one flesh' level.[9] They are both expressions of total and complete mutual giving (including physical giving) between the actors which become a union of 'one flesh' – but also of rejoicing, celebration and pleasure in the crucial relationships between the actors.

Moreover, sexual relationships and the associated pleasure are gifts from God in the celebration of a mutual self-giving relationship. In a way, the relationship and the pleasure involved is a sort of wonderful 'party-gift' from God to enjoy in the relationship that a husband and wife have together though, as we have seen, this may not always be physically possible with certain married couples. But this sexual act between man and wife is something which is similar to the celebration of communion in church in which there is a rejoicing in the relationship between Jesus Christ and the church.

The direction of the relationship of love

Having glimpsed the strength of the inter-dependence which exist between the husband-wife and the Jesus-church relationships, it is also possible to suggest that both relationships of love have a sort of 'direction' between the female actors (the woman or the church) and the male actors (the man or Christ) which are complementary. In other words, it is not only the identity of the two different actors that form a complementary unity but also the different directions of their loving relationships.

For example, the 'direction' in the relationship which exists between the husband and his wife gives the man an opportunity to make room for the woman and to let her come to herself in the fullest and most complementary way. In doing this, the man has the role of a 'loving and servant leader', but in such a manner that the mutual complementariness of himself and his wife as well as the different ways in which they love each other comes into expression.

---

8   This is just one aspect of communion among many others.

9   Communion in the Old Testament was also expressed by 'sacrifices to God' which were also expressions of a deep giving.

However, the inherent mutual association of man-woman relationships with the Christ-church relationship means that if the 'direction' in a relationship is distorted, then the relationship between Christ and his church would also be undermined, in that a relationship of equals would be forced upon it. In a homosexual relationship, there is no longer a 'direction' because the two individuals have the same gender, and so it would be trying, in a mysterious way, to either make the church take the role of Christ, a form of idolatry, or make Christ take the role of the church, whereby he would lose his deity. And this could only be a complete distortion of who God really is.

It can be noted, in this regard, that idolatry in the Bible always involves a strong element of role-reversal (Rom 1:21-32); the creature perverting nature by making the Creator in his own image. This is seen as a part of man's rebellion by which he seeks to be as God (Gen 3:5) or to call God into judgement (Gen 3:10-13).

The aforementioned argument may, therefore, be seen as one of the most relevant arguments against homosexual relationships since it emphasises the crucial nature of the different relationships of love and their directions between the female actors (the woman or the church) and the male actors (the man or Christ).

This correspondence can also help to understand Hosea 1:2-9 and the manner in which God asked his prophet to express Israel's unfaithfulness to himself. Indeed, since the exclusive relationship between God and Israel was already being undermined by the prostitution of Israel to other gods, the undermining of the relationship between Hosea and his wife through her prostitution was only another expression of the same reality. In a sense, these two relationships were inter-dependent and expressing the same mutual reality of brokenness.

The suffering of the homosexual person

It is interesting to note that a minority of homosexual persons have indicated that they were already aware that something was deeply 'wrong' with them, well before they were introduced to any Christian, moral or social expectations, because of the acute pain and suffering that their attractions caused. Therefore, their wish to resist homosexual relationships did not originate in the teachings of the Bible. Instead, these teachings came as a kind of confirmation of what they had already known and experienced since early childhood.

But how do these homosexual persons, including children, explain their deep experience of suffering when confronted with homosexual attractions?

Obtaining an answer to this question is very difficult though a glimpse of a solution may be suggested by first looking at heterosexuality and the manner in which heterosexual persons 'see' one another when they are attracted to each other. In a way, heterosexual persons who are neuro-psychologically attracted to one another, are attracted to the whole sexual identity of the partner which 'enters into them' as a 'complement' to their own sexual identity, thereby becoming a unity of one flesh (Gen 2:24).

For some homosexual persons, on the other hand, who are neuro-psychologically attracted to a person of the same sexual identity, this identity does not 'enter into them' as a 'complement' to their own gender (they are already of the same gender) but as a 'competition' to who they already are as a specific sexual being. This is because there is no possibility of a peaceful cohabitation of sexual identities or genders in a person, when they do not 'complement' each other.[10]

In addition, the very manner in which a person is (heterosexually or homosexually) attracted to another person then comes into operation. This means that a person is very likely to 'see' the other as being very beautiful or 'perfect' in his or her sexual identity.

For some homosexual persons, however, this may result in deep despair. This is because they are aware of their own limitations and will often feel that, in the competition of the two same sex identities which are present in them, they will always result in being conquered by the 'perfect' foreign identity. As a result, their own original identity will often be completely defeated, crushed and even denied existence by the new 'perfect' identity which has entered into them and taken over. In this case, the homosexual person will feel the denial of his or her own identity very deeply. And as a result, he or she may often consider his or her own destruction, including through suicide,[11] in order to comply with the new foreign identity that has taken over in his or her being.

In other words, when a same sex identity enters into some homosexual persons, this new identity completely overpowers their own sexual identity.

10　In any 'sexual relationship', be it between two human persons or between Jesus Christ and his church there is indeed no room for anything else apart from complementariness and exclusivity.

11　Because of the battles in the minds of homosexual men, they are about 12 times more likely to commit suicide than heterosexual men.

Moreover, this is happening through the neuro-psychological attraction of the homosexual person and often against his or her will. This means that, in a very similar manner to what is happening during a heterosexual rape in which the whole sexual identity of the rapist enters and overpowers that of his or her victim, in some (but not all) forms of homosexuality, the sexual identity of a person is also entering and overpowering the same sex identity of the homosexual person.

Conclusion

As a homosexual Christian in the Church of Scotland, I am becoming increasingly aware of the pressure to remain silent in society because of the strength of the vocal homosexual lobby, which emphasises that it is now unacceptable to believe that same sex relationships can be wrong. Even in the Church of Scotland, there appears to be some kind of intimidation campaign going on which has made some homosexual Christians deeply afraid of stating publicly that they are opposed, for reasons of conscience and faith, to homosexual relationships.

These Christians are people who have decided to prioritise their love for God and what they believe is his opposition to same sex relationships, no matter how attracted they are to other people of the same sex, because they believe that this love for God should come before any sentimental love of men and women. They have decided to love God with all their hearts, and with all their souls, and with all their minds, and with all their strength, and so are prepared to give up lives of sexuality and physical affection for him. It is by no means an easy life, and deep suffering and loneliness are often very present, but they believe that it is worth living for God.

If the Church of Scotland's General Assembly decides that the purpose and values of these celibate Christian lives are effectively meaningless, it is difficult to see how they could then feel safe as members, elders and ministers in the Church of Scotland. It will, therefore, make their presence in the Church of Scotland increasingly insecure. These are men and women who have a very profound love for God and who are deeply aware of the cost of loving him more than anything else in the world. The loss of such people to the church would be immeasurable.

Chapter 13

Matters of the heart: James E. Loder on homosexuality and the possibility of transformation

Mark S. Koonz

Mark Koonz has been involved in pastoral ministry for over twenty years, and is currently serving as pastor of Emmanuel Lutheran Church, Walla Walla, Washington. His journal articles have appeared in Theology in Scotland, Princeton Theological Review, CSL, and Edification: Journal of the Society for Christian Psychology.

1 Introducing James Edwin Loder (1931-2001)

James E. Loder received his Ph.D. from Harvard University's Graduate School of Arts and Sciences. In his dissertation he integrated the insights of Freud and Kierkegaard on "reality restoring" therapeutic experience and the therapeutic power of the imagination in religious experience.[1] He did his clinical training at Massachusetts Mental Health Center, a hospital affiliated with Harvard Medical School. He was a scholar at the Menninger Foundation (1961-1962), and did postdoctoral work at Piaget's *Institut des Sciences de l'Education* in Geneva (1968-1969). For almost four decades he taught at Princeton Theological Seminary until his unexpected death in November 2001.

In addition to his seminary teaching, Loder devoted much time, free of charge, to counseling. His counseling work involved seminary and university students, as well as others from the wider community. Some were referred by other counselors and therapists. It was Loder's intention to write more completely on his counseling ministry upon retirement, but his death prevented this and others must now bring forward information to fill in the inevitable gaps. Loder's earlier interviews with this writer provide

---

1   *Redemptive Transformation in Practical Theology: Essays in Honor of James E. Loder, Jr.*, edited by Dana R. Wright and John D. Kuentzel, (Grand Rapids: Eerdmans, 2004), 14.

supplemental information used here.[2] Loder's primary publications include *The Transforming Moment*,[3] *The Knight's Move*,[4] and *The Logic of the Spirit*.[5]

2 The question of homosexuality

In our focus on Loder's therapeutic work dealing with homosexuality, we will examine two basic questions. Firstly, does the condition of the human spirit play a significant role when homosexual desire arises in the course of personal development? Secondly, is a life transformation possible which renders homosexual inclination reversible? (If so, what facilitates that transformation?) Loder answered "Yes" to both questions, based on his years of counseling experience.

At the outset it should be made clear that Loder did not impose an agenda on people who came to him for help. For example, 'Christina' in *The Transforming Moment* came to him with her own desire to change. She was troubled about her inability to have an emotionally empathetic relationship with a man, and specifically asked Loder whether he could help her. This was not a case of Loder trying to change another person. His therapeutic exploration did not focus much on her lesbianism but went to earlier matters in her life, particularly the important relationships she had with her mother and father. These key relationships (including her personal interpretive response) were central to her self-understanding and identity. In the process, she went through a transformation that eliminated lesbianism from her life, beginning with her desires.[6] Others came and

---

2   Prof. Loder allowed me to interview (and audio-record) him several times about his counseling work: March 13th & 27th, April 24th, November 30th, 1990, and June 10th, 1993. The topics were varied and not always on sexuality. Here I only cite what is quoted from his books. All other quotations which are not referenced will be from these recordings; occasionally I will cite 'Interviews' to remind the reader of this source. The vignettes he used in *The Logic of the Spirit* were previously discussed in these sessions, and so statements he made then can shed light or add detail to some of the sentences in the book. Finally, the use of this material was given to a member of Loder's family for review prior to publication.

3   James E. Loder, *The Transforming Moment* (Colorado Springs: Helmers & Howard Publishers, second edition, 1989) [hereafter TM]. This edition is to be preferred to the 1981 Harper & Row edition.

4   James E. Loder and W. Jim Neidhardt, *The Knight's Move: The Relational Logic of the Spirit in Theology and Science* (Colorado Springs: Helmers & Howard, 1992).

5   James E. Loder, *The Logic of the Spirit: Human Development in Theological Perspective* (San Francisco: Jossey-Bass Inc., Publishers, 1998) [hereafter LS].

6   *The Transforming Moment*, 60-62.

asked for help in exploring their life story, inclinations, and possibilities for change. Some people involved with homosexuality did not seek or desire change of sexual inclination, and Loder never tried to force on them any attempt to change.

3 What did Loder mean by 'transformation'?

For Loder, the term 'transformation' refers to much more than positive change in attitude or behavior. "Rather, transformation occurs whenever, within a given frame of reference or experience, hidden orders of coherence and meaning emerge to replace or alter the axioms of the given frame and reorder its elements accordingly."[7] When one's conceptual frame of reference is altered or replaced, one cannot think of the world only in the previous way. The new frame of reference may be broader in scope and far richer in explanatory power, opening up new possibilities of meaning and understanding. Previous conflicts which could not be resolved in the old frame of understanding may be resolved within the new one.

Loder observed a transformational pattern (or logic) in his therapeutic work.[8] The pattern involves (1) a person in conflict; (2) a scanning process in search of resolution; (3) reception of an insight with convictional force, in which a new perception or perspective provides resolution of the conflict; (4) a release of energy in which the person discovers new implications of the insight – these may carry the person more deeply and richly into his or her world; and (5) a time of interpretation, as the knower searches to find congruent connections between the imaginative construct and the original conditions of the conflict. Truth is tested to determine whether the significant insight both "fits the terms of conflict and resolves it with maximum sufficiency and without excess".[9]

When this therapeutic goal has been reached, new freedom opens for the patient. Freud said, "Analysis does not set out to make pathological reactions impossible, but to give the patient's ego freedom to decide one way or the other."[10] Thus a person successfully helped by therapy is not rendered incapable of choosing for a neurosis. Rather the person has also become capable of choosing against it. There is new freedom to make

---

7   *Ibid.*, 229. This is discussed more fully in chapter two, "Knowing as Transforming Event."

8   *Ibid.*, 35-63.

9   *Ibid.*, 59; the latter part is from the glossary's definition of 'congruence', 222.

10   Sigmund Freud, *The Ego and the Id*, trans. Joan Riviere; revision ed. James Strachey (New York: W.W. Norton, 1962), 40 n. 1.

a choice for or against the neurosis, or make a choice for or against the former construction of reality. Therefore, in Loder's thought, the person is given the ability to live in the light of the transforming insight which reconfigures the self and the world.

4 The presence of a wounded human spirit

Loder did not approach questions of sexual behavior or orientation as though everything were genetically predetermined. Nor did he follow only a neo-Freudian model when he studied human development and the formation of personal identity. He paid special attention to matters affecting the human spirit, because the human spirit impacts the formation of self-understanding in the context of interpreting life-experiences and relations with other people.

In counseling settings he was willing to explore painful memories, yet knew that pervasive patterns in family dynamics were also important. The human spirit may be affected by undercurrents in human relationships as much as by specific painful incidents.

For example, Jill Faulkner Summers was interviewed about her father, William Faulkner. The famous novelist had good personal qualities, but was an alcoholic who might drink for days on end. Once, as an adolescent, Jill asked him not to drink. "It was just before my birthday and I knew that Pappy was getting ready to start on one of these bouts. I went to him – the only time I ever did – and said, 'Please don't start drinking.' And he was already well on his way, and he turned to me and said, 'You know, no one remembers Shakespeare's child.'" These hurtful words wounded Jill and left an imprint on her memory. Yet before the words were ever spoken, her alcoholic father had probably shown enough emotional distance to wound his daughter's spirit. It is often in the dynamic of a child interpreting that emotional distance, day after day, that the human spirit is adversely affected.[11]

Of the people who sought out Loder in order to talk about their homosexuality, in spite of diversity in background and family dynamics, he observed a common thread: their human spirit had been wounded. In many cases there were problems in their relationships with significant people – often parents (but not always) – in the course of their development from childhood to adulthood. In some cases parents were neither

---

11 Albert I. Bezzerides, William Faulkner: *A Life on Paper* (Jackson: University Press of Mississippi and Mississippi Authority for Educational Television, 1980), 92. Jill said, in reminiscing of her relationship with her father, "I think he cared about me. But, I also think I could have gotten in his way and he would have walked on me," 67.

intentionally nor overtly cruel. In others the physical absence of a parent impacted a child, or the parent was physically present but emotionally distant.[12] Yet with others there was overt and perceived cruelty experienced in the parent-child relationship.

The power of an absence to wound a young person's spirit indicates that we are into something deeper and more profound than trying to pinpoint some aspect of 'poor parenting'. This is particularly true where a parental absence is due to death. There may be conflicts in a child's mind and spirit that are not the result of any intentional antagonism directed towards the child. Yet those conflicts may be accompanied by sorrow, fear, or anger in the life of the growing child.

There is relevant literature on the connection between childhood molestation and adult homosexuality.[13] Sometimes Loder dealt with people who had been molested. "In one case, this boy was raised on a farm in the middle of nowhere. And he was raised to be a little girl by two grandparents . . . he was taught to tap dance. He was given skirts. And when he would

---

12 "If one factor influences the character development and emotional stability of a person, it is the quality of the relationship he experiences as a child with both of his parents. Conversely, if people suffering from severe non-organic emotional illness have one experience in common, it is the absence of a parent through death, divorce, time-demanding job or absence for other reasons. A parent's inaccessibility either physically, emotionally, or both, can exert a profound influence on the child's emotional health." Armand Nicholi, "The impact of parental absence on childhood development: an overview of the literature," Journal of Family and Culture, 1 (1985): 19-28. Cf. T.L. Trunnell, "The absent father's children's emotional disturbances," Archives of General Psychiatry 9 (1968): 180-188; R. Aseltine, "Pathways linking parental divorce with adolescent depression," Journal of Health and Social Behavior 37 (1996): 133-148.

13 One study reviews clinical literature on the molestation of boys, and notes that adolescents who were sexually molested by men were up to seven times more likely to identify themselves later as homosexual: W.C. Holmes et al., "Sexual Abuse of Boys," Journal of the American Medical Association 280 [1998]: 1855-1862. Cf. Stanton L. Jones and Mark A. Yarhouse, *Ex-Gays? A Longitudinal Study of Religiously Mediated Change in Sexual Orientation* (Downers Grove: IVP Academic, 2007), 82-83, concerning a NARTH (National Association for Research and Treatment of Homosexuality) study of 882 persons who answered retrospective questions: "The average age of awareness that they had 'homosexual tendencies' was 12.4 years. Interestingly, 520 (almost 60%) reported having had a childhood homosexual contact at an average age of 10.9 years, with the person initiating that contact being an average age of 17.2 years." For a related discussion, on the problem of older men seducing young men and then abandoning them, initiating a spiral of promiscuity, see Donald M. Joy, *Re-bonding: Preventing and Restoring Damaged Relationships* (Nappanee: Evangel, 1986), 87-88.

ride on the tractor with his grandfather he was subjected to homosexual experiences . . . from day one. It was so deeply ingrained in him . . . this was the most intense psychogenic form of homosexuality that I've ever dealt with."[14] But not everyone testified to a history of sexual abuse. For others the underlying tensions were less apparent to both the counselee and the outside observer (therapist).

Loder worked with a variety of people who met with him about their homosexuality, and he came to realize that in every person's life there was a deeply wounded human spirit. For him, the connection could not be ignored. The human spirit searches for meaning in our lives. The spirit is involved in all self-interpretation. The strength or weakness of the human spirit tremendously impacts the meaning-making process that includes self-identity. When the human spirit is wounded in the depths, it becomes distorted, twisted, interpreting everything very differently than would otherwise be the case. Therefore, in its wounded and distorted form the human spirit must receive grace and healing from the Spirit of Christ.

Loder said, "And in every case my concern, if I'm talking to a homosexual, is not to say, 'Well now look, you're a sinner. Unless you change you're going to hell. And I love you. But if you don't change it's goodbye.' Now the reason I don't want to do that is that . . . in all the cases I've worked with in terms of persons who are homosexual (not all from the seminary, some from the outside), they have all become homosexual because – (and there are other cases that we could talk about, types of cases) – but they became homosexual because there was a cruelty administered to their human spirit. It was twisted."[15]

David Seamands, of Asbury Theological Seminary, was another counselor who saw connections between certain types of sexual desires, including homosexual desires, and matters of the human spirit. In many of his counseling contexts the sexual problem was connected to a very wounded human spirit. After describing one such case scenario in reference to homosexuality, he advises: "When dealing with sexual matters, make sure that you discover the real issues that need facing and healing. So often the sexual injuries are closely intertwined with hurts that originate from a different area. There can be no lasting healing and change until those memories are uncovered and adequately dealt with. The real issue is often the association and relationship between the two.

---

14 Interviews.
15 Interviews.

In order to accomplish this, you need to be sensitive to the discernment of the Spirit."[16]

5 The presence of anger as a secondary emotion

Apart from any one incident, it is in and through various life experiences and family dynamics that a growing child constructs meaning about herself or himself. Regardless of the original context and the intentions on the part of others who participated, once a wounded spirit develops it can produce an incredible amount of anger. However, this does not make it possible to predict the outcome in a deterministic sense. That a youth has a wounded spirit does not mean that he or she will necessarily resolve the sexual aspect of his or her identity in a homosexual direction. Nor does it mean that the parents are to blame in a simplistic and naïve sense. It does, however, indicate the presence of something beyond the individual's genetic makeup, a spiritual matter in need of spiritual resolution.

In counseling Loder never thought it was sufficient to note the presence of anger. Anger is not a primary emotion. The deeper issues of the human spirit that often underlie anger are grief, sadness, loss, fear, yearning, or confusion. These were the deeper matters that Loder wanted his counselees to explore.

When probing the anger of the wounded human spirit, Loder often found a deep sense of yearning for intimacy with another human being, together with a terrible sense of frustration that that yearning was not fulfilled. Ultimately that yearning can only be satisfied by the Spirit of God.[17] Loder's prayers were for his counselees to have their yearning for intimacy met by the presence of the One who truly knows and loves them.

6 From rage to aggression and despair: negative results led to a re-evaluation of Loder's counseling approach

Loder's initial understanding of the nature of homosexuality seems to have undergone change over time, particularly due to the aggressive and

---

16 David A. Seamands, *Redeeming the Past: Recovering from the Memories that Cause Our Pain* (Colorado Springs: Victor Press, 2002) 175.

17 The information in this section comes from Loder's former doctoral student Daniel Reese. Loder would say "Studies show in nine times out of ten with men, and in four out of ten with women, when you see anger in a counseling situation it's a secondary emotion rather than a primary emotion. Beneath it is a whole layer of primary emotions."

destructive aspects of homosexuality which he observed in the lives of his counselees. For example, he talked in our conversation of his early work with one man who began to have nightmares as their sessions progressed. At first Loder worked with him so that he could accept or come to terms with his homosexual feelings. He seemed to come to terms with his homosexuality because the man indicated he was willing to accept it, but then the nightmares began and continued with severe intensity. "He began to have these dreams over and over again. And in the dreams someone will come out of the dark and start to attack him." Why was he experiencing this kind of violent attack against himself? "We had to deal with the anger that is under the surface: the rage. What's the rage come from? It comes from this twist put on the human spirit somewhere back there."[18]

Loder thought of this case when another man talked with him about his previous homosexual lifestyle, a man "who actually changed, became a heterosexual." In *The Logic of the Spirit* Loder says: "One with whom I worked for some time and who eventually married and had a family said that homosexuality, as he experienced it, was a form of necrophilia, a love of death."[19] Loder found this comment illuminating when he thought about his earlier work with the man distressed by violent nightmares. When he discussed this with me he said, "I could see in this other person, in this first person's dreams, to accept the homosexuality was releasing anger and aggression." This is not exceptional, but rather fits a pattern. "One of the stereotypes of the homosexual boy is the best little boy that ever lived. He's so good. But he's so good because all of this anger and aggression has been repressed and turned against his own sexuality."

As he reviewed his work with these two men and connected their stories with others he had worked with, he summarized, "So I've come to think about homosexuality as having a very deeply embedded, a deeply entrenched aggressive component that must be somehow dealt with. So I'm not of the school that says, 'Well, this is just a matter of sexual preference.' I do think there's something wrong in the human spirit that gives rise to this difficulty."[20] There was a link between the homosexuality and the inner aggression: the rage was evidence of a deeply wounded, troubled human spirit.

Thus his concern was to help each person enter the presence of Christ in prayer, that Christ's Spirit be invited to bring healing to every wounded

---

18 Interviews.

19 *The Logic of the Spirit*, 222; this vignette was discussed earlier in Interviews.

20 Interviews.

human spirit. To encourage a person to accept homosexuality is to ignore spiritual issues that are in need of resolution. "It has appeared to me in subsequent work that it is doing such a person no favor to say that homosexual expression of this aspect of his identity is just one choice among others. If he is not attacked in the night through his dreams, he will turn the powerful negative at the base of his psyche on others – heterosexuals, the church, society at large – or on himself in depression and dependency."[21]

Thus Loder learned during his earlier work that some counseling goals, even when reached, did not lead to the desired outcome. Shortly before his death, he referred to one of the ways his thinking had changed: "In the course of counseling, I have worked with some persons to help them come to an acceptance of their homosexual feelings and with others to help them change their lifestyle. What I discovered, in my counseling experience, was that those who continued to practice homosexuality were not truly content even after accepting the practice. They continued in despair, though it was pushed down deeper. Later in my practice, I realized that helping them to accept this condition was not doing them a favor, and I had to take it up from a more profoundly spiritual standpoint."[22]

---

21 Also in *The Logic of the Spirit*.

22 James E. Loder, "The Great Sex Charade and the Loss of Intimacy," Word & World 21, no. 1 (Winter 2001): 85. Whereas Loder found that individual acceptance of homosexuality did not lessen despondency, a recent study focused on societal acceptance of homosexuals and came to a similar conclusion. In the Netherlands society is very tolerant of homosexuality. Yet a 2001 study of homosexual and heterosexual men and women in the Netherlands found that homosexual men were about three times more likely than heterosexual men to suffer in the past year mood disorders(39%) and anxiety disorders (32%) and to have two or more DSM-III-R diagnoses (38%), while homosexual women were almost five times more likely than heterosexual women to suffer substance abuse disorders (26%): T. Sandfort, et al., "Same sex Sexual Behavior and Psychiatric Disorders: Findings From the Netherlands Mental Health Survey and Incidence Study (NEMESIS)," Archives of General Psychiatry 58, no. 1 (2001): 85-91. There is no western society more openly welcoming of homosexual practice than the Netherlands. It is significant that even there, with societal acceptance supporting personal acceptance of homosexual inclination and practice, homosexual males have a high rate of inner turmoil and depression. This finding supports Loder's insight that helping homosexuals accept their condition does not alleviate their personal despondency.

The U.S. Center for Disease Control and Prevention in Atlanta conducted a study on homosexual lifespans, concluding that diseases, organ failures, psychological and mental problems associated with homosexual sex develop early and hit hard among participants. These factors cannot be dissociated from the reasons why homosexual

7 The intimacy that liberates

> The principal point of my observation is not an attack on persons who practice homosexuality, but it is in opposition to what this practice does to persons. The issue forces us to realize that homosexuality is not ultimately fundamental to anyone's nature; it lives too close to death for that. The condition of homosexuality is, however, provocation to look deeper and discover that the real issue is not sexuality at all. It is intimacy.[23]

All sexuality, heterosexual or homosexual, "is a proximate and deficient longing for a deeper intimacy that only the spiritual life can provide."[24]

Among the wide spectrum of people whom Loder worked with, he witnessed again and again the power of Christ's Spirit to transform lives. In the case of 'Christina', she was set free from her lesbian desires and given the possibility of responding emotionally to the man who wanted a relationship with her. She was able to marry and have a family. Loder counseled and prayed with some men who were also set free from homosexual inclinations and promiscuity, and set free for marriage and fatherhood. However, Loder never claimed that all his homosexual counselees were set free from homosexual inclinations, nor did he claim that all of them wanted to change, for some counseled with him about other matters. Loder was guided by their requests, not his own agenda. He did claim that some of his counselees were freed of their homosexual inclinations, based on their testimony and resultant life-changes, and his follow-up work with them.

Did these changes come about overnight? Loder did not maintain there was an immediate cure for any problem. There are decisive turning points, when cognitive frames of reference are altered. There are accompanying

---

persons live 20 years less on average than heterosexual persons. The report is in Psychological Reports 96 (April 2005): 693-97. Those who blame these pervasive negatives on lack of societal approval of homosexuality must confront the findings of the Sandfort study. The inherent instability of relationships in the homosexual lifestyle, particularly the discovery of a partner's unfaithfulness, is the chief factor in suicidal ideation. An older study discovered that the major reason for suicide attempts among homosexuals was the breakup of their relationships, often with the discovery of unfaithfulness. The second most common reason was the person's own inability to accept oneself. See Alan P. Bell and Martin S. Weinberg, *Homosexualities: A Study of Diversity Among Men and Women* (New York: Simon and Schuster, 1978).

23 *The Logic of the Spirit*, 222.

24 *Ibid.*, 223.

inner changes that bring a sudden awareness of new-found freedom. Yet this often happens in a process that takes time, and one may unpack the meaning of transformational insight for a life-time. If and when the new cognitive insight and sense of freedom comes suddenly, it still needs to be affirmed by attending to all it means and living in harmony with it.

Each person's transformational pattern had unique elements. What may have happened quickly or slowly for one person could not be exactly replicated or determinative for another person. This is said because we don't know how long it took any person to counsel and pray with Loder, before they experienced the inner change that freed them from homosexual inclinations. The time involved probably varied from person to person.

Had Loder lived to write his book on counseling, it would have been interesting for him to interact with Robert Spitzer's study of 200 people who wanted change from homosexuality and achieved their goal. These wanted change passionately and worked with counselors in reparative therapy, but found it took two years, on average, before their behavioural changes were matched with changes in their inner life, in their feelings and fantasies.[25] Yet this study does not provide a normative time frame. Apart from the obvious fact that no two people respond exactly alike in therapy, the people reflected in this average were involved in differing types of reparative therapy. Some were able to enter into heterosexual relations with heterosexual feelings more quickly than two years, while some took up to seven years.

---

25 Robert L. Spitzer, "Can Some Gay Men and Lesbians Change Their Sexual Orientation? 200 Participants Reporting a Change from Homosexual to Heterosexual Orientation," in Archives of Sexual Behavior, Vol. 32, No. 5, October 2003, 403-417. See Warren Throckmorton's interview with Robert Spitzer for contextual information and reflections on this study, at the blog at wthrockmorton.com. While a predominant number of people included in this study were involved in religious-based reparative therapy, a number of them began their search with secular counselors and therapists. When the secular therapists or liberal religious counselors told them there was nothing to be done, that they would just have to live with the fact that they were "born homosexual," many of these people became suicidal. The fact that so many secular therapists do not want to work for change is indicative of prevailing attitudes in our current society, not of what is psychologically possible though difficult to achieve. A few decades ago a number of secular therapists did offer reparative therapy for homosexuals, without moral or religious motivation, as was done much earlier in Sigmund Freud's practice. Today political pressure makes such work unpopular in professional circles, but political pressure does not make it morally wrong or impossible to assist men and women who want to be free of homosexual inclinations.

Even when a person has received a cognitive insight that comes with power to transform his or her life, that same person can hesitate to explore all of the implications that go with it. By Loder's own admission, this was the case in his own life after his remarkable 'transforming moment'. He admits, "I resisted the implications of this experience for over two years."[26]

Therefore, with people struggling with homosexuality, we do not have enough information to posit any normative time-frame for the inner changes they seek. Of those who worked with Loder, if we could but ask them, some may testify it took a longer time than they hoped. Others may testify that inner changes came surprisingly sooner than they anticipated.

Once I asked Loder about one of the anecdotes concerning a remarkable transformation in his counseling ministry, which seemed to come into place quickly. He responded that in his counseling with individuals, he often put a lot of time and energy into "preparing the way of the Lord, as it were," before anything happened that seemed sudden or remarkable and brought healing changes or transformation. Whether Loder's counseling sessions with people were short-term or long-term depended on many variables. With this in mind, let us consider further the spiritual dimension of his counseling, which focused on the quest for spiritual intimacy in the presence of Christ's Spirit.

Loder worked on 'two fronts' at the same time, as he once put it. He worked on the first front regarding psychological problems related to a person's sense of self and identity, as well as other relevant factors in their personal history. He worked on the second front, as it were, to help the

---

26 *The Transforming Moment*, 13. Yet the gift does not have to be lost because of hesitation in exploring the full ramifications which inhere in it. It was not lost to Loder because he resisted its implications for a time. The power of the cognitive insight in the transformational process endures with vitality because it is not the prisoner of time, and because the truth liberates ("You shall know the truth, and the truth shall set you free," John 8:32). Theologian Hugh Ross Mackintosh advised Christians not to become dismayed if a process of moral or spiritual renewal takes time, and we can apply his words to many contexts: "When a man first kneels at the Cross there is coming to birth in him a new unprecedented element or principle, which may be reckoned on to transform his character from end to end. That the process may be a long one in no way alters its intrinsic nature; whether it takes minutes or days or years, in essence it is still the same. Always it implies that a human life has taken a new start, of a kind which only Divine power can explain." H.R. Mackintosh, *Life on God's Plan* (London: Hodder and Stoughton, 1909), 49.

person enter into prayer and invite the Spirit of Jesus to minister to his or her human spirit. For in Loder's understanding, a human person can strengthen another person's ego (sense of self), but only the Holy Spirit can heal the human spirit. Loder found that cognitive changes came first, before behavioral change. In his work with each individual, how long it took before the significant cognitive changes came into play, or any sense of freedom and new beginnings developed, cannot be determined. Each person presented a unique and individualized situation, and Loder was not searching for an average. What is important is that the cognitive changes were not just the result of his psychological focus, but were also impacted by the Holy Spirit's outpouring of love on the human spirit.

In Loder's understanding, transformation is facilitated wherever the Spirit of God establishes an intimacy between Holy Spirit and human spirit. This liberates and leads to transforming reconfigurations that impact one's self understanding and identity. "A careful examination of sexuality reveals that no one's identity is ultimately determined by sexuality; rather it comes from their walk in the Spirit of God. Whatever permits Spirit-to-spirit intimacy in that walk is gracious, and it empowers and truly liberates the human spirit. Moreover, that intimacy works toward the transformation of the whole person, including the sexual aspect of identity."[27] In such a transforming context sexual orientation can change. Loder saw it happen more than once and testified to this in both public lectures and in his books.

Insofar as some were set free of homosexual inclinations in Loder's counseling much sooner than the two year average in the Spitzer study, in many of these instances Loder would have pointed (as in fact he did) to one chief reason: when the Holy Spirit visits a human spirit bearing the gift of God's love and healing presence, the Holy Spirit brings to the human spirit the deepest and richest sense of intimacy the heart has ever longed for. It is that experience of intimacy that liberates and makes all things new, for other proximate and inadequate forms of intimacy cannot compare or hold greater power. Former attractions can diminish or disappear. That divine gift of intimacy with the human spirit is truly liberating and life-enhancing.

While this aspect of Loder's work cannot be presented in an easily-replicated formula or human technique, each of us can enter into the presence of the same Holy Spirit whose love and power Loder relied upon in his counseling, especially after his own transformation. The Holy Spirit,

27 *The Logic of the Spirit*, 223.

who taught Loder in the school of prayer, welcomes our entrance into this healing and learning context. In prayer we come into dependent and receptive contact with the One who knows us inside-out, and still loves us, and always loves us. In the presence of Christ's Spirit, we can support and intercede in prayer for those who counsel with us about sexual concerns or other matters, reminding them that they are known through and through, and always loved, because the risen Jesus Christ endures and always loves (Romans 8:31-39). We can pray for the visitation of Christ's Spirit to visit their human spirit, bringing the intimacy which heals, renews, and transforms.[28]

8 On the importance of cognitive change preparing the way for behavioural change and intrapsychic reorientation

First, we note one difference with the 200 men and women in the Spitzer study who waited, on average, about two years for their inner changes to harmonize with their behavioral changes. Rather than working on behavioural changes first and waiting for inner changes to 'catch up' and harmonize, Loder worked for inner changes first, and then saw that behavioural changes followed more readily. Both changes working together moved the person towards a total reorientation.

When Loder reviewed his own counseling work, he wrote very succinctly about the process that led to a new freedom and new identity.

---

28 See Loder's discussion on the intimacy of prayer in the Presence of the Holy, in *The Transforming Moment*, 89-91. This intimacy is often resisted because it revolutionizes life: "The absolutely unique claim of Jesus that one could be on 'Abba' terms with the Holy, and the same claim made by St Paul, is based on simple trust; yet it is highly complicated by its offensiveness to two-dimensional existence and the demoralized outlook of three-dimensional atheism." By "three dimensional" Loder means an understanding of the self and the world which is aware of the Void, or that which threatens the annihilation of the self. The threat of destruction brings fear, confusion, anger, denial, and distortions of life, as does the threat of absorption. Only the fourth dimension, called the Holy, which is God's presence, can overcome the Void and negate the negation of life. Loder affirmed that when the intimacy of God's presence is welcomed in prayer, all things can become new. "When serenity comes up out of anxiety, joy out of depression, hope out of hopelessness; when good is returned for evil, forgiveness replaces retaliation, and courage triumphs over fear; then we recognize the movement of something beyond the personality and mental health. Such profound manifestations of the human spirit are the faces of the fourth dimension, which I have called the Holy." Cf. Loder's *The Logic of the Spirit*, 264-268. See also the forthcoming article by Mark Koonz, on the use of prayer in Loder's counseling ministry, to appear in the journal *Edification*.

"Cognitive change appeared first, then behavioral change, and finally intrapsychic reorientation. Thus, even when homosexual behavior was transposed into a personal identity, a change was not thereby inhibited."[29] We want to unpack the meaning of this statement.

As stated above, transformation is more than a positive change in attitude. It includes a cognitive change that results in a new composition of the self and the world, a new frame of reference, and manifests its power in a new freedom to make choices. Vital cognitive shifts may have a powerful impact on self-identity.

Loder replied to a question on homosexuality, "Well, let me tell you how I think about this. This comes out of having worked with, over the years, students who have come to me with varying degrees of intensity of homosexual inclinations and so on. And always the first thing, for me, is to separate the person's identity from their sexual preference, so to speak. As soon as somebody has a homosexual inclination, they say, 'I am a homosexual.' And I say, 'No. You are a human being, and you have homosexual desires. But you are first and foremost a human being.'" Whenever an individual came to see Loder about homosexual issues, the clarification and affirmation of that person's fundamental identity as a human being was his first priority: as a human being you are created and valued by God, and invited to live in relationship with God. Firstly, you are a human being. Secondly, human beings have sexual desires, but their identity is not determined by those desires.

Loder continued, "See, the big move here can be described in terms of Kegan's picture of the shift, because you're disembedding the person from the homosexual matrix so that homosexuality is something they have rather than something they are, you see. The question is not, first we've got to get rid of this problem. You have to have a self there, a self that has enough strength of its own to begin to recompose the world however, okay."[30]

Robert Kegan's book *The Evolving Self*[31] is on the dynamics by which the self makes meaning and constructs an understanding of self in relation to the surrounding world, beginning with infancy and continuing throughout life. The self can be 'embedded' [totally immersed] in a certain way of meaning-making, and then strive to break out of that way of

29 James E. Loder, "The Great Sex Charade and the Loss of Intimacy," *op. cit.*, 86.
30 Interviews.
31 Robert Kegan, *The Evolving Self* (Cambridge: Harvard University Press, 1982).

understanding. When the self 'breaks free' from the old way of making meaning, it becomes 'disembedded'. When that happens, there is a search for a new understanding of the self in relation to the world. Then when a new understanding is constructed, the self becomes 're-embedded' in a new form of meaning making.

In Loder's understanding the human spirit searches for meaning and order in one's life. When the human spirit is strong it is better able to compose a sound understanding of the self in relationship with others. A strong human spirit helps one to break free from false meanings that distort the self and truncate its freedom.

His reference to Kegan in our discussion had to do more with the 'meaning that is constructed' than the process by which it comes about. One of the significant ways in which a human being develops and grows to maturity is by learning to distinguish the difference between who she or he is and what she or he has. A basic example is the infant who grows and comes to understand "I have a mother; I am not one with my mother". This differentiation helps form self-understanding and self-identity. And this type of differentiation needs to take place again and again throughout one's life. As it does, the maturing person comes to recognize the full range of what it means to be a self, a self distinct from but living in relation to others.

Can individuals with homosexual inclinations recompose their world? Yes, by being helped to recognize that their inclinations are something they have, not what they are. This distinction is crucial for all of us.

You are not your memories, memories are something you have. You determine the way in which your life today will or will not be defined by those memories. You are not your feelings; feelings are something you have. You are not your desires; desires are something you have. Because thoughts and desires are something you have, you can choose for or against them. You can choose to welcome and embrace them. Or you can choose to reject them as unworthy to define the meaning and purpose of your life. This distinction between who a person is and what a person has prepares the way for the important cognitive change that helps people to recompose the meaning of their lives.

"You are a human being and you have homosexual desires. But you are first and foremost a human being." Having homosexual desires does not make one a homosexual, because desires are something one has, not what one is. Loder saw that cognitive recognition of this distinction was crucial and often brought freedom to individuals so they could begin to recompose their world, so they could become "disembedded from the homosexual matrix" or way of making meaning about the self. In that freedom they can more readily see that "homosexuality is something they have rather than something they are." With this freedom (inherent in the 'new' meaning) there often comes a newfound ability to make choices for or against the homosexual inclination. None of this belittles the serious struggles some individuals may still endure, but a new way of making meaning does open up new possibilities, including the diminishing power of the homosexual attraction. Everything changes when you realize you have a choice to make, a choice about how you will respond to something you have, and also realize you have the power to choose.

One caveat is necessary. This important cognitive insight was of great importance for a number of people, but not necessarily the only one that they discovered. Each individual may have received additional insights unique to his or her life, which initiated or helped complete the transformational process. These other very personal cognitive insights were also Loder's focus, as he helped each person examine and test a given insight in fulfillment of the transformational process. Thus the role of the therapist or counselor was not set aside in Loder's work, but fully engaged with other issues beyond reaching this understanding that personal identity is not determined by our desires.

9 Response to criticism

For the above reasons Loder came to believe that it was possible for a homosexual orientation and identity to be reversed, and he testified to this publicly. However, since Loder's death a couple of writers have criticized his work in this area. Kenneth Kovacs recently published book, *The Relational Theology of James E. Loder*, is a rewarding read on many levels. This book is valuable for any who want a greater understanding of Loder's intellectual and spiritual contribution. Kovacs presents Loder's theologically-based interdisciplinary work with both depth and clarity, as he seeks to make Loder's ideas more accessible to a wider audience. Kovacs includes an important section on Loder's "Counseling in the Spirit", and applauds the way Loder used his skills as a therapist to "awaken faith in individuals" as he helped them with specific concerns. This process brought to Loder's practical theology a depth of insight about the human condition, as he helped people live life in the Spirit so they could become authentically human, that is, to discover "what it means to be a redeemed creature in the presence of God."[32] Yet, in spite of his great appreciation for Loder, he critiqued Loder's therapeutic work regarding homosexuality in the content of two endnotes. Here I will give responses to a couple of his comments.

The first example is only an implied criticism, yet for some reason the author connected it to his critique on Loder's therapy with homosexuals. Kovacs reports that Kenda Creasy Dean, a professor at Princeton Seminary, told him "she knew people who had been in counseling for years with little success until they met with Loder." Others could report the same, but Kovacs added, "This was certainly not the case with everyone who worked with him."[33] Here Kovacs' statement is as obvious as it is unnecessary. Loder never claimed that he had helped every person with homosexual inclinations any more than he had helped every person with marital problems; in fact he spent time counseling with some who did not even want help with their homosexuality. Yet a little more should be said on this point.

Loder knew that even when an individual Christian desires to grow spiritually, there is a counter-desire to go slowly, or a counter-drift that says, "Wait! I'm not ready for this." The same individual who is open to help in a counseling session may also experience a counter-drift that makes him or her hold back in hesitation. The same person, who prays one morning to be set free of homosexual inclinations, may later that same day choose to spend time with titillating pornography.[34] This counter-drift is a real factor, an aspect of the 'death instinct' in psychological discussion.[35] Søren Kierkegaard's insight that not every sufferer wants to receive help or relief, holds true for many contexts.[36] Furthermore, Loder never thought the worth of his theory on transformation was based on percentages, but

---

32 Kenneth E. Kovacs, *The Relational Theology of James E. Loder: Encounter and Conviction* (New York: Peter Lang, 2011), 175-182.

33 *Ibid.*, 258 note 107.

34 There are other possibilities regarding failure in counseling. One factor might include the counselee's lack of bringing up pertinent information. Another factor might have been the imperfections of Loder himself, either in his response to a given individual or in his lack of knowledge. All of which may apply to any counselor-client cooperation in therapy.

35 Karl Menninger, *Man Against Himself* (New York/London: Harcourt Brace Jovanovich, 1966, 1985), 5-8.

36 Søren Kierkegaard, *The Sickness Unto Death*, ed. and tr. by Howard V. Hong and Edna H. Hong (Princeton: Princeton University Press, 1983), 71-74.

rather on the fact that individuals engrossed in a wide range of human dilemmas had received spiritual healing and transformation.

Without going into specific case histories, the fact that some people were not helped in this area of Loder's counseling, or that some did not want to pursue any change in sexual orientation, does not indicate they could not be helped. At least, in my interpretation, Loder would not have concluded these people could not be helped. He was aware of the impulse to resist personal transformations, and other important personal factors. Therefore, Loder would not have seen these people as special cases or exceptions to his transformational theory, nor would he have concluded they were "just born that way." Rather, he would have seen them as people with personal and spiritual problems still in need of resolution. In the end, the fact that some were not helped cannot detract from the fact that others were indeed helped to be free of homosexual inclinations. Loder's testimony about those who were helped remains important and relevant.

Kovacs also said, "For Loder, homosexuality originates in adolescence as an expression of arrested human development, a diagnosis rejected by the psychoanalytic community."[37] Yet this is not accurate. Psychoanalysts see significant factors even before adolescence which have power to distort ego development. While Loder did at times work with the concept of "arrested development," he did not work exclusively with it, nor did he see it as deterministic regarding the development of homosexual inclinations. It can exist as a consequence of a deep spiritual problem rather than a cause, and may exist concurrently with other important developmental factors. Loder actually used at least twelve different scenarios or models which guided his ideas on how homosexuality developed in individuals, none of which were applicable in every case.

Loder's own testimony was that a deeply wounded human spirit was present in every case of homosexuality that he encountered. This discovery led him to recognize the deeper spiritual dimension of the problem. The importance of this cannot be minimized, for the human spirit affects all forms of meaning-making from childhood to adulthood, and to the end of life. In responding to the spiritual needs which this insight illuminated, Loder saw many positive results. Therefore we must ask the question, if Loder's position was so flawed, why was his therapeutic work so effective?

Finally, Kovacs presented an anecdote of a conversation he had with Loder, in which he strongly disagreed with Loder's statements

---

37 Kovacs, *op. cit.*, 262 note 154.

on homosexuality in *The Logic of the Spirit*. He claims that Loder "acknowledged that if he had the chance to re-write TLS, he would temper his comments on the subject, as his understanding of homosexuality and the Christian experience was still evolving."[38] This account, however, does not tell us much we can build on. Kovacs only says Loder considered tempering his language on the subject, not that his position had changed in any significant respect. Loder did not write loosely in that section of the book, rather he demonstrated carefully chosen wording, so even if we accepted this anecdote, it is unclear which of Loder's sentences he considered "tempering." Many of us wish he had not been so succinct and had elaborated more fully on what he said there, but it is still clear that Loder wrote with intentional precision.

Kovacs gives no reason to believe, other than this ambiguous comment about their conversation, that Loder was in any way retracting or modifying his overall evaluation of homosexuality. The proof that Loder did not change or modify his position can be seen in one of the last things he wrote before his death. Following his November 2000 conversation with Kovacs, he published in the Winter 2001 edition of Word & World, his article "The Great Sex Charade and the Loss of Intimacy." In this article Loder makes it clear that his position had not changed, for he affirmed that homosexuality is not life-enhancing in the human quest for intimacy, which is one reason the biblical prohibitions are in place. Loder also gave an example from his 'reparative therapy' with an individual, in a way that shows he still thought such work was appropriate.[39]

While Loder is not the end of the discussion, his testimony may provide an opening for further discussion and comparison with other work, including that of Joseph Nicolosi,[40] Warren Throckmorton, Stanton Jones and Mark Yarhouse.[41] Loder sometimes referred to the Pattison study

---

38 Kovacs, *ibid*.

39 Loder, "The Great Sex Charade", *op.cit.* (see note 22 above). Concerning the biblical prohibitions, the standard text remains *Robert A. J. Gagnon, The Bible and Homosexual Practice: Texts and Hermeneutics* (Nashville: Abingdon Press, 2001). Gagnon has continued to answer his critics, including writers recommended by Kovacs, and his website can be consulted for many aspects of the debate. Cf. Richard Hays, *The Moral Vision of the New Testament* (San Francisco: HarperCollins, 1996), 379-406.

40 Joseph Nicolosi, *Reparative Therapy of Male Homosexuality: A New Clinical Approach* (Northvale: Jason Aronson, 1991); Joseph Nicolosi and Lucy Freeman, *Healing Homosexuality: case studies of reparative therapy* (Northvale: Jason Aronson, 1993).

41 Jones and Yarhouse, *op.cit.*

as confirmatory of his insight that cognitive change precedes behavioral change, followed by intrapsychic reorientation.[42] While the Pattison research affirmed Loder's conclusion, each reached their conclusion in a context completely independent of the other.

Donald Capps, Loder's former colleague, and Nathan Carlin wrote a critique of the Pattison study. Insofar as they imply that Loder relied heavily on the Pattison study, they do not relate the facts well. The Pattison study did not initially guide Loder in his therapeutic practice. He had already worked with people with homosexual inclinations and activity, as well as saw some set free from their homosexual orientation, prior to receiving any insights or confirmation from the Pattison study's publication. For example, 'Christina', discussed in *The Transforming Moment*, was prior to his accident in 1970, hence prior to the Pattison study which was published ten years later. What can be said is that the Pattison study offered some confirmation for the conclusions he had already arrived at independently in his own work. Capps and Carlin also allege that Loder's citation of the Pattison study had a "considerable influence on the general ethos of Princeton Theological Seminary throughout the 1990s and early 2000s." [43] Their conclusion comes as a surprise to many of us who were there, and we see it as a distortion. What impacted the seminary and wider

---

42 E. Mansell Pattison and Myrna Loy Pattison, "'Ex-Gays': Religiously mediated change in homosexuals," American Journal of Psychiatry 137, no. 12 (December 1980), 1553-1562. Cf. Loder, Logic, *op.cit.*, 223.

43 Donald Capps and Nathan Carlin, "The 'Religiously Mediated Change' of 11 Gay Men: A Case of Unexceptional Sublimation," in Pastoral Psychology, 57 (2008), 128. Capps and Carlin also complain that Loder's counseling with seminary students may "be viewed as a violation of boundaries between one's professional and counseling roles," *ibid*. They make this charge without explaining in what sense Loder violated boundaries, and without providing a rationale for that accusation. Whether this criticism can even bear weight also depends in large part on what one thinks the proper role of a seminary teacher is in the Christian context. Is he or she a mere purveyor of information, or also a member of Christ's community who is available to listen, discuss, and pray with other members of the community when they are hurting or perplexed? Many people are grateful that Loder used his counseling gifts and was willing to pray with them for guidance or for the transformation of their lives. Furthermore, Capps and Carlin fail to mention that Loder never attempted to help anyone 'change' his or her 'sexual orientation' unless that person first asked him for such help. He did not impose an agenda contrary to their wishes. Loder may have seen his teaching work and his counseling work as two significant aspects of his one pastoral ministry, both roles being part of God's call on his life. In both teaching and counseling, he was operating within the classical tradition of pastoral care, as portrayed in the surveys by Thomas Oden.

community was not one citation occasionally mentioned or appearing in print, but rather the full burden of Loder's testimony concerning the results of his own therapeutic work, his recognized competency, and the transformations that were exemplified in the lives of some of the people who had worked with him.

Yet we can agree that there are serious limitations regarding the Pattison study. Had Loder lived long enough to publish a book on his counseling method, he would have had to interact with additional studies. One criticism of the Pattison study is that numerically their study group was quite small. A second criticism was that they did not add a longitudinal study that tracked the lives of the men who left homosexuality for heterosexuality, to verify that the changes were abiding long-term. However, longitudinal research with a larger group was done by Jones and Yarhouse which is not open to these criticisms, offering confirmatory weight to the conclusion that homosexuality can be reversible, at least for some. They also conclude that the changes were not negative or harmful for the persons who sought them, but in many cases were actually beneficial according to standard measurements of psychological health.[44] The Jones-Yarhouse study provides significant areas for comparison and reflection.

In all of the vast modern discussion on homosexuality, the work of James Loder serves to remind us that matters of the human spirit often play a key role, and cannot be ignored by the counselor, priest or minister of the gospel. Loder's reflections on his counseling work led him to affirm that the logic (or pattern) of transformation may operate even where homosexual inclinations seem deeply entrenched in a person's life.

---

44 Jones and Yarhouse, *op.cit.* (see note 13 above). The Jones-Yarhouse study met the standards set by the American Psychiatric Association for documenting the claim that change of sexual orientation in a heterosexual direction is possible, undermining the argument that homosexuality is immutable. This book also analyzes the Pattison study, giving a balanced response to criticisms of it, as well as analyzes the work of Robert Spitzer and others.

Chapter 14
A pastoral letter in defence of marriage

Philip Tartaglia

Bishop Tartaglia wrote this 'Pastoral Letter to the Clergy, Religious and Faithful' of the Roman Catholic Diocese of Paisley in October 2011, in response to the Scottish Government Consultation on Same Sex Marriage. It is reprinted here by kind permission.

"God created man in the image of himself, in the image of God he created
him, male and female he created them" (Genesis 1:27)

My dear brothers and sisters in Christ,

The Scottish Government has launched a consultation in which they propose that same sex marriage should be introduced in Scotland.

The Catholic Bishops of Scotland have expressed their unanimous opposition to this proposal. I have made public my own submission to the Scottish Government. You can read it on the website of the Diocese of Paisley at www.rcdop.org.uk. I have also given radio and television interviews in which I have defended the institution of marriage as uniquely the union of a man and a woman, and stressed the foolishness of the Government's proposal to re-define marriage to accommodate same sex unions.

I now ask you to respond individually to the Government Consultation and say that you are against the introduction of same sex marriage.

Same sex marriage is wrong in principle

Nature, reason and religion concur that marriage is uniquely the union of a man and a woman, which, by its very nature, is designed for the mutual good of the spouses and to give the children who may be born of that union a father and a mother.

For obvious reasons, a same sex union cannot do that. A same sex union should not therefore be called marriage. Same sex unions are different in nature and purpose from marriage. Same sex marriage is therefore not an issue about equality or human rights. It is an issue about the nature and meaning of marriage in our society.

It is very important to realise that opposition to the introduction of same sex marriage is not, as some so stridently assert, 'homophobic bigotry', but is the assertion and defence of the nature and meaning of marriage which has been universally recognised by all cultures and all the great religions, and which has sustained humanity since time immemorial. It is therefore wrong and foolish to undermine this understanding of marriage.

Same sex marriage is unnecessary

The State recognises same sex unions in the form of civil partnerships. In law, same sex partners have all the rights and privileges of marriage, except the right to be called a marriage. Same sex marriage is therefore unnecessary. Moreover, to call a civil partnership a marriage is to play a childish but dangerous game with language, in which people make something mean whatever they want it to mean.

Same sex marriage will have undesirable consequences

1 Same sex marriage will change the nature of parenting. The normal mother and father model of parenting will be replaced in law and then gradually in culture by a non gender-specific model of parenting which will deprive children of their right to have a mother and a father, and which will have negative implications for the sexual identity of children, creating in the long run a society in which more and more people will not be able to identify their sexuality, something which will further damage marriage and family, and be to the detriment of the common good.

2 The introduction of same sex marriage into law will have detrimental effects on education. The new models of sex education, of marriage and of parenting will certainly become mandatory in public schools. While Catholic schools in Scotland have autonomy in religious education programmes, the ideological and bureaucratic pressure on teachers and schools to conform to the new coercive orthodoxy could become unbearable, creating a climate of confusion, mistrust and fear in education and in schools, as teachers and educators are cajoled and bullied into teaching what is contrary to faith, reason and common sense.

3 Once the definition of marriage is changed to accommodate same sex unions on account of equality and human rights, Government will have no good reasons not to extend the definition of marriage to other combinations, such as three or more partner marriages. The problem will be that Government will not be able to give a principled answer to requests for polygamous marriage. It will not be able to say, "This is not allowed

because it is not right". It can only say, "This is not allowed because it's not allowed", and this is clearly unsatisfactory and ultimately unsustainable.

4 The redefinition of marriage to include same sex unions will bring with it State-sponsored discrimination and penalties in the courts and in the workplace against anyone who dares to question the rightness of same sex marriage, thereby riding roughshod over freedom of speech, freedom of religion and freedom of conscience.

Civil partnerships and same sex marriages in church

The Government's assurance that it will not require religious bodies to register civil partnerships or conduct same sex marriages is disingenuous. The Government could not require the Catholic Church under any circumstances to conduct civil partnerships or same sex marriages. In a democracy, any such attempt would be a serious infringement of religious liberty. So as far as the Catholic Church is concerned, this assurance is worth nothing. It is a complete red herring.

However, what the Government's assurance may do is to create the expectation that religious bodies will register civil partnerships and conduct same sex marriages, thereby heaping pressure on religious bodies which are uncertain which way to go and sowing the seeds of dissent and disunity among Church memberships. It would have been much wiser for the Government not to have attempted to interfere in the legitimate freedom and self-regulation of religious bodies.

Conclusion

The Government Consultation remains open until 9th December 2011. Please contribute to the consultation and tell the Government that you do not want same sex marriage to be introduced in Scotland because it is wrong in principle, it is unnecessary in practice and will have damaging consequences for the common good.

Yours devotedly in Christ,

+ Philip Tartaglia

X Philip Tartaglia, Bishop of Paisley

Chapter 15

Compassion and community

Jock Stein

Jock Stein is a retired minister and erstwhile warden of Carberry Tower; he has been the editor of the Handsel Press for the past twenty years.

Many years ago I shared a flat for two years with a Christian man with a strong same sex orientation. I became aware of the huge struggle life is for such a person, and how much they deserve our compassion. Later in life, my friend decided to marry, but his marriage did not last.

We care for our neighbours because they are neighbours, because they are made in God's image, and because God sent his Son into the world for them as well as for us. Our identity is formed by what God declares to be true about us, as well as by the nation into which we are born, and the communities to which we choose to belong (or which are chosen for us) as we grow up. Choice may be a significant part of what makes us who we are, but it is not the fundamental part, which belongs to God himself and his providential care.

One of those communities is the Christian church. The Church of Scotland, like other mainstream churches, is divided by the question of homosexual practice. The Bible section of this book explains why this is such a serious issue, and why Christians should give it the time and attention which we would far rather devote to mission and the many demands of service in today's world. This is a moral and spiritual issue which cannot be brushed aside by talk about human rights. Neither can the values by which we choose to shape our behaviour be decided by science, although empirical research can raise important issues for us to consider.

In the New Testament, Acts 15 describes at length the process and content of the Jerusalem Council. It met because of a dual concern for the teaching and the unity of the church. Paul and James and others took great trouble over this, and the Council shows the young Christian community struggling to discern what militates against the gospel on the one hand,

and what is only a secondary issue on the other. If a solution was to be found, they believed that the Holy Spirit would lead them to it, and so it proved. The issue was soluble because each party listened to Scripture and listened to a new experience of the work of God's Spirit which they found, after all, was in agreement with Scripture.

When John Knox issued the Scots Confession of Faith, he said that if any reader felt that what he and his fellow Reformers had confessed or published was wrong, they would consider the matter and diligently search the Word of God, to discover whether the objection was valid. In the present situation, where there is such division concerning same sex relationships and ministry, the only way forward is for both sides to state what they believe in the light of God's word. What has happened, sadly, is that traditionalists have carefully studied Scripture, while revisionists have qualified their reading of Scripture by arguing:

(a) "If Paul had known what we now know, he would not have written what he did." Gagnon and even revisionist commentators think this is unlikely to be true.

(b) "Surely this is one of the minor issues, on which Christians may legitimately disagree (*adiaphora*) compared with 'weightier matters of the law'."[1] Gagnon looks at this in detail (see chapters 10–12).

This second argument is sometimes put differently, by saying that this is a matter of church practice rather than doctrine. The problem here is what such a conclusion implies about the authority of the Bible, and in particular on the importance, as well as the right understanding of Bible passages such as Genesis 1:27 and Ephesians 5:31-32.

Understanding the division

Traditionalists hold to the Bible as the supreme rule of faith and life, and the Bible clearly teaches that marriage is the only right setting for sexual practice. Jesus himself upheld this, and while questions of homosexual practice did not arise in his ministry,[2] he was known to take a

---

1 Matt 23:23. William Placher in his recent theological commentary on Mark says, "Though matters of war and torture seem surely more important than the sexual orientation of our ministers, it is the latter question that threatens to divide several of our denomination at the national or worldwide level." (Westminster John Knox Press 2010, 7)

2 As far as we can tell, Jewish opinion (unlike Gentile opinion of the same era) was solidly 'traditional' on this, so the question would not have arisen within the context of Jesus' ministry.

stricter position generally than the liberal rabbis (Matt 19:3ff.), and a more forgiving position than the conservatives (John 8:1-11).

Revisionists, because they believe that a significant minority of people are homosexual by nature,[3] feel that it is unjust to exclude civil partners from leadership in the church. Over the past twenty years, the debate between nature and nurture has swung in the direction of 'nature' – although all efforts to isolate a 'homosexual gene' have proved fruitless, and no one cause of the homosexual condition has been shown to be dominant; all cases are different, and complex. Fashions in both science and therapy change.[4] One can go back and look at Freud's views, which in some respects are wildly out of date but in other respects are interesting.[5] His testimony was, that out of those who came to him seeking change of orientation (a wider cross-section than might be the case today), one third did change, one third got 'some help' and the other third changed not at all.

The scientific literature review in chapter 2 shows that whereas in the middle of last century opinion was unfairly biased towards seeing homosexuality as a pathological condition with psychiatric causes, now it is just as unfairly biased towards seeing homosexuality as purely a biological condition, with even the possibility of change denied outright.[6] By contrast, Jones cites a recent study of attempts to change orientation, done by Exodus International; out of 98 participants, 61 completed the survey properly. Of these, 23% reported successful change of orientation

---

3   See chapters 1 and 9 for a proper discussion of the vexed meaning of 'nature'. There is a brief consideration later in this chapter.

4   Harsh controversies in science, philosophy and life typically seem to require one of two very different solutions. Yet sometimes, a both-and solution (like the wave and the particle theory for the nature of light) may be the best way forward; other cases – as C. S. Lewis used to say – may require the uncovering of some underlying wrong assumption which hitherto have been made by both sides. It was said, "God hath more light to break forth from his word." God has also more light to break forth from his world – if biology was in its infancy before Darwin, and in its childhood before the discovery of the human genome, it is perhaps still in its adolescence today.

5   The story of Sabina Spielrein, made into a recent film (A Dangerous Method) because of her relationship with Freud and Jung, shows that in contrast to those two, even then there were people who started from biology and anticipated theories like 'the selfish gene'. The book is by John Launer.

6   The Scientific Literature Review in the Special Commission's Report to the 2011 Assembly was a combination of reviews commissioned from two different people, and the Report concluded (5.2) that "science has not yet produced a clear answer as to the causes of different sexual orientations."

and practice, 30% reported some change, and greater stability of behaviour, 17% no change, and 20% decided to embrace a gay identity. This is remarkably similar to what Freud reported, suggesting that among those seeking change (at least) there is a considerable variety in both the cause of homosexuality and of the outcome of seeking change.

So on the one hand, it is not possible to argue that we can interpret the Bible in a way favourable to homosexual practice. On the other hand, it is not right glibly to say that all homosexual orientation can be changed simply by therapy and/or prayer.[7] That leaves revisionists accusing traditionalists of being unfair, even harsh to individuals, and traditionalists accusing revisionists of being unbiblical (as well as perhaps naïve in thinking that changing social views will have no harmful consequences).[8] That in turn encourages revisionists to say, "now we know better than the Bible, and we think . . ." and traditionalists to maintain, "the only authentic choice for all is the biblical one between heterosexual marriage and celibacy".

There is a clear division between those who take the whole Bible seriously and those who do not. The latter generally argue that Jesus tells us that love of God and neighbour are supremely important; so, once we have these two commands, we can then interpret what love means without paying attention to the rest of the Bible, which gives us the context and background to understand the ministry of Jesus. "Love your neighbour as yourself" is typically understood as "Do for others as you would wish them to do for you, were you in their position" – but unfortunately this simply begs the question, since a revisionist thinks of the homosexual as seeking a natural relief which we can give simply by saying, "Homosexual behaviour is OK", while a traditionalist thinks of him or her as seeking a false dawn which will be good neither for them nor for society.[9]

Therefore the traditionalist views the revisionist, in the light of Scripture, as superficial and disobedient, while the revisionist views the traditionalist as poorly informed and cruel. Is it surprising the church is divided?

---

7 There has been controversy over 'ex-gay' programmes. The Christian Medical Fellowship recently produced a booklet, *Unwanted Same-Sex Attraction*, by Goddard and Harrison, which looks in a professional way at such pastoral and therapeutic issues.

8 See *God, Gays and the Church*, ed. Nolland, Sugden and Finch (Latimer Trust 2008), 201ff.

9 This whole debate concerns 'virtue', which is a wider subject well treated by N.T. Wright in *Virtue Reborn* (SPCK, 2010).

What is the position of the State?

We know that in our Western society today, children are sexualised from a young age, and that this has been one factor contributing to a high rate of teenage pregnancies. There is now a widespread assumption that sex is for recreation, and an acknowledgment of sexual activity among those who are under age. People who choose to remain celibate until marriage are now considered unusual, whereas a hundred years ago this was the norm in most parts of society (and still is in most parts of the world). Furthermore, people who choose to remain celibate all their lives are considered odd.

There have been novels and films exploring the hypocrisy of Victorian and Edwardian society. They were written and scripted because a norm was being broken in secret, not because adultery and promiscuity were the norm. Whereas today promiscuity in many Western countries has become acceptable and even expected. We know also that because of this, sexual diseases are increasing among both sexes, and that this is a particular problem wherever people practise anal or oral sex. Given these factors, people for different reasons may accept that there is merit in a government making provision for the ordering of homosexual relationships within civil partnerships.

A few European countries, some American States, and Canada have legalised 'gay marriage', thus declaring publicly that marriage is open to people of the same sex. This is a solution that goes further than simply saying that homosexual relations are permissible, and would be unacceptable to any traditionalist, and probably also to some revisionists.

Civil partnership, whatever its merits or otherwise, is a compromise which seeks to meet the demands of financial justice, provide for some ordering of same sex relationships, and still allow for the distinct place of marriage as between a man and a woman. The difficulty about any compromise, however, is the pressure to go further. At present, both Westminster and Scottish Governments are debating whether to enact that same sex unions should enjoy the same status as marriage, and that therefore marriage be redefined.

Traditionalists differ when it comes to how they view the wider provision in society for those who wish a homosexual relationship. Some would view civil partnership simply as bad legislation which shows how far the West has fallen from Judaeo-Christian morality. Others would recognise that in a democratic society, civil partnership does offer the prospect of a more stable framework, and fulfils the demands of natural justice in several areas. All traditionalists would agree with some passion that for homosexuals and others to further demand that marriage should be open to people of the same sex is unacceptable: a sad illustration of Nietzsche's dictum that if God is dead, ethics no longer has a foundation and all that remains is a struggle for power.

There is one more thing to be said at this point. When civil partnerships were introduced, it left long-term friends who shared a house or flat (but not a sexual relationship) in a strange and unhappy position. They might also have wished for certain financial advantages like being able to leave property to one another without tax, but they certainly would not wish to be thought of as engaging in a sexual relationship. In our sex-conscious society, few seem to imagine that people can live together in a celibate manner – but of course they do, for a whole variety of reasons.

What is the way forward for the church?

Is it possible that a practical solution could be found which allows both sides to hold to their convictions with some integrity, without causing such a deep division within the church that some of the most highly motivated ministers and elders leave, while others remain, uncomfortable with the situation?

Are there 'weaker brothers and sisters' in this dispute?

In Romans 14, the weaker brothers are those who will not eat meat because it has been purchased in the market, and such produce has been dedicated to false gods. But it is not clear how this would help the current controversy. Are the weaker brothers those who cannot accept that homosexual relations are allowed (in which case, the revisionists should keep quiet for the sake of the conscience of the traditionalists)? Or are the weaker brothers those who can neither relate sexually to women nor remain celibate (in which case the traditionalists should keep quiet for the sake of the revisionists)?

Or is Acts 15 a better example? The Jewish brothers were willing to allow the Gentile brothers not to undergo circumcision (since keeping the Jewish law in this way was no longer necessary for salvation) but they still insisted on no sexual immorality, which brings us right back to the question, "What constitutes immorality?" Traditionalists rule out homosexual behaviour (as both Jewish and Gentile Christians would have done in those days),[10]

---

10 See chapters 9 and 11.

revisionists argue that faithful (i.e. non-promiscuous) homosexual behaviour is not immoral.[11]

In both Romans and Acts, the accommodations recommended were between different cultural groups, or concerned individuals with scruples. The dispute over homosexual practice is not essentially about this, although in the Anglican communion there is a significant difference between, say, churches in Nigeria and in the USA.[12]

Neither side is willing to concede that the issue is sufficiently unimportant to adopt a 'weaker brother' line. Both sides wish to affirm that they are speaking and acting in accordance with the will of God.

Possibly we all wish we could simply follow Paul's advice to "stop judging one another" (Rom 14:13). But in the context he continues, "Instead, decide never to do anything that would make your brother stumble or fall into sin" – and immediately we are faced with the question, "What is sinful?" Clearly none of us should take a proud pleasure in thinking we are right, but equally we cannot dodge this issue as if it were unimportant, especially if it might, as Paul claims, have eternal consequences (1 Cor 6:9-11). We will all stand before the judgment seat of Christ. His penetrating word, which Scripture identifies with the word of God himself, is already at work in us (Heb 4:12-13, Rev 1:16).

Is there danger of hypocrisy?

Yes indeed! We make a fuss about same sex relationships while married clergy commit adultery, drop out for a year, and then find a call to another church, carrying on with a new partner as if nothing had happened. Arguably this is an even bigger scandal, which Presbyteries have not had the courage to address.[13] And we turn a blind eye to ministers who openly

---

11 Paul, at least, clearly had in view the creation texts in Gen 1:27 and 2:24 behind his two main indictments of homosexual practice, Rom 1:24-27 and 1 Cor 6:9 (cf. 1 Tim 1:10). There are eight points of correspondence, in a similar relative order, between Rom 1:23, 26-27 and Gen 1:26-27: human, image, likeness; birds, cattle, reptiles; male, female (see Gagnon).

12 It is often claimed that Western Christians are mainly revisionist, while African and Asian Christians traditionalist. This is an over-simplification – see *Other Voices, Other Worlds, The Global Church Speaks Out on Homosexuality* (ed. Terry Brown, Darton, Longman and Todd 2006). Desmond Tutu, for example, is a prominent Anglican revisionist. The situation is complicated because there is also concern about the draconian measures taken by some African governments against homosexuals.

13 My own Presbytery gave a practising certificate to such a minister before he had even married his new partner – no one bothered to investigate!

say they do not believe in the virgin birth or bodily resurrection. Because the church was excessive and sometimes mistaken in its discipline in past years – think of the expulsion of John McLeod Campbell just because he insisted that the Westminster Confession should be checked against the Bible – we have now become a gumsy church with no teeth.

While this may be more of a challenge to revisionists, who are typically theologically and ethically more liberal, there is a different challenge facing traditionalists. If we wish to help someone with same sex attraction live a happy and fulfilled celibate life – and we believe that is possible with God's help – we must do more than simply talk about compassion![14]

Compassion is not simply a matter of caring for an individual. It goes beyond that to the kind of laws and norms we have in the wider community. Do they reflect God's will? Here traditionalists and revisionists clash. To revisionists it is obvious that compassion means allowing people to 'do what they feel they need to do'. To traditionalists it is equally obvious that the liberalisation of sexual norms over the past fifty years does not by and large reflect God's will. It has brought huge damage to the health and social well-being of the nation (let alone the public purse), which is not an outcome that compassionate people should welcome.

Revisionists then say, well let's limit the damage by giving homosexual couples the fairest wind possible, i.e. marriage, whereas traditionalists say that this is only compounding the damage.

That is not to say that all homosexual relationships are equally damaging, far from it. As with married couples, there is a wide spectrum! Further, there is now a recognition by many male homosexual couples that anal intercourse (also practised by some heterosexuals) is dangerous to health, so that their sexual relationship is more restrained. We do not and should not know what goes on behind closed doors – Christians by and large value a more open and democratic society compared to the theocratic societies of yesterday and today. We are rightly reluctant to make judgments unless we have to, for the good of individual, church and society.[15]

We should all tremble before Jesus' warning to any town which would not receive his disciples and their message about God's rule. The citizens of Sodom and Gomorrah would find more mercy on Judgment Day than they would.

---

14 1 John 3:18 – the comparison between 'rich' and 'poor' brothers is very apt.

15 Compare Matt 7:1-5 and 1 Cor 5:12-13.

What about a 'conscience clause'?

This is a traditional Presbyterian remedy, but it relies on the church not only being willing, but having the authority to grant exemption to ministers on grounds of conscience from performing duties which in general belong to a parish ministry.

The Church of Scotland had a long tradition of running its own show, free from State interference. However, this is no longer true in general. The willingness of the church to settle in the Helen Percy case,[16] and the opening of church accounts to the requirement of OSCR,[17] are each significant milestones.[18] Further, the European Court of Human Rights has already said[19] that it would uphold the right of a same sex couple to marry in church if such enabling legislation had been passed by the national government concerned.

The church still gives a degree of 'protection of conscience', for example in not requiring ministers to remarry divorced persons. This holds because the church has a view on marriage, and recognises that divorce, where allowable on biblical grounds of adultery, is still not God's first choice for couples. It has been suggested that ministers would likewise not be required to, say, provide a church blessing for a civil partnership as part of their parish duties (or 'marry' such a couple, were the church to allow same sex marriage).

This liberty would be difficult to uphold if in fact the church adopted a revisionist view. At the time of writing, the Scottish Government talks about building in safeguards for religious bodies with scruples, were it to pass legislation allowing same sex marriage. But it is for the church itself to decide what may or may not happen, and if a church adopts a revisionist view, safeguards for individuals would be worth little, for two reasons:

(a) Two civil partners wishing to prove a point could challenge in court a minister refusing to bless their union (or their marriage, were the church to allow same sex marriage).

---

16 A complex case some years back where the Revd Helen Percy was accused of immoral conduct, and resigned (it was claimed, under improper pressure and when she was unwell). A case was later brought against the Church under civil law. Since the matter was settled out of court, it was never legally tested whether the accusation was false, or whether the procedure was simply irregular.

17 Office of the Scottish Charity Regulator.

18 Some indication of the uncertainty is given in section 9.16 of the Special Commission's Report.

19 This is yet to be actually tested in the Court. But see http://www.christianconcern.com/our-concerns/social/churches-will-be-forced-to-marry-same-sex-couples-european-court

(b) As time passes, pressure to conform increases. When the ordaining of women elders was first discussed, I recall an assurance given in General Assembly that a Kirk Session not wishing to ordain female elders would always be free to take that line. Yet some years later, a Principal Clerk chose to argue that it was now against church law to object to female elders!

Pressure to conform

Traditionalists face the common argument that Christians used to argue for slavery from the Bible, and had to learn to change – or that people used to make left-handers use their right hand, because it was considered to be 'against nature'. So in another generation or two, it is suggested, we will all see how foolish it was to oppose homosexual practice. Although such views are presented as arguments, it is not of course reasonable to argue that because Christians changed their minds on one thing they should automatically change their minds on another! Such views actually rely more on the spirit of the age, which tolerates everything except conviction, but they do increase the pressure on traditionalists to conform.

This is explored further by Fearghas MacFhionnlaigh in the Epilogue, writing from the Dutch theological tradition. We have become so used to living in what was once called 'a Christian country' that we find it hard to realise that the Western world today is much closer to the world of the early Christians than it has been for centuries.

While we must resist pressure to conform, and seek to adhere to what we judge to be the mind of Christ, we must equally seek to inhabit the heart of Christ, and continue (the best we can) to love those who disagree with us, and take care 'to play the ball and not the man' in our debates.

The demand for 'resolution'

Christians are as inclined as anyone in the modern world to rush towards solutions at all costs, and to try to resolve matters primarily by votes rather than consensus. It is now widely assumed that consensus on this issue is impossible, as the two sides seem far apart. It is as if the ghost of Nietsche has invaded church as well as society, with his dictum that when the traditional source of morality dies, only power is left to decides things.

So we may find the liberal seeking to cut the knot by urging homosexuals just to accept their sexuality and the conservative equally wanting to 'fix' people by promising a change in orientation. Scripture does promise us resolution of all our difficulties, but only when our Lord returns in glory –

till then we have to live with a 'not yet'. That is not an excuse for putting off hard decisions, but we do well to heed the warning of the late Alan Lewis:

> We may misrepresent the pace of the biblical story, hurrying on to the end, impatient with its periods of slowness and waiting: we may silence some of its most painful and puzzling questions because we feel we already know its answers; we may ease its agonizing tensions through foreknowledge of their final relaxation.[20]

Explaining ourselves

Somewhere in one of Walter Scott's novels comes the choice observance, "Gie a Scot a theological explanation, and there's naethin' he winna' dae fur ye!" Well, Scotland has changed, but traditionalists have not done a very good job of explaining themselves, which is one reason for compiling this book.

It may sound very pious to say, "I do this because the Bible tells me to", but that has been the route to acts of terror and cruelty in the past, and dangerously close to reasons which, say, the Taliban might give for their behaviour. We are commanded to love God with our minds, and that means not only working hard to understand *what* the Bible really does say (and what it doesn't), but also seeking to understand *why* the Bible says what it does – and in an age where the Bible is no longer respected for its own sake, we are bound to do that if we have any concern to persuade others of the relevance of Christian faith and the importance of a relationship with a personal, living God.

Calum MacKellar explores such deeper reasons at the end of chapter 12.[21] While what he says stands on its own merits, I am far happier for him to express this from a same sex perspective than for a married heterosexual like myself to do so.

Compassion and morality

When the General Assembly is debating moral issues, I have observed that, often, all it takes to win a debate is for someone to produce a story of pain which is resolved by someone breaking the rules, whereupon people for compassionate reasons take the side of what is presented. Jesus is often presented as a campaigner for freedom against the wicked rule-bound Pharisees; however, this is a caricature – the best example of his balanced

---

20 Alan Lewis, *Between Cross and Resurrection* (Eerdmans 2001), 29-30, also cited in "R.S. Thomas, Poet of Holy Saturday", The Heythrop Journal Nov. 2011.

21 *See also God, Gays and the Church, op. cit.*, as well as chapters 7 and 8.

attitude is shown by how he treated the woman taken in adultery, where he prevents her being stoned, makes her accusers face their own guilty lives, but also tells the woman to "go and sin no more".

Ministers are trained to be pastors rather than prophets, so perhaps it is unsurprising that 'compassion' trumps 'morality' in debates. But is it really compassionate to say that anything goes, as long as it doesn't seem to harm other people? Also, the Church of Scotland is used to being 'chaplain to the nation', and so finds it hard to grasp any nettle which might threaten that cosy relationship, and thereby disturb the position of the parish minister from whom we ever expect a show of compassion.

One of the reasons why some traditionalists have moved to the other side of the debate is their family experience. If you have a daughter who says she is a lesbian, and moves in with a female friend, how do you react? Do you invoke sanctions and break off your relationship? The immediate biblical examples do not apply directly, since 1 Corinthians 5:2 is directed against incest, and 1 John 3:10 is directed at teachers who have a false view of who Christ is. So, do you simply say, 'You are still my daughter, but don't bring your friend back here'? Or do you carry on as if nothing has happened?

This not a unique problem. In different contexts, it is faced by the Jewish parent whose son or daughter 'marries out', it is faced by the parent whose son does something which is either criminal or regarded as highly anti-social, indeed it is faced by the parent whose child enters any relation-ship which is judged to be extremely foolish if not outright wrong. These situations can all result in much pain and misunderstanding. Yet we love someone because of who they are, not because of what they have done or not done. And we share in the pain of God who knows more than any of us what it is to watch and wait for a wayward human race.

God is patient, and amazingly, does not lose hope for the human race. He also sees things more clearly than we do. It is easy for traditionalists to get angry at a culture which not only tolerates but seems to revel in complete freedom of relationships – Los Angeles, or the Findhorn Community, for example. If we do, we should remember that many people in such communities are only too aware of what it is to be weak and wounded, and may be more open to God's mercy than many of the 'strong'. Let us beware of being like Jonah!

There is a long Scottish tradition of balancing compassion and morality, shown in how doctors used to help a family with a terminally ill member. They would eschew euthanasia, but not hesitate to give pain-reducing medi-cation which might have the side-effect of shortening life. While such an approach can easily be defended, doctor and family alike would not welcome scrutiny by, say, a hostile legalist. Would that translate into a 'don't ask, don't tell' approach? Probably not, since the latter is now regarded as unacceptable by both traditionalists and revisionists – revisionists because they think the time for secrecy is past, traditionalists because they do not wish to be accused of inconsistency.

Love and 'nature'

If same sex attraction is like kleptomania (whose cause is also unclear), then it is not compassionate simply to say 'indulge'. If same sex attraction is 'natural', then the situation might be different. But this just pushes the debate to another level. It is true that Paul, for example, appeals to 'nature' in at least two contexts. One of them we do not follow today – where he claims that nature teaches that long hair on a man is a disgrace, while on a woman it is a thing of beauty. We say instead that Paul is using 'nature' as an expression for 'the culture of his day', which has this view of what is natural', or we say that in any case, this matter is not essential, and best left to individual judgment. The other is Romans 1:26-27, where Paul argues that same sex relations are unnatural acts; and we note that Paul has Genesis 1 and 2 in mind (see footnote 11).

At this point, traditionalists and revisionists part company. The former say, it is still obvious that men and women are biologically shaped for intercourse, so anything else is unnatural; the latter say, a small percentage of same sex attraction is natural, so out of compassion for minorities we should accept that and allow homosexual practice. So there is still disagreement about what is right in God's sight.

An illustration which perhaps shows the limitations of the 'it's my nature' argument for homosexual practice is to point out that nearly all men (including most homosexuals) are capable of fathering a huge number of children, yet we do not make that an argument for polygamy, let alone promiscuity.

Sometimes the language of 'human rights' is brought in at this point, as if every human being somehow had a 'right' to a sexual relationship, or as if sexual gratification was a basic human need like food. Currently, the language of rights is used in relation to same sex marriage. This has confused the issue, but perhaps explains why, especially in America, the debate sometimes sounds like a re-run of the human rights issues of the 1960s.[22]

---

22 The Special Commission's Report clearly says in section 8.2, "The issue for the Church is not a matter of human rights . . . it is essentially a theological issue."

Robert Gagnon near the end of chapter 11 cites how Augustine explained his original version[23] of the modern saying, 'all you need is love', contrasting the love of a father who disciplines his son with the 'love' a paedopohile might have for that same child. Augustine is not of course talking about same sex love in general – nor is he even saying that paedophiles are homosexual, which we know is not generally the case – but he does remind us that love is not the same thing as attraction.

The primary question is whether God has declared homosexual practice to be sinful. If so, it cannot properly be described as loving behaviour, whatever the degree of emotion felt, and tolerating it cannot be properly an act of compassion.

In practice

One good outcome of this controversy has been that traditionalists have been faced with their acute lack of compassion, and indeed with the hostility and persecution that people of a homosexual orientation have faced for generations. As Paul Burgess says at the end of chapter 9, our lack of good pastoral care for the homosexual means that the traditionalist apologetic must be considered a work in progress. However, at last speech and attitudes have begun to change for the better. Given traditionalist conviction that homosexual behaviour is wrong and not to be encouraged, are there practical ways of showing compassion? Here are a few suggestions:

1 **Create a culture in congregations where people are not shocked** by personal struggles, and can be open about their problems knowing that they will be accepted and supported.[24] Most congregations have people who are struggling with addictions to pornography and alcohol, and it is a disgrace that often organisations like Alcoholics Anonymous are the only places where they can find real fellowship and 'tough love'. Congregations have people who are struggling with loveless marriages, and with singleness as well as same sex attraction. Are there families and groups who give safe, caring space to such strugglers?

---

23 "Love, and do what you want."

24 Eph 5:3 has sometimes been understood out of its context to prevent Christians ever talking explicitly about sexual issues. In fact, verse 4 indicates that what is in view is flippant talk and crude jokes. Significantly, greed is put alongside fornication as a sin putting us right outside our future in God's kingdom. Greed concerns money and power and status, and in this context I fear the church is often greedy for the approval of society, which used to be named simply as 'the world'. In a previous generation this desire may have led us to shun sexual offenders without discernment, now it leads us in the opposite direction.

2 **Give positive but balanced teaching about healing and change.** Many ministers are afraid to talk about healing, because not all who are sick are healed – yet it was a large part of Jesus' ministry. Likewise, because many who have sought change in their sexual orientation have been disappointed, ministers are afraid to pray positively for such change, even if the person is seeking it.[25]

Let us not lack courage. Ministers often want their teaching and pastoral practice to be 'cut and dried', perhaps under the guise of being 'professional'. Jesus cared for people, and took risks. We can of course take refuge in saying "but we are not Jesus", yet that is evading the issue, since we are called to minister 'in his name', and we have a model in the gospels of disciples who themselves were scared about going out "to preach and to heal", yet commanded to do it.

3 **Train pastoral care groups** in care for single people.

4 **Find good one-to-one mentors** for those who may find that helpful.

5 **Treat single people who remain celibate with honour**, understanding and compassion, whatever their orientation, whatever their circumstance. Never make single people the butt of any joke.

6 **Create a culture in which single people are invited to join families** for meals, holidays, and in other ways.

7 **Recognise the sheer variety of human relationships.** For example, is it not possible for men to live with men, and women with women, in a permanent but celibate relationship – as indeed some married couples do? And why should civil partnership, in this context, not be allowed, to provide security?

Conclusion

Sadly, the Church of Scotland is no more likely to find a satisfactory solution to this controversy than other mainline churches. Our understanding of God's will on these issues reflects deep differences in the way that we understand God, what he is saying in Scripture, and in our understanding of the Christian life. As Christians we may be reduced to finding ways of maintaining 'fellowship at a distance', if such is possible.

No Christian can take delight in this outcome. We still have a duty of care for those with whom we disagree. It is God who removes lampstands,

---

25 Chapters 12 and 13 look at this in more detail from different viewpoints.

not we; it is not for us to mentally or practically 'unchurch' those on the other side of this debate.

We all live before God only because he is merciful and kind. While we disagree on what it means to be 'kind' to someone with a same sex orientation, we happily recognise that the Bible does not label people in this way, and that our identity is found in being made in the image of God, and having that image restored to us in Christ. Every person deserves our respect. We are called to "do good to all, especially to those of the household of faith" (Gal 6:10), and to live in peace with all, "as far as it depends on us" (Rom 12:18).

The churches in Scotland have not been conspicuously successful in demonstrating how to live in community. Relationships between them are friendly, but fall short of a willingness to seek union, as the seventh Declaratory Article of the Church of Scotland requires, "with other churches in which it finds the word to be purely preached, the sacraments administered according to Christ's ordinance, and discipline rightly exercised." One reason for our unwillingness is that we know full well that we ourselves are divided and fall short of what that seventh article expects.

Therefore this book is published not with any spirit of pride, but with an acknowledgment of our weakness, our failure both to teach and practise true compassion and community, and our prayer that God may have mercy on his people.

> The law of the Lord is perfect; it gives new strength.
>
> The decrees of the Lord are trustworthy, giving wisdom to those who lack it.
>
> The precepts of the Lord are right, and those who obey them are happy.
>
> The commandment of the Lord is clear, and gives understanding to the mind.
>
> No one can see his own errors: deliver me, Lord, from hidden faults!
>
> Keep me safe also from wilful sins; don't let them rule over me.
>
> May my words and my thoughts be acceptable to you, O Lord my strength and my redeemer!
>
> (Psalm 19:7-8,12-14)

Epilogue
Drawing a Line in Shifting Sands

Fearghas MacFhionnlaigh

The author is a retired art teacher, writer and Gaelic poet

Suddenly I find myself stumbling along a storm-smudged strand of churning, crashing waves and windborne, stinging sand. What am I doing here? This was not on my itinerary. Yet here I am. Squinting into the horizons. Leaning into the squalls. Time defeating me. One *volte face* already . . .

I thought my proposed answer to the Scottish Government's Consultation on Same Sex Marriage was settled. It was to be 'Yes'. And for good reasons. Scripture censures homosexual practice, sure, but a democratic Christian should nonetheless concede space to diverse groupings. Anticipating reciprocity, of course. Our pluralist society is in various stages of theological freefall. Some spectacular. So what's new? Why attempt a 'line in the sand' on this fraught issue in particular?

What changed my mind? The realization that my notion of 'reciprocity' was an illusion. I had made a serious category error. This was no exercise in pluralism. Far from it. This was liberalist despotism. The proposed law would not reinforce choice in society but reduce it. That was its entire, if sotto voce, point. Ecclesiastical opt-out clause? As well inscribed on tidal sand. And a diversion from the real deal on the street where opt-out would be outlawed. So do I fault our politicians? Not really. I think by-and-large they are being honourable and high-minded. They are simply doing what politicians do. Conforming to a changing landscape. Democracy in action, folks. The bigger question then is: what subterranean dynamics have so strikingly transmuted our landscape? Ah! The fascinating 'plate-tectonics' of Western Thought! How deep does it all go? Very.

Dooyeweerd's 'ground-motives' [*religieuze grondmotieven*]

I suggest we take as our 'speleological' guide the great Dutch Christian philosopher Herman Dooyeweerd (1894-1977). His central insight was that all thought is ultimately 'religious' in the sense that it betokens a pre-commitment of one's deepest selfhood to God or a false god (the latter being any absolutisation of that which is relative). Idol summons counter-idol, as reality resists dis-equilibrium. Entire civilizations can thus become gripped by a dialectical *dunamis* (to use a Pauline word – cf. Rom 1:16), oscillating between the polarities of absolute and counter-absolute, spellbound by each in turn. Deeper even than philosophy, such a dialectic is uncritically premised as self-evident reality. Dooyeweerd identifies four major 'ground-motives' (three are dualistic):

1 Matter-form

First we are led down to the fractured bedrock of Hellenistic thought with its irreconcilable polarities of 'Matter' and 'Form':

> The Aristotelian view of nature was no more independent of religious presuppositions than any other philosophical view. It was completely ruled by the dualistic religious basic motive of Greek thought, namely, that of form and matter . . . It originated from the meeting between two antagonistic Greek religions, namely, the older nature religion of life and death, and the younger cultural religion of the Olympian gods. Nietzsche and his friend Rhode were the first to discover the conflict between these religions in the Greek tragedies. Nietzsche spoke of the contest between the Dionysian and the Apollonian spirit. But in fact here was at issue a conflict in the religious basic motive of the whole Greek life and thought. The pre-Olympian religion of life and death deified the ever-flowing stream of organic life which originates from mother earth and cannot be fixed or restricted by any corporeal form. It is from this formless stream of life that, in the order of time, the generations of beings separate themselves and appear in an individual bodily shape. The corporeal form can only be maintained at the cost of other living beings, so that the life of the one is the death of the other. So there is an injustice in any fixed form of life which for this reason must be repaid to the horrible fate of death, designated by the Greek terms *anangkè* [inescapability] and *heimarmenè tuché* [arbitrary fate] . . . This is the original sense of the Greek matter-motive . . . The religious form-motive, on the other hand, is the central motive of the younger Olympian religion, the religion of form, measure and harmony, wherein the cultural aspect of the Greek polis was deified.[1]

---

1 Herman Dooyeweerd, *In The Twilight of Western Thought*, Craig Press, Nutley, New Jersey, 1968, 163, 164.

The Greek Tragedies reference is indeed pertinent, since the 'dunamis' (power, influence, authority) of drama over our consciousness impinges on our discussion. For example, we can even glimpse, I would suggest, these form-matter polarities in 21st century cinema's genres of superhero (neo-Olympian 'deified cultural forces') and zombie (pitiless, dreadful, *anangkè*).

2 Creation, fall, and redemption

The second ground-motive which shaped the landscape is the non-dualist one of 'creation, fall, and redemption through Jesus Christ in the communion of the Holy Spirit':

> Already in its revelation of creation the Christian religion stands in radical antithesis to the religious ground-motive of Greek and Greco-Roman antiquity. Through its integrality (it embraces all things created) and radicality (it penetrates to the root of created reality) the creation motive makes itself known as authentic divine Word-revelation. God, the creator, reveals himself as the absolute, complete, and integral origin of all things. No equally original power stands over against him in the way that Anangkè and Moira (blind fate) stood over against the Olympian gods. Hence, within the created world one cannot find an expression of two contradictory principles of origin.[2]

Historically, however, Christian thought has struggled to escape the prevailing dualistic ground-motive of society at large.

3 Nature-grace

A new dichotomy arose from the attempted synthesis of the two preceding ground-motives by Thomas Aquinas (1225–1274). Most obvious in Catholicism,[3] this motive also pervades much evangelical thinking (through a stalling of reformational philosophy):

2   Herman Dooyeweerd, *The Roots of Western Culture: Pagan, Secular, and Christian Options*, Wedge Publishing Foundation, Toronto, 1979, 28. Free book download at: www.reformationalpublishingproject.com

3   But note Dooyeweerd's comment regarding mid-twentieth century developments: "And now, now the nouvelle théologie arose ... they spoke about the religious center of man. Yes, so at once Vol. II of my book Reformation and Scholasticism immediately lost its basic foundation, for the Roman Catholics would be able to say, 'What do you mean? We live in a changed time, and neo-scholasticism has for quite some time grown out of that old standpoint." (Center and Periphery: The Philosophy of the Law-Idea in a changing world, Herman Dooyeweerd, 1964 Lecture at the annual meeting of the Association for Calvinistic Philosophy. Provisional translation by Dr J. Glenn Friesen). http://www.members.shaw.ca/hermandooyeweerd/1964Lecture.html

Like the Greek form-matter motive, the ground-motive of nature and grace contained a religious dialectic which drove life and thought from the natural pole to the supranatural pole. The naturalistic attitude summoned the ecclesiastical truths of grace before the court of natural reason, and a supranatural mysticism attempted to escape 'nature' in the mystical experience of 'grace'. Ultimately this dialectic led to a consistent proclamation of the unbridgeable rift between nature and grace; nature became independent, losing every point of contact with grace.[4]

Of particular interest to us, given our current consideration of 'State' and 'marriage', are Dooyeweerd's following comments:

In conformity with Greek thought, Thomas held that the State was the total, all-inclusive community in the realm of nature. All the other life spheres were merely its subservient parts. Thomas therefore conceived of the relationship between the State and the other natural spheres of life in terms of the whole-part relation. Certainly he would not defend a State absolutism that would govern all of life from 'above'. The modern totalitarian regimes of national socialism and fascism would have met an unwavering opponent in Thomas, as they did among the modern Thomists . . . Both the individual and marriage (in its sacramental superstructure) participated in the supranatural order, and the jurisdiction of the State did not extend beyond the natural.[5]

The Thomistic synthesis prevailed insofar as papal authority was able to suppress dissent. However, the incisive critique of English Franciscan William of Ockham (c. 1280-1349) initiated a profound and ongoing split:

Denying any point of contact between nature and grace, this movement exposed the deep rift between the Christian religion and the Greek view of nature. Western culture seemed presented with two options: it could either pursue the 'natural' direction which ultimately would lead to a complete emancipation of man from the faith of the church, or return to the pure ground-motive of Scripture, namely, creation, fall, and redemption through Jesus Christ. The Renaissance movement, the early

4   *Roots of Western Culture*, 117.
5   *Ibid.*, 124.

forerunner of humanism, followed the first path; with more or less consistency, the Reformation followed the second.[6]

To better grasp the crisis provoked by Ockham, we should here note the key conundrum of 'normativity'. If the laws of physics, for example, are creational rather than consensual, what of the laws of logic? Physical? Hmm. Consensual? Problematic. They can clearly be infringed. But fruitfully? Alright, so are there creational laws or principles with a bearing on 'State' and 'marriage'? Dooyeweerd would maintain there are:

> In his common grace God first of all upholds the ordinances of his creation and with this he maintains 'human nature'. These ordinances are the same for Christians and non-Christians. God's common grace is evident in that even the most anti-godly ruler must continually bow and capitulate before God's decrees if he is to see enduring positive results from his labours.[7]

As essentially a nominalist (denying 'universals'), Ockham would disagree. He emancipates 'nature' from Aristotelian metaphysics, but crucially also uncouples it from the Creator's ordinances, deeming these to be arbitrary rather than integral. Nature is brute. Hence our unease when hearing the great reformer Martin Luther (1483-1546) assert: 'I am of Ockham's school':

> Luther, however, was influenced by Ockham's dualism which established a deep rift between natural life and the supranatural Christian life. In Luther's case this conflict expressed itself as the opposition between law and gospel ... With respect to the truths of faith reason was hopelessly blind. But in matters of secular government, justice, and social order man possessed only the light of reason. It was Ockham's rigorous dualism that sustained Luther's separation of natural reason and the Christian religion.[8]

---

6   *Ibid.,* 149.

7   *Ibid.,* 37. Cf. Dooyeweerd, *New Critique,* Vol. II, 237-240: "From the logical sphere onwards the modal laws are only given as regulative principles which cannot be realized on the subject-side without rational consideration and distinction ... In the pre-logical aspects of reality the modal laws are realized in the facts without human intervention ... We must hold fast to our insight into the nature of a normative principle. In the historical and post-historical aspects the laws acquire a concrete sense through human positivizing of Divine normative principles ... The distinction between 'absolute' and 'empirical' norms is untenable ... Arbitrariness can never be elevated to a norm, to an obligatory rule of conduct."

8   *Roots of Western Culture,* 140-141.

Dooyeweerd argues that the 'nature-grace' dichotomy is discernible in (mainly the early) Karl Barth (1886-1968) and Emil Brunner (1889-1966):

> Whereas the Roman Catholic Church accepted the Greek view of nature in a positive sense by attempting a reconciliation with the Christian creation motive [scheppingsmotief], [the early] Barth allowed the creation motive to recede from sight, sacrificing it to the motives of fall and redemption in Jesus Christ. The great master of dialectical theology had no use at all for creation ordinances that might serve as guidelines in our 'natural life'.[9] According to Barth the fall corrupted 'nature' so thoroughly that the knowledge of the creation ordinances was completely lost. Brunner was of a different mind on this point. He believed that the creation ordinances were valid as expressions of 'common grace'. At the same time, however, he depreciated these ordinances by placing them in a dialectical polarity with the divine love commandment which he understood as the 'demand of the hour' [Gebot der Stunde]. Because of their general character, the creation ordinances are cold and loveless. They form the realm of the law which stands in dialectical opposition to the freedom of the gospel in Jesus Christ who was free from the law. In Brunner too one clearly sees the continuation of the Lutheran contrast between law and gospel. This contrast is merely a different expression of the dialectical opposition between nature and grace which in this form – gospel vs. law – had made its first appearance already in late-medieval scholasticism. For Brunner the law, the cold and rigid framework in which God confines sinful 'nature', must really be broken through by the evangelical commandment of love. This commandment knows no general rule and is valid only in and for the moment. For example, marriage – a creation ordinance – cannot be dissolved; but the command of love can break through this rigid, general structure as the 'demand of

---

9 Dutch: "Deze grootmeester der dialectische theologie wil nets meer weten van scheppingsordinantiën, die ons in het „natuurlijk leven" tot richtsnoer zouden kunnen strekken." It should be noted that Dooyeweerd significantly tempered this view in subsequent years: "In his *Kirchliche Dogmatik* Barth has relinquished the extreme dualism of his earlier writings ... There are really masterly and magnificent traits in Barth's reflections on Christian faith" (*New Critique*, Vol. II, 301-02). Nonetheless, Dooyeweerd's perspective continued to constrain him from any plenary acquittal of Barth.

the hour' [*Gebot der Stunde*]. Brunner held that God is indeed the author of the creation order, but as 'law' the creation order is not the authentic will of God, which manifests itself only in the evangelical love commandment. Thus it is still the same ground motive of nature and grace which brought division even within the camp of dialectical theology.[10]

It is conspicuous that in Romans 1 Paul does not fault homosexual behaviour for being contrary to Scripture (i.e. no mention of Leviticus) but rather for being contrary to nature (cf 1 Cor 6:11 – "For such were some of you"). This attests creational parameters, and also arguably 'common grace'. It was in the context of the latter that Dooyeweerd interestingly commended historical Humanism for its record on human rights. Indeed Paul himself endorses 'humanist' thinking, as it were, when in his Acts 17 Areopagus speech he favourably quotes pagan poets. And John Calvin[11] forcefully argued that all Truth comes from God, whatever the conduit:

> Therefore, in reading profane authors, the admirable light of truth displayed in them should remind us, that the human mind, however much fallen and perverted from its original integrity, is still adorned and invested with admirable gifts from its Creator. If we reflect that the Spirit of God is the only fountain of truth, we will be careful, as we would avoid offering insult to him, not to reject or condemn truth wherever it appears. In despising the gifts, we insult the giver. (*Institutes* 2:2:15-16).

Paul was invited to speak by the opposed Stoics and Epicureans. Dooyeweerd suggests a Semitic influence[12] behind the Stoic emphasis on the natural freedom and equality of all men, a strand of Hellenistic philosophy picked up by Roman civil law and thence adopted by Germanic countries in the late middle ages with lasting effect on Western jurisprudence. Of course the Biblical revelation that all men are made in the image of God, and therefore equal before God, also informed more directly, for example, the anti-slavery movement.

---

10 *Ibid.*, 146.

11 "The scholastic motive of nature and grace is not found in Calvin's thought, nor is there any trace of the spiritualistic contrast between the divine Law and the Gospel, found in Luther." (*New Critique*, Vol. II, 517)

12 *Roots of Western Culture*, 26.

4 Nature-freedom

> The fourth [ground-motive] is that of Nature and Liberty, introduced by modern Humanism, which originates in an insoluble conflict between the religious cult of human personality in its liberty and autonomy and the desire to dominate reality by modern natural science, which seeks to construe it as a rational and uninterrupted chain of causes and effects. This humanist motive has absorbed into itself the three earlier fundamental motives, secularising the Christian motive and the [Thomistic] Catholic motive.[13]

We now enter strikingly familiar terrain. In the wake of Ockham, modern Humanism is born. Autonomous humanity harnesses natural laws. But if Man himself is a product of deterministic laws, whence his freedom? Enter Immanuel Kant (1724-1804) with his 'fact/value distinction'. A sensory realm of 'science' (*phenomena*) is sharply distinguished from a suprasensory realm of 'freedom' (*noumena*). The latter is the domain of ethics. Freedom is not provable by science, but is a 'reasonable idea' in which 'to have faith'. Dooyeweerd summarises: "In Kant's thought the chasm dividing science and [humanistic] faith runs parallel to the chasm separating nature from freedom."[14]

Let us now relate this more closely to our discussion. Christianity, which still in the second half of the twentieth century retained at least a tenuously formal status as 'fact', has in our day been re-assigned to the subjective 'value' side (in a ragbag labelled: 'Faith Groups'). In contrast, homosexuality has been re-categorised from the 'value' side, i.e. from being a subject about which public opinion could legitimately differ, to the 'fact' side of objective scientific truth. In other words, it is no longer deemed to be a 'moral' matter but one of physics and chemistry ('just how I am made'). Any attempt to treat it as if in the 'ethical' arena (i.e. as a subject for debate) is an anachronism which State legislation must therefore address forthwith. In the run-up to the last Westminster general election, Liberal leader Nick Clegg stated that homosexuality is "normal and healthy". On which basis dissent cannot be a moral choice, only immoral prejudice. But note also that the current campaign is about far more than the normality of

---

13 Herman Dooyeweerd, "Introduction to a Transcendental Criticism of Philosophic Thought", Evangelical Quarterly XIX/1, Jan. 1947.

14 *Roots of Western Culture*, 172.

homosexuality. It is about the normality of homosexuality, heterosexuality, and everything in between (i.e. every transgender condition and transvestite whim).[15] The Fall is of course forgotten – and with it the perspective that in the light of creational normativity we all without exception struggle with personal 'abnormality':

> Cultural education cannot change the male structure into a female one, nor the other way round. Only a fundamental encroachment upon the biotic structure of the human body would be able to accomplish such a structural alteration because sex difference has a typical biotic foundation. As long as psychology continues to speak of a male and a female feeling-structure, it will be in need of a normative structural principle which itself is independent of the concrete historical development. To point out effeminacy in a man's emotional life implies a normative structural principle lying at the foundation of this statement.[16]

If nothing can conceivably be abnormal, normativity vanishes. Society becomes entirely self-referential. This is post-modernism. Dada revisited. Historicism. Heraclitus. Reality is but a flux of shifting sands. Dada was an irrational ('freedom') reaction to the authoritarian and mechanistic ('nature') carnage of the First World War. Freudianism and Surrealism ensued, truth sought in dreams, the subconscious, drugs. Then followed World War 2. The Holocaust. Hiroshima. Vietnam. Apocalypse Now.

Film is *dunamis*. Broadcasting is spellcasting. From Neo-Classical versus Romanticist painting, to the machine versus human in the Terminator and Matrix trilogies, the nature-freedom motive pervades. The nature polarity generates cinematically jaw-dropping but insistently materialist television. The freedom polarity interrogates normativity via postmodernist multi-narrative labyrinths, as in Reservoir Dogs, Inception,

---

15 Cf. a recent France Culture radio discussion citing a 2009 international athletics gender-testing case as evidence of the "arbitrariness" and "absurdity" of sexual norms ("Qu'est-ce qu'un test de féminité?"). It is "very difficult to submit all our bodies, all our ways of existing, to only two categories defined in opposition". The suicides of young homosexuals suggest "an inability to define themselves in terms of these dominant norms". Imposition of this problematic "binarité", or bi-categorisation, is an impoverishment which neglects "la plasticité de nos corps, la perversité de nos désirs". (Les Nouveaux chemins de la connaissance: Transgression 2/4 : la norme du sexe - travestissement et transgenre, France Culture, 06.12.2011)

16 Herman Dooyeweerd, *New Critique of Theoretical Thought,* Vol. III, 326-7.

Source Code. Electronic mediation (screening) of reality fast approaches 'total immersion'. Humanism's reductionist materialism, internalized by society, is 'lived' as default actuality. Through the media it has become the arena, the very 'boxing ring' of life. There is no 'pluralism' in this sense. To be allowed to 'slug out' ideas on mainstream radio or tv, participants must bow and enter the confines of humanistic ropes and accept the arbitration of humanistic referees. These are the rules. The alternative is marginalisation. Off mike. Off air. Talked about rather than to, by gurus and guests who **do** respect the rules. Scripture is unacceptable. Incomprehensible. Offensive. Out of kilter with society not just in terms of content, but also as a category of discourse. Thus the virtue of homosexuality is no longer in question. That of Christianity most certainly is. As for Dooyeweerd, he bids us find footing within a Christ-rooted, non-dualistic reality; within a creational normativity deeper than self, than society, than physics:

> The ground-motive of the divine Word-revelation is an indivisible unity. Creation, fall, and redemption cannot be separated . . . Did God reveal himself as the creator so that we could brush this revelation aside? I venture to say that whoever ignores the revelation of creation understands neither the depth of the fall nor the scope of redemption. Relegating creation to the background is not scriptural. Just read the Psalms, where the devout poet rejoices in the ordinances that God decreed for creation. Read the book of Job, where God himself speaks to his intensely suffering servant of the richness and depth of the laws which he established for his creatures. Read the gospels, where Christ appeals to the creational ordinance for marriage in order to counter those who aimed at trapping him. Finally, read Romans 1:19-20, where the creational ordinances are explicitly included in the general revelation to the human race. Whoever holds that the original creational ordinances are unknowable for fallen man because of the effects of sin, does basic injustice to the true significance of God's common grace which maintains these ordinances. Sin changed not the creational decrees but the direction of the human heart.[17]

The shoreline seethes. The dunes are browbeaten, winnowed by the winds. But eventually we all must reckon with the rock beneath the sands.

---

17 Herman Dooyeweerd, *Roots of Western Culture*, 59.

General and Scripture Index